"Doing *Breakfast with God* is the gre_____ _____ hope for each day of our lives. [The auth___ ____ ____ _____ out meals for us to munch at as we look to enjoy God and harness each day for his purposes in our lives."

Matt Bird, Joshua Generation

"Fresh, immediate, in-yer-face, like OJ with the bits in, *Breakfast with God* is a really good starter for your day... Read the Bible this way – it'll do you good."

David Bruce, Scripture Union in Northern Ireland

"Living in the age of the mobile phone, internet cafés and on-line shopping must mean living better, not faster. [These] light-hearted but provocative insights give us 366 positive ways to achieve this. This is a must for those wanting to engage with the issues surrounding living in the twenty-first century."

Steve Chalke, Oasis Trust

"With its sporting stories and analogies, this book will prove to be a great resource in my work with professional footballers. The bite-size pieces mean it can be read by anyone in a spare moment; yet its clever and creative style means it will be remembered long after breakfast time has finished. Reading one page leaves you hungry for more and more and more."

Graham Daniels, Christians in Sport

"There are some ideas I wished I'd had first. *Breakfast with God* is definitely one of them. A brilliant read, and especially for anyone who loves collecting good quotes."

Joel Edwards, The Evangelical Alliance

"Filled with sound-bite sized insights, challenges, scripture and prayer, this book will kick-start many into daily spiritual feeding and be an injection of refreshment to the spiritually hungry."

Trev Gregory, Author of Serious Prayer

"*Breakfast with God* will refresh the parts other Bible-reading guides cannot reach! It's creative, stimulating material. It's an insightful and pithy treatment of both familiar and unfamiliar passages. It will help any reader mine nuggets of wisdom from God's word for today's world."

Andy Hickford, Maybridge Christian Fellowship

"*Breakfast with God* is all about serving the Bread of Life fresh to you. Feed on it and it will nourish you, sustain you, fill you, satisfy you, delight you and make you hungry for more."

J John, Philo Trust

"*Breakfast with God* is an unexpected approach to meeting the Almighty ... which opens up the rich truths of Christian discipleship in an exciting way. I am delighted to commend this book for Christians wrestling to work out how to get time with God each day."

Rev. Richard Kew, Episcopal Priest and Writer

"This is fresh, sizzling stuff – don't miss it."

Jeff Lucas, Evangelical Alliance UK

"*Breakfast with God* is ... brilliant!"

Rob Parsons, Care for the Family

"*Breakfast with God* is chunky for chompin' on – so eat it, baby."

Dawnie Reynolds, Soul Survivor

"I love the idea of browsing for spiritual nuggets ... It's so suitable for young adults rejecting a one-size-fits-all authoritarian approach ... Packs more discipleshipping punch in amongst the eclectic references and titbits. Excellent."

Geoffrey Stevenson, Centre for Christian Communication, Durham

"They reckon there are two types of people, those who say 'Morning God', and those who say 'God, it's morning'. *Breakfast with God* is for both types. Whether you are after orange juice, a big breakfast, a continental option or just a strong coffee, *Breakfast with God* nourishes a biblical spirituality for those standing in the foyer of the new millennium."

Steve Taylor, Postmodern Church Planter, New Zealand

"*Breakfast with God* is funny, flexible, friendly, deep, and full of the Bible... A varied diet of truth and honesty for the hungry disciple."

Pete Ward, King's College, London

"God used these thoughts to show me more of Jesus and more of myself. Short, to the point and profound – just what I needed to read."

David Westlake, Tearfund

DUNCAN
BANKS

GERARD
KELLY

ROZ
STIRLING

SIMON
HALL

BREAKFAST
WITH GOD

SPIRITUAL FOOD FOR EVERY DAY

ZONDERVAN

ZONDERVAN.com/
AUTHORTRACKER
follow your favorite authors

Breakfast with God
Copyright © 2002 by The Zondervan Corporation
The following titles, from which selections in this volume were taken, were first published in
Great Britain in 2000 and 2001 by Marshall Pickering
Breakfast with God Copyright © 2000 Duncan Banks
Breakfast with God Volume 2 Copyright © 2000 by Gerard Kelly
Breakfast with God Volume 3 Copyright © 2000 by Roz Stirling
Breakfast with God Volume 4 Copyright © 2001 by Simon Hall
Duncan Banks, Simon Hall, Gerard Kelly, and Roz Stirling assert the moral right to be identi-
fied as the authors of this work.

A catalogue record for this book is available from the British Library.

Library of Congress Cataloging-in-Publication Data

Breakfast with God: spiritual food for every day / Duncan Banks ... [et al.].
    p. cm.
    Originally published: Great Britain: Marshall Pickering, 2000.
    ISBN 0-310-24831-0
    1. Devotional calendars. 2. Bible—Devotional literature. I. Banks,
Duncan.
BV4810 .B68 2002
242—dc21

2002010351

Introduction

Breakfast. I got off the early morning express train at London's Marylebone station, took a black cab past Buckingham Palace getting out just before Piccadilly Circus. My appointment was an 8 a.m. breakfast meeting with one of London's most influential and wealthy businessmen. The venue was the famous Ritz Hotel. I sat with him amongst London's finest and we ordered food that came disguised as a work of art. I caught a glimpse of the bill as the waiter presented it to my friend. I gasped. It looked more like the annual budget of a small South American country and as I caught the train home I thought to myself, "Now that's what you call breakfast!"

Breakfast. It was early and jet lag was still playing games with my body. I was sitting in the board room at Willow Creek Community Church in Chicago with a bunch of leaders from across the globe, trying to prop open my eyelids with matchsticks when in came the food cart. I headed fast for the coffee. Forget international unity and Christian love, we are talking coffee here and if I didn't get some soon there was no telling what damage I was capable of. However, as I elbowed past a huge German I caught a glimpse of the muffin basket. My English eyes had never seen such outrageous baking. They were massive. The size of Florida. I grabbed a coffee and a blueberry muffin. It took two hands to carry the muffin whilst performing a clever balancing act with the hot coffee that a Russian gymnast would have been proud of. And as I ate and the tiredness slipped away I thought to myself, "Now that's what you call breakfast!"

Breakfast. The early morning sun was hot and already putting my sunscreen to the test. I had driven for hours along dusty tracks and then further through nothing but bush land. My breakfast appointment was spontaneous and it was with a ten-year-old boy called Alex. The jeep pulled up in one of the remotest parts of southern Uganda in a region where Compassion, the child sponsorship agency, had just begun working with some of the poorest children I had ever seen. Alex beckoned for us to visit his family. We climbed a dusty, barren hillside and sat outside his house. Well, not so much a house, more of a hut made of mud and covered with a banana leaf roof. Inside it was empty. No pots, pans or any possessions, just shelter from the sun and it was all they had. Alex offered me a banana as we sat together. I knew it was a very expensive gift for him to offer me. I saw the look of shock on his mother's face that quickly turned into a proud smile. I peeled it, took a small bite and held it up to Alex's mouth. He looked into my eyes as he bit into the fruit and as I looked back I saw the face of Jesus. And as I put my arms around that frail boy I realised that out of all the breakfasts I had ever had in my thirty-eight years on planet earth, this morning I was actually having breakfast with God himself. And I thought to myself, "Now that *really* is what you call breakfast!"

Are you hungry for breakfast with the divine today? The book you hold right now is your personal invitation.

Don't shelve it; don't lose it.

Respect it and I guarantee your very soul will be satisfied.

Duncan Banks
England 2002

Orange Juice

When Jesus saw the crowds, he went up on the side of a mountain and sat down.

Matthew 5:1 CEV

Choose the Vital

The Big Breakfast

Now hold on. Stop filming. Time out. This just can't be right. What on earth was Jesus doing, ignoring the crowd and wandering up a mountainside for a sit-down? Surely it was for the crowd that he came to earth in the first place. That crowd would have been full of sick people who needed healing and confused people who needed setting free. The crowd would have been bulging with lost people who needed saving. So what's with the hike up the hill?

I guess the answer is blatantly clear. In that moment Jesus saw what was pressing but chose what was a premium. In our own lives there will always be people and their demands crowding in, pressures and deadlines that scream at us. Unless we choose premium mountaintop moments with ourselves and our Creator we will come to ruin. We need a daily dose of peace and perspective or we will burn out fast.

Phone calls, emails and deadlines will always demand our immediate response. Choosing to stand daily on the mountain top with God and breathing in the fresh air of his kingdom will give us new energy to face the madness of the market-place. If Jesus himself needed to schedule regular appointments with his Father...

Continental

Bill Hybels is one of the world's most successful ministers. He leads Willow Creek Community Church, the largest church in America. Yet he confesses, "If I do not set aside a time for a private meeting with God at least once every 24 hours, I tend to drift way off course spiritually."

Coffee

Choose the vital right now. Choose to sit at the feet of Jesus. Choose a private meeting with God before the marketplace comes crashing in today.

DB

Orange Juice

Jesus answered, "I am the way and the truth and the life. No one comes to the Father except through me."

John 14:6

The Power of One

The Big Breakfast

If you distil fruit juice, you get alcohol. If you boil down a carcass you get bones. If you reduce a perfume to its essence, you get a single, powerful, concentrated fragrance. What do you get if you take 2,000 years of Christianity and similarly reduce it?

According to theologian Hans Küng, you get Jesus. Küng writes: "Christianity does not stand or fall by an impersonal idea, an abstract principle, a universal norm, a purely conceptual system ... Christianity stands and falls by a concrete person, who represents a cause, a whole way of life: Jesus of Nazareth."

No matter how religious those who follow Christ become, no matter how complex their systems of theology, the heart of the matter remains a tangible person. It is this that has made the Christian faith so durable, so adaptable, so attractive over 2,000 years of exploration and diversity. And it is with this that the 21st century must do business – not the system of *Christianity* but the person of *Christ*.

Continental

How much of your spiritual investment is in the system of Christianity, and how much is in the person of Christ?

Coffee

"To you we come, O Lord, the true goal of all human desiring. Beyond all earthly beauty, gentle protector, strong deliverer; from first light be our joy."

Celebrating Common Prayer, *London, Mowbray, 1994*

GK

Orange Juice

As Jesus was walking beside the Sea of Galilee, he saw two brothers ... "Come, follow me," Jesus said.

Matthew 4:18-19

Make Following Worth It!

The Big Breakfast

Some years back there was a man from the United States who tramped round the world with a huge wooden cross. He was called Arthur Blessit and he caused quite a stir. I remember him coming to our town. Everyone was talking about him. Loads of people turned up to hear him speak. Some even began to travel with him. It was a bit like that scene in the movie *Forrest Gump*. Forrest was running across the United States, and people fell in behind him and started running with him. It was all a bit silly, really, but following is something we humans do. Take a look at the shoes you're wearing. Who started that fashion craze? Mr Nike? Now look how many of us are following it.

Jesus reaches out to the part of us that wants to follow, the part of us that gets excited about great causes. Jesus is the greatest cause of all. Follow him and you will find yourself in a relationship that makes the hike worth it.

Continental

Jesus has a load of competition these days. Voice after voice yells at us every day: "Buy me!" "Love me!" "Indulge me!" Be smart enough to follow Jesus *all* the way, not just part of it.

Coffee

I have been a Christian for many years. I think the most important thing I've learned is that following Jesus is often a struggle, but it's always the best road.

RS

Orange Juice

The heavens will disappear with a roar; the elements will be destroyed by fire, and the earth and everything done in it will be laid bare. Since everything will be destroyed in this way, what kind of people ought you to be?

2 Peter 3:10-11

The Secret Place Revealed

The Big Breakfast

Read the verse above and imagine you are sitting in the soft seats of a multiplex cinema, eating popcorn and listening to a Hollywood-epic voice previewing the latest sci-fi blockbuster: It could well be a trailer to a modern-day movie, but the question that Peter asks in his 2,000-year-old letter is bang up-to-date: "What kind of people ought we to be?" It is one we would do well to try to answer in this millennium. Peter's next few words give us a good answer to be going on with:

You ought to be people of good and holy character (PHILLIPS).

Do you get his drift? If the world is going to come to an end and our lives fade away quicker than we imagine, let's invest now in the really important things of life. Not so much in our outward appearance, but on what our characters are like. The question being asked is, "Who are you really, when no one else is looking?"

I guess we all have a clever public image carefully fashioned. We know who we are with others around us. The more painful and probing question is, "What goes on under the surface and behind closed doors?" Answer that and you get a pretty good idea of how your God relationship is going.

Continental

I once stood in a packed tube train in London overhearing a conversation between two businessmen. One was attempting to describe a great new office colleague to the other. He quickly ran out of adjectives and said, "I can only say, she has a beautiful soul."

Coffee

I desperately want my soul life to be far more memorable than my public life. Take some time to consider your progress on your inner journey.

DB

Orange Juice

O Lord, you have searched me and know me. You know when I sit and when I rise; you perceive my thoughts from afar.

Psalm 139:1-2 NIV

Inside Out

The Big Breakfast

We used to laugh at our mother. When she wanted to get hold of one of us, because there were six for her to choose from, she would often go through all our names before she got to the person she really wanted. She would then tut at herself in frustration. Poor lady. She always had far too many things on her mind. To get the right name straight off was a struggle.

God knows our names, and he gets them right every time. That's a good feeling, isn't it? He also sees what we get up to. Scary as that may be, it is actually very, very good news. Nothing can shock him. He's beyond that. Nothing can put him off. There is also plenty that excites him. We have so much potential! All he wants is to get into partnership with us.

Continental

Matthew 10:30 reminds us that even the hairs on our heads are counted. Now that is amazing.

Coffee

How do you feel about yourself today? Do you feel special? You are, and that's a fact. You are known and accepted inside and out. You belong.

RS

Orange Juice

Just then a woman ... came up behind him and touched the edge of his cloak. She said to herself, "If I only touch his cloak, I will be healed."

Jesus turned and saw her. "Take heart, daughter," he said, "your faith has healed you."   *Matthew 9:20-22*

Wholeness

The Big Breakfast

I once had a friend who received an unusual package from abroad. A certain preacher had sent him a handkerchief, sealed in a plastic bag and marked with the words, "Only to be opened in case of emergency". This handkerchief had apparently been blessed and was available for use when my friend needed a miracle. If the plastic packaging was opened, the blessing would be lost, the spiritual freshness dissipated. I wish I was joking, because such an idea is profoundly silly and conflicts with my idea of how the world works.

Yet here we are with a story about a woman who gets healed by touching Jesus' cloak. How offensive that is to my rational sensibilities. What does Jesus say to this woman? "Don't be so superstitious, you stupid girl." Nope. He says her faith has healed her. The odd thing is, the Greek word for "healed" can also be translated "saved". It seems that salvation might include the whole person, not just their soul or spirit.

Continental

It is often said that most Western Christians separate the "sacred" and the "secular", whereas the Bible doesn't make this distinction and treats the whole world as one – as God's.

Coffee

If our salvation covers the whole of life, not just "the spiritual bit", that makes a big difference to all kinds of stuff – our lifestyle choices, our home life, our work ... Is there anything in your own life which you have separated off from God? What do you need to do about it?

SH

Orange Juice
The world did not recognize him.

Blind Date

The Big Breakfast
Austin Powers, International Man of Mystery, is among other things a master of disguise. Like other super-agents before him, he must know how to insinuate himself into a new and foreign situation without being detected.

This is not true of that other man of mystery, Jesus. God's "disguise" was not deliberately chosen to deceive us. The reverse is true – the Incarnation is an act of self-exposure: it makes God more visible, not less.

But the idea of God becoming a human being is so audacious, so strange to our eyes, that when he comes we don't see him! So perfect is God's act of taking on humanity, so complete is his adoption of our nature, that we fail to recognize him. Even in a police line-up, we could easily pass over Jesus as just another human. Only when God opens our eyes do we begin to see who Jesus really is.

With a number of significant exceptions, those who witnessed the life of Christ did not see him as God. But those who did were so changed by what they saw that they went on to change the world.

Continental
Like a *Blind Date* winner, Jesus waits behind the screen of our perceptions. Only when the screen is rolled back do we begin to see the truth.

Coffee
I open my eyes, Lord, to see you. I open my heart to receive you. I open my life to be your dwelling-place.

GK

Orange Juice

No discipline seems pleasant at the time, but painful. Later on, however, it produces a harvest … for those who have been trained by it.

Hebrews 12:11

Training That Works

The Big Breakfast

For the past few summers, I have travelled to Atlanta, Georgia, with a Christians in Sport team. We take a group of professional footballers each year to lead a soccer camp. ("Football" in the UK is "soccer" in the US.) Being a big footy fan, I love the chance to get to know the players and to play football with them. On my first visit I was stunned to be asked to play on the team. I even managed to convince an ex-Queens Park Rangers and Wolves soccer player to lend me his boots for the game. I laced them up, convinced that with these boots on my feet I would soon be playing for England. The truth was, I was terrible. Wearing the boots made no difference whatsoever.

I learnt the lesson. The reason my footballing buddy plays at the highest level is because he has disciplined himself to train hard every day, to work out in the gym, to eat the right food and to get the right amount of rest. The disciplined life has turned him into a top sportsman. For me to wear his boots and expect to play like him was pure comic-book fantasy.

When it comes to the word "discipline", I think we get the wrong idea. It conjures up images of school teachers or angry parents. If we are ever to achieve our dreams in life – dreams to be a success, to be a better friend, a better partner, even dreams to live as the Christian we have become – it will mean making discipline a close friend.

Continental

Proverbs gives this sound advice: "He who ignores discipline comes to poverty and shame" (Proverbs 13:18 NIV). It must be worth taking this seriously. To choose not to must be to choose ruin.

Coffee

Make a mental list of at least one place in your life where you need to begin to apply some discipline. The list may include food, leisure, entertainment, time, etc.

DB

Orange Juice

After that, he poured water into a basin and began to wash his disciples' feet.

John 13:5

God on the Dole

The Big Breakfast

I was one of those people who left college and went straight into my first teaching job. After a few years I left and took up work with a charity. It was a short-term contract and three years later I found myself on the dole. I will never forget the experience of those few months. To get into the system, I had to go through the humiliation of answering a load of personal questions, which were put to me by a girl I had once taught. She never once lifted her eyes from the page. The next ordeal was the weekly dole queue. There was another past pupil at the counter. I felt like a piece of discarded rubbish.

One day I looked back down the queue. There was someone I recognized. What was he doing here? It was the headmaster of the school where I had taught. I felt so embarrassed for him. How was he going to feel when he got to the counter?

This verse reminds me of a situation like that. Instead of God peering at us from behind the glass screen, he is in the queue with us.

Continental

There is no position lower than that of a servant. Yet that is how far down Jesus chose to go.

Coffee

Who do you need to serve today? No matter how difficult it is for you, do it. It will change your life.

RS

Orange Juice

From the fullness of his grace we have all received one blessing after another.

John 1:16 NIV

Shakin' the Tree

The Big Breakfast

Shake an apple tree in winter, and what do you get? A lone leaf might float to the ground or a twig might break loose. Or maybe nothing. Shake a barren tree, and the result is much the same.

But shake a fruitful tree at harvest time, when the apples are ripe and ready, and you will have a different experience. Apples falling on your head. Apples rolling across the grass. Apples piling up at your feet. Newton might never have explained gravity if he had not picked the right tree in the right season. It is from fullness that fruit falls – where there has been growth, where each fruit has ripened until it is almost too heavy for the branch that holds it.

So it is, John tells us, with grace. Jesus came into the world so full of grace, so heavy with fruit, that all who know him are blessed. Not just one blessing, nor the occasional blessing, but one blessing after another, a torrent of blessings tumbling down like ripe apples on our heads. When you shake the tree of Jesus, blessings fall.

Continental

With the coming of Jesus, the tide has turned. The walls of our sand-castle lives are breached – and in flows grace.

Coffee

Where there is barrenness, where we are tired and dry, *let grace fall*. Where there is anger, where bitterness is the only fruit of our lives, *let grace fall*.

GK

Orange Juice

Peter and his companions were very sleepy, but when they became fully awake, they saw [Jesus'] glory.

Luke 9:32

Wake Up!

The Big Breakfast

What I wouldn't give to see the glory of God right before my eyes. You tell me anything that could beat that.

My good friend Ian is a big Formula I motor racing fan. He had watched every race in the season and, like millions of others, stayed up to the early hours to watch Damon Hill win the 1996 world championship in Japan. He kept awake until the warm-up lap at 3 a.m. Then he closed his eyes for what he thought was just a blink – and opened them again to the chimes of Big Ben ushering in the six o'clock morning news. He had missed out on one of the most memorable races of the decade.

Jesus had taken his closest friends, Peter, James and John, up a mountainside to pray. The Master gets down on his knees, while the disciples curl up under the stars for a doze and nearly miss out on the fireworks as heaven touches earth. "As he was praying, the appearance of his face changed, and his clothes became as bright as a flash of lightning" (Luke 9:29). Imagine missing out on that!

So where do you feel dozy in your spiritual life? Once the passion burnt like a bolt from heaven. Nothing would stop you making your life dreams come true. Now, your passion lies dormant, fast asleep, waiting for a spark to set the fire burning again.

Continental

The British Chief Rabbi Jonathan Sachs once said, "Death is more universal than life. Everybody dies but not everybody lives." Wake up before you fall asleep for good!

Coffee

Wake up! Don't sleep through the race of life and miss out on seeing the glory of God.

DB

Orange Juice

When the disciples heard this, they were greatly astonished and asked, "Who then can be saved?"

Jesus looked at them and said, "With people this is impossible, but with God all things are possible."

Matthew 19:25-26

Salvation: Hard or Easy?

The Big Breakfast

This verse comes after another of those rather annoying hard sayings of Jesus. He's just been talking about rich men getting into the Kingdom, camels and the eye of a needle.

I once heard that there was a gate in Jerusalem that was so narrow that it was called "The Needle's Eye". It was so narrow, in fact, that a trader coming through the gate would have to take all his baggage off the camel in order to get it through.

Whether or not this is true, the disciples react as one by saying, "So what do we do, then? Just 'cos UK pop guru Cliff Richard's got a Rolls, does that mean he can't get into heaven?"

Jesus responds by saying something frightening: God can break the rules, maybe even his own rules. Because he wants everyone to be saved (see 1 Timothy 2:4), he can make it possible for us to be saved despite our own sinfulness. So, big cars and cheesy singles notwithstanding, Cliff is a friend of God – saved – because he trusts in God to forgive him.

Many of us, just like the Pharisees, want to make our own rules about who's in and who's out. I, for one, am profoundly grateful to God that his love and salvation stretch out beyond any rule and grab me wherever I am, whatever I'm doing.

Continental

If there is anything in your life that you feel bars you from God's presence, *you're wrong!* The Bible says all you need to do is turn away from it and ask God's forgiveness and help. If you feel that God likes you because of something you've done, *you're wrong too!* Being saved is all down to God.

Coffee

Why not take a moment to thank God for the one unique thing about Christianity: you are saved not because of something you did, but because of something God did.

SH

Orange Juice

Love must be sincere. Hate what is evil; cling to what is good. Be devoted to one another in love. Honor one another above yourselves.

Romans 12:9-10

No Fakery

The Big Breakfast

I read the following letter on an agony page of a magazine recently:

"My boyfriend says he loves me, but he has trouble showing it. I always do special things for him, like sending him surprise love letters, but he only does nice things for me when I complain that he is not expressing his feelings. He says he is just very laid back and that he's never felt about another girl the way he feels about me."

How are you doing on the "expressing your feelings" front? Do your friends and those special people in your life know that they are loved?

Jesus has a great plan for the people who get into his type of love. It is love that isn't afraid to be real, that doesn't need to be prompted to show up. It is about being devoted to one another – caring so much about one another that somebody else always comes first. Now that's the kind of love I want to experience.

Continental

Whenever I talk to people who have no time for church, I am always interested to discover how fascinated they are with religion. Everybody wants some kind of spiritual reality. Is this a search for real love?

Coffee

This lovely verse tells us what people in church are like. Do you recognize anyone?

RS

Orange Juice

Just as iron sharpens iron, friends sharpen the minds of each other.

Proverbs 27:17 CEV

Let the Sparks Fly

The Big Breakfast

Do you ever feel powerless to chop your way through the jungle of life? Sometimes I feel so blunt when it comes to standing strong in the face of deep temptation. I can so often feel I've lost my cutting edge when it comes to resolving those damaged relationships. So how do I get sharp again? Spend more time praying? Read a few more chapters of my "Every-Other-Day-with-Jesus" daily devotional? Put on a Delirious? CD? All good stuff, but the Bible is clear on the best way to sharpen up. Read the verse again. We need to involve other people.

Of course, sparks fly when two bits of metal clash with each other. It is not an easy experience, but it's the only way to beat being blunt. Answer honestly. Who is passionately committed to your growth and development? When did you allow someone else you trust to open the door of your life and take a wander through?

The Salvation Army evangelist Phil Wall once said, "Fewer might fall to the arch-enemy of Christian believers – money, sex and power – if only they had protected themselves with the honesty and accountability that any good relationship demands."

Continental

The Beatles were so right when they sang, "I get by with a little help from my friends." We need to pursue sharpening relationships. The author Virginia Woolf made this profound statement: "I have lost friends, some by death ... others through a sheer inability to cross the street." Make the effort!

Coffee

I love the wisdom of Proverbs. It is said of Billy Graham that he lives in the Proverbs. I once heard a preacher say that there are 31 chapters in Proverbs and 31 days in most months. It would do the soul good to read a chapter a day.

DB

Orange Juice

For the law was given through Moses; grace and truth came through Jesus Christ.

John 1:17

The Last Piece of the Puzzle

The Big Breakfast

There are few figures in the history of Israel who loom larger than Moses – founder of the nation; giver of the Law; leader of the people through the most significant 40 years of their history. Of all the Hebrew giants, Moses is the tallest.

In Christian history, too, he plays a huge part. The Jewish/Christian co-operation over the filming of Steven Spielberg's *Prince of Egypt* bears witness to this shared regard for this shepherd, politician, theologian and military leader.

Moses is important in God's plan of salvation. But he is not the whole picture. Stop with Moses, John tells his Jewish audience, and you have half a story. You have a puzzle with the final, crucial pieces missing. You have an unfinished symphony. You have a lottery ticket with only four numbers chosen. You have a quiz that asks the questions, but goes off air before the answers can be given.

It is Jesus who completes the picture. Jesus brings grace and truth – the last two pieces without which the puzzle makes no sense. Jesus is the completion of Israel.

Continental

If the Law of Moses told us how we should behave, it is the grace and truth of Jesus that enable us to do so.

Coffee

May Jesus who brings completeness to an ancient Law bring the same completeness to my faith. May the Christ who brings fulfillment to the words and works of Moses bring that same fulfillment to my life.

GK

Orange Juice

If you declare with your mouth, "Jesus is Lord," and believe in your heart that God raised him from the dead, you will be saved.

Romans 10:9

Can It Be *This* Easy?

The Big Breakfast

Imagine you are a Christian man in the Roman Empire, circa AD 50. Every man in the Empire has to serve in the army at one point, and as part of your induction there is a quasi-spiritual ritual to go through. It's a bit like Members of Parliament in the UK declaring their allegiance to the Crown or American school-kids saluting the US flag. Only there's one problem: you have to acknowledge that Caesar – the Emperor – is a god and that you will worship him as "Lord". The alternative is a horrible death.

But you are a Christian, and you believe that there is only one Lord, Yahweh, the great I AM. Worshipping Caesar would be idolatry, a sin against God. Well, what would you do? Would you confess with your mouth, "Jesus is Lord", or would you mumble away with your fingers crossed, hoping that you won't get them chopped off?

Shouting out "Jesus is Lord!" in the safety of your bedroom isn't much of an acid test. Try shouting it in the local shopping centre. On second thought, don't – you'll embarrass everyone, including other Christians, probably. Why not try living in a way that shows that Jesus is the Lord of your life?

Continental

The Bible includes an ongoing debate about whether anything we do gets us into heaven. The clear answer is "No", but if God really has saved us, then it should be obvious in the way we live our lives.

Coffee

Talk to God about how you would feel if you were a Roman and had to choose between Caesar and Jesus. Be honest with God about your fears and weaknesses, and leave space for him to speak to you.

SH

Orange Juice

If we confess our sins, he is faithful and just and will forgive us our sins and purify us from all unrighteousness.

1 John 1:9

Not Guilty!

The Big Breakfast

Have you ever woken up on a winter's morning and seen the pure white snow transform your grubby neighbourhood? Have you ever felt your whole body sigh with relief as you take your heavy rucksack off after a long hike? Have you ever known the indescribable joy of hearing your Father in heaven declare you "not guilty" as you confess your failure to him?

Sin and guilt are responsible for crippling both Christian and unbeliever alike. The head of one of London's largest psychiatric institutes said, "I could release half of my patients today if only they could be assured of forgiveness." So how do we get rid of sin?

Sin leaves the body through the mouth. John says that "if we *confess* our sins", then God will rush in with wave after wave of purifying snow. If we let the words of wrongdoing out of our mouths then the rucksack of past failure can be abandoned at the foot of the cross and we can stand tall once again.

Why do we hang on to our sin like some security blanket when the freedom of forgiveness is just a confession away?

Continental

I have made it my aim to begin reducing the gap between the time I mess up and the time I say sorry, until one day the gap will get so small I can almost catch myself before I fall. Remember that God is never shocked with us. We shouldn't put off our confession to him out of embarrassment.

Coffee

If you let unconfessed sin pile up, it will only drive a wedge between God and your soul. Open your mouth and get it straightened out right now.

DB

Orange Juice

Bless those who persecute you; bless and do not curse. Rejoice with those who rejoice; mourn with those who mourn.

Romans 12:14-15

Robben Island

The Big Breakfast

"Mother, I've done it! I've got the part. They're going to let me play Nora, the leading role. I can't believe it! And that gorgeous Nick will play my oppressive, controlling husband. I'm over the moon!" It will be easy for this mother to rejoice with her girl. It's her daughter's first big part, and she plans to go to drama school.

"Rejoice with those who rejoice." Sure, I can do that. Most people can. "Bless those who persecute you." Hmm. If you're anything like me, you will fume and puff and plan a tactical revenge – and that's only for minor persecutions. Bless? Not on your life.

Then there's the serious stuff, when someone is really out to get you – the kind of thing that's about destroying you or some part of you. The Bible makes it clear. Our job as Christians is to bless. To return good for evil. To find ways of doing good to those who mean to harm us. This kind of response, while it is the obligation of every Christian, can only be done with the help of God's Spirit.

Continental

In his book *A Witness For Ever,* South African Michael Cassidy tells of the power of such a Spirit-filled response. One African National Congress leader who had spent time on Robben Island with Nelson Mandela spoke of a moment when he took courage and reached out in friendship to a brutal and cruel warden. The warden was reduced to tears.

Coffee

Lord Jesus, your power to transform the most brutal, cruel person is still around today. Give me the courage to bless those who persecute me.

RS

Orange Juice

Moses said to God, "Suppose I go to the Israelites and say to them, 'The God of your fathers has sent me to you,' and they ask me, 'What is his name?' Then what shall I tell them?"

Exodus 3:13 NIV

Whom Shall I Say Is Calling?

The Big Breakfast

This verse is often quoted as evidence for Moses' lack of faith, as if he is using his questions to put off the dreadful moment when he must simply believe God. There is another possibility. These questions may in fact be evidence of the great wisdom of Moses.

Even as he asks, he is demonstrating why it is that God has chosen him above all others. Wisdom tells Moses that it is all very well *him* meeting God in a bush – but if those to whom he goes have no grasp on that experience, he will simply appear mad.

With the bush still burning, and the encounter in full swing, Moses is already thinking ahead to the cold light of tomorrow, when he will have no such props to help him. He needs not only to encounter God, but also to be able to explain. He asks God for a spiritual currency that is *transferable*.

How much fuller might our churches be if those of us who seek to encounter God worked as hard at seeking to explain?

Continental

What qualities make our experience of God *transferable?* What makes it easier – or harder – to tell others about the God whom we have encountered?

Coffee

God may meet you in divine confrontation at the Burning Bush – but can you explain it in mundane conversation at the Boring Bus Stop?

GK

Orange Juice

Love the Lord your God with all your heart and with all your soul and with all your mind.

Matthew 22:37

Embrace the Emotion

The Big Breakfast

So, Jesus says that the command is to "love God with all your heart". The heart is the centre of our emotion. Ever heard a sports coach shout, "Put your heart into it!" or a ditched lover say, "She broke my heart!"? In the Old Testament, it wasn't the heart but the bowels the writers used to describe our emotional centre. It's a good job Graham Kendrick wasn't writing songs back then.

Jesus is saying that the kind of relationship he wants with his followers is an emotional one. Trouble is, for many of us the emotional side of our lives has been sucked dry. For me, being British meant that I had to keep my upper lip stiff in all circumstances. I was always told as a kid that "big boys don't cry", and then on my first trip to church I was told to keep my emotions separate from my faith and my worship.

I guess my wife could prove her love for me by constantly showing me a copy of our marriage certificate. However, I for one am much keener to discover the emotional side of our relationship. I would swap a bit of paper for a passionate kiss any day! Loving God with all our heart means loving with all heartfelt passion and romance. Only then do we move on to our souls and our minds.

Continental

Someone once asked this question: "Why is it that if a film produces laughter it's regarded as successful, or if a football match thrills the spectators it's reviewed as exciting, but if the congregation are moved by the glory of God in worship it's excused as emotionalism?"

Coffee

It is said that "experience is not what happens to someone; it's what someone does with what happens to them". So what will you do with that experience of holy, heartfelt emotion?

DB

Orange Juice

If my people, who are called by my name, will humble themselves and pray ... then will I hear from heaven and will forgive
their sin and will heal their land.

2 Chronicles 7:14 NIV

The Return

The Big Breakfast

I once saw a biker motoring down a road with this verse
written on the back of his leather jacket in studs. It must have
weighed a ton! Still, it is a great verse, the kind that really gets
people praying. But what for? How many people realize that
this verse is about the land getting healed? It is as if there's a special part of our brain
that processes bits of the Bible that are too hard (miracles, anything about money,
etc.) and sort of calms them down. This is one such verse: we get the bit about
praying and that it leads to something good, but we ignore the fact that this verse is
specifically about dealing with famine and plague in the land.

Still, it is good to realize that God takes seriously the needs of the land. In the UK,
where I live, the land is quite a big issue, with a raging debate about genetically
modified food and an active Green movement, but Christians are generally very quiet
about these issues. I don't really know why.

There is clearly a challenge here for us to pray for our land – not just as the place
where you live, but as something in itself. It all sounds a little bit – dare I say it? – New
Age. But in an era where capitalism and industrialization have ripped us out of our
environment, maybe we need to get back to nature a bit, eh?

Continental

The laws, life and beauty of the material part of God's creation
are as eternal and sacred as virtue and praise are in the spiritual
realms.

Coffee

Jesus told us to pray for our daily bread. Pray today for the land
that grows your food, and for those who bring it to you in such
wonderful condition.

SH

Orange Juice

I am the good shepherd. The good shepherd lays down his life for the sheep. The hired hand is not the shepherd ... he abandons the sheep and runs away.

John 10:11-12

Cultural Misfit

The Big Breakfast

A few years ago, Ben Johnston, of MTV, was quoted as saying, "We don't influence 11 to 14-year-olds, we own them already." That's a pushy statement. I guess he was saying MTV has been so good that kids drink in every word. It is more than an influence. It's a bible. It tells us how to think, dress and behave. I get very bothered by that, because I know Ben Johnston is right.

Take a look at the magazines in the newsagents. Watch the TV soaps. Some of it's just a laugh, certainly, something to relax in front of in the evening. But look again. It is put together very carefully with you in mind. Well, maybe not you, but definitely the money you'll feed into it. It tunes into the issues that mess you up. It tells you what's cool, hip, exciting, what must be had at all costs. So you keep buying the magazines, you keep watching the TV. Do you want to be owned by Ben Johnston? I don't think so. As the American rock star Larry Norman sings: "Why don't you look into Jesus, he's got the answer ..."

Continental

There are two people in Jesus' story – the shepherd and the farm labourer. The shepherd has invested in these sheep, so he cares about them. Jesus has invested in you.

Coffee

Don't become so well-adjusted to your culture that you fit into it without even thinking. Instead, fix your attention on God.

Romans 12:2 MSG

RS

Orange Juice
Blessed is the man who does not walk in the counsel of the wicked ... But his delight is in the law of the Lord, and on his law he meditates day and night.

Psalm 1:1-2 NIV

The Big Mac Bible

The Big Breakfast
One of the McDonald's in my town has a "drive-through" window. From the comfort of the driver's seat you can order a Big Mac, fries and a drink – it only takes an instant. And it doesn't take much longer to consume it.

In Paris there is a restaurant called La Parisian where I once had a meal with some friends. We spent four hours enjoying the cuisine and the company – course after course of delicious delicacies.

Why is it that we so often reduce the essential food of the faith to a Big Mac meal that only ever gives us a dose of spiritual indigestion? How do we turn the "law of the Lord" into our delight? How can it become as appetizing as a fine French meal?

The answer must be to do all we can to dust off the Bible on the bookshelf and make it our manual for life. We must do all we can to make time to digest it – after all, we always seem to find time for food, our friends and even our favourite TV shows. We must create an inspirational environment in which to read it, write a journal to help apply it, and find a suitable translation to understand it.

Continental
The psalmist goes on to tell of the results of making God's Word a delight in our daily lives. We will become like a tree that yields fruit (character growth) and a leaf that doesn't wither (perseverance), and whatever we do will prosper. Good, eh?

Coffee
So what translation of the Bible do you read? Take C.S. Lewis's advice: "A modern translation is for the most purposes far more useful than the Authorized [or King James] version." Try the NIV – it works for me.

DB

Orange Juice

Jesus replied, "Very truly I tell you, no one can see the kingdom of God without being born again."
"How can anyone be born when they are old?" Nicodemus asked.

John 3:3-4

Inherit the Wind

The Big Breakfast

Nicodemus might well ask. He was not only old; he was also educated, wealthy, powerful, significant, competent and respected. He was everything a religious leader of his generation might want to be – and everything a new-born baby is not. He was so scared of change that he went to see Jesus under cover of darkness.

Jesus issued a direct challenge – he called him to swap his competence for newness, his knowledge for ignorance, his certainties for mysteries and his faith in a static, unchanging God for a living relationship with "the wind that blows wherever it pleases". Jesus asked him to give up religion and inherit the wind.

How many of us in today's religious institutions – who call ourselves "born again" and are as sure of our faith as Nicodemus was of his, until he met Christ – stand in just as much need of such a change as Nicodemus did?

Continental

"The things that have got you to where you are today are not the things that will get you to where you need to be tomorrow."

George Barna

Coffee

Blessed are you, God of compassion and mercy. In the darkness of my life, let your light break forth in new birth.

GK

Orange Juice

But you will receive power when the Holy Spirit comes on you; and you will be my witnesses in Jerusalem, in all Judea and Samaria, and to the ends of the earth.

Acts 1:8

The Mission

The Big Breakfast

We all know the story about Pentecost – flames, wind and tongues – but sometimes we forget why God did it. Well, here is what Jesus said: we are to tell everyone about him *everywhere in the world*. But that's what we send missionaries for, isn't it? So we don't have to worry about all those billions of people who don't know Jesus, do we...?

Unfortunately, Jesus never said, "Peter, James and John, you're going to Kenya and the rest of you can stay at home." Nope, he said *everyone* would be his witnesses, and they were. After AD 70, the church in Jerusalem was scattered throughout the Roman Empire and beyond. All the Christians would have had to give an account of themselves, because their strange beliefs meant they would not worship the emperor.

And what happened? The more they got thrown to the lions, the more people joined them. Makes you think something might be missing nowadays, doesn't it? I don't know exactly what's missing, but I do know that things would change if Christians would start going where God wants them to go and simply be witnesses to what Jesus has done in their lives.

Continental

"Jesus commands us to go. It should be the exception if you stay."

Keith Green

Coffee

Is there anywhere God wants you to go? It doesn't have to be Africa; it could be a quick visit to a lonely neighbour. Is there anyone you need to talk to about Jesus? You don't have to understand deep theology; you just have to be able to talk about your friend Jesus.

SH

Orange Juice

Jesus went up on a mountainside and called to him those he wanted, and they came to him. He appointed twelve *that they might be with him* and that he might send them out to preach.

Mark 3:13-14 (emphasis added)

More Than a TV Show?

The Big Breakfast

Jesus' first reason for calling twelve followers was "that they might be with him". If the Son of God needed people around him, then how much more do we need key relationships feeding into our lives?

Over the years I have discovered that the kind of friend we are dictates the kind of friends we attract. If we are not finding those "soul mate" kinds of friendships, then maybe we need to take a long hard look in the mirror.

We must develop a close network of relationships if we are ever to stand strong in the tough times of life and create memories in the good. I love my Silverstone moments with Dave, and my Stratford moments with Leon.* I love laughing with Chris, Sheena and Caroline. I love travelling everywhere I go at the moment with Dan. I love summer days with Alastair and Debbie. Then of course there's Rob, Andy, Nigel, Pete and Gerard, Dawn, Ben, Joel and Steve ... the list goes on. The names mean nothing to you but everything to me. They have taken a lifetime to find and will take a lifetime to keep.

*Silverstone is the British Formula I racing circuit, and Stratford, of course, is Shakespeare's birthplace!

Continental

Back in the 1980s, the world watched as nine paraplegic Olympians lined up for the 100 metres, each with a passion to win. The race began and one runner, out in front, tripped and fell. He expected to see his competitors leave him behind, but they all stopped, picked him up and ran over the finish line together. Who picks you up when you fall?

Coffee

Philip Zimbardo, a world authority on psychology at Stanford University, said, "I know of no more potent killer than isolation. There is no more destructive influence on physical and mental health than the isolation of you from me." Get together with a friend today.

DB

Orange Juice

One of the Pharisees invited Jesus to have dinner with him . . .
A woman in that town who lived a sinful life learned that Jesus
was eating at the Pharisee's house, so she came there with an
alabaster jar of perfume.

Luke 7:36-37

Ketchup

The Big Breakfast

A friend of mine told me a wonderful story. He was in church,
when halfway through the service a homeless man came in.
The man was restless. He moved from seat to seat. Perhaps
he was looking for a warm spot. He eventually settled down.
A few people stole glances at him, but mostly he was ignored. Then he brought out
his dinner – fish and chips. The smell was distracting and the man was a noisy eater.
An elder of the church got up to investigate. After a few minutes he left the man,
walked to the front of the church and out through the door. He returned a few
minutes later with a bottle of ketchup.

This verse in Luke 7 is about an unusual guest arriving at a dinner party. Like the
homeless man, she stood out. She also took a great risk. The dinner party host had
the power to have her stoned to death. She was a prostitute and death by stoning
was often their fate. Why, then, did she come? Jesus was the reason.

Continental

Jesus is a very special man. People all around you need to meet
him, but they don't realize it. They have often confused fame
and the attention of a crowd as the reasons for Jesus'
popularity. You need to show them the real Jesus.

Coffee

Jesus will be seen more easily when those of us who know him
learn how to fetch the ketchup!

RS

Orange Juice
But when the set time had fully come, God sent his Son.

Galatians 4:4

An Idea Whose Time Has Come

The Big Breakfast
The "Pregnancy Principle", used in management training, states that it takes one pregnant woman nine months to produce a baby – but nine pregnant women given one month won't do it. Some things just have to take their course. Once they have taken their course (ask any mother), nothing can stop them. There is no power on heaven or earth that will stop a baby being born once the time is right.

For Jesus, Paul is saying, the time was right. Heaven was pregnant with mercy. God was longing for the day – it was the moment that the whole cosmos had been moving towards. When the time came, nothing would be the same again.

Never, until Jesus, had such an audacious idea been proposed. Far from forcing men to seek him, God himself would seek them. The great gulf between God and humankind would be bridged not from the human side but from God's. Once the moment was right, nothing could hold back the flood. The Cross was an idea whose time had come.

Continental
The coming of Christ was God's initiative, God's intervention and God's idea. While religion is so often about women and men seeking God, Jesus embodies the very reverse.

Coffee
Jesus, born of Mary, I welcome your initiative of mercy. You made the choice to seek me out – I make the choice to receive.

GK

Orange Juice

As evening approached, the disciples came to him and said, "This is a remote place, and it's already getting late. Send the crowds away, so they can go to the villages and buy themselves some food."

Jesus replied, "They do not need to go away. You give them something to eat."

Matthew 14:15-16 (emphasis added)

Give Up Your Lunch Box

The Big Breakfast

If only the Church could grab this one, we would really begin to live as God intended and the world would sit up and take note.

The crowd was large and the hour late. The disciples felt it their duty to let Jesus know that they had heard one or two rumbling tummies, with their own sounding the loudest. The nearest burger joint was quite a distance away.

The Master's answer showed them, as it shows us, who is responsible for feeding the hungry. It is not primarily governments or aid agencies. "They do not need to go away. You give them something to eat."

It is your responsibility to feed the hungry in our world. I know you don't have enough to solve the problem. Neither did the disciples.

"We have here only five loaves of bread and two fish." Jesus didn't need them to have enough – they just had to be willing to give what they had. What can you give today to the man on the street or the project in your town? The axiom is true: if you're not part of the solution, you're part of the problem.

Continental

When the disciples gave of their little, the Master gave of his abundance. He turned a packed lunch into a feast for thousands of hungry people. The miracle went so "above and beyond" that they collected 12 basketloads of leftovers. A friend of mine suggested that would make one for every disciple to take home!

Coffee

The great wartime British prime minister Winston Churchill said, "The price of greatness is responsibility". Aspire to greatness, and make feeding the hungry your responsibility.

DB

Orange Juice

Take up the shield of faith, with which you can extinguish all the flaming arrows of the evil one.

Ephesians 6:16

You Gotta Have Faith

The Big Breakfast

Oh, it is such a slippery word, "faith". I know the picture with the cuddly kitten and the motto "Faith isn't faith until it's all you're holding onto". And I know the bit in the last Indiana Jones movie where he has to step out onto what appears to be nothing, but is in fact a computer-effects bridge (smart people, these Knights Templar).

Sometimes an organization will have a "statement of faith" that lists a whole load of stuff that you have to believe in order to be a Christian. I don't want to say that these things don't matter, just that believing certain things and having faith are different.

Faith is about how we respond to the voices in our head that say, "You can't do that, you'll make a fool of yourself. You'll get hurt. God will let you down. You can't trust him. You're useless, anyway – why do you think *you* can do it? You can't even sort out your own life! Just give up ..."

How do you respond to those voices? Most people in this world listen to them, and give up on life before it's even started. Our job is to reject these "flaming arrows of the evil one" and to step out into the unknown. Whoaaa!

Continental

In his book *Life after God,* Douglas Coupland has a character commenting on some blind people asking him to take their photograph. "They couldn't see, but they still believed in sight," he says. "I think that's a pretty cool attitude."

Coffee

Is there an area in your life where you need to step out in faith?

SH

Orange Juice

Now Peter was sitting out in the courtyard, and a servant girl came to him. "You also were with Jesus of Galilee," she said … "Your accent gives you away."

Matthew 26:69, 73

God Don't Make Junk

The Big Breakfast

God spoke with an accent. Have you ever thought about that? Jesus' home district, perhaps even the town of Nazareth that he came from, would have been identified immediately by those who heard him speak, because of his accent.

He was a Galilean. That meant Jesus was judged by some as a person of low position. He had a "common" accent. It gave away the fact that he was a very ordinary man. The religious leaders had decided it was impossible for a prophet to come from such common roots.

God may not have called you to be a prophet, but he has called you to be his child and that gives you enormous value. Don't ever believe you're a nobody, or that you're second-rate. There is no second-rate with God. Whatever your background, whatever your accent, you are very special. God has made sure of that by sending Jesus to die for you.

Continental

A kid from the New York Bronx wrote the following words on a card and set it on his desk: "I'm me, and I'm okay, 'cause God don't make junk!"

Coffee

Accept yourself today for who you are. Don't measure yourself by other people or what they expect of you. "God don't make junk," so feel special today. God thinks you are.

RS

Orange Juice

Delight yourself in the Lord and he will give you the desires of your heart.

Psalm 37:4 NIV

The Discipline of Delight

The Big Breakfast

I'm sure you've got a whole stack of excellent desires for your life. Some very laudable ones even – desires to find the right person to marry, to find the right career to do, even desires to serve God in some shape or form. We must never let these desires fade as age grows, lest we give in to mediocrity.

However, the flip side of having a heartfelt desire or vision is invariably frustration and disappointment. I read recently of one lucky tourist who inadvertently won 2,000,000 francs for being the 2,000,000th visitor to the Eiffel Tower. How must the person behind him in the queue have felt? Total disappointment, no doubt.

Maybe today you are disappointed with God because he just doesn't seem to make a difference. You've failed an exam that you worked and prayed so hard about, you didn't get that promotion, a special relationship has failed, you prayed for the sick on Sunday and they got a whole lot worse.

Truth is, you can't talk about being a Christian without talking about disappointment. Maybe the key is to put those good desires to one side for a period and get back to where that verse from Psalms starts: "Delight yourself in the Lord." Maybe … just maybe, God will pick those desires up and make them his desires for you.

Continental

The evangelist Smith Wigglesworth once said, "Great faith is a product of great fights. Great testimonies are an outcome of great tests. Great triumphs can only come after great trials." The reality is that the victory crown Jesus wore was a crown of thorns.

Coffee

The Bible says "don't be afraid" 366 times. That's one for every day of the year – even in a leap year! What a great place to start this new discipline of delight.

DB

Orange Juice

He reached down from on high and took hold of me; he drew me out of deep waters.

Psalm 18:16 NIV

Incarnation Street

The Big Breakfast

Ever dropped your car keys down a drain? More often than not, Mercy's Law dictates that they are not washed away, but land on a shelf not far below the drain-cover.

But Murphy's Law follows closely behind, dictating that they are too far away to reach. You can see them glinting in the shadows, but nothing you can do reaches them. A coat-hanger isn't long enough to hook them. Physical contortions aren't enough to get your arm through the grill of the drain-cover. And shouting at them generally achieves nothing.

You have only two options. You can abandon your keys. Or you can prise open the drain-cover and climb down. Only the second option will get your car started.

Even before Christ, the Bible anticipates the notion of God "reaching down" for us. When nothing else will save us, God himself takes the initiative to reach us. In the verse above the psalmist gives a trailer for the miracle of incarnation, when God not only lifts the drain-cover, but climbs down the ladder himself.

Continental

There is no place so low that God can't reach us. There is no water so deep that he can't draw us out. There is no current so strong that his grip will fail us.

Coffee

God of rescue and redemption, Christ of salvation and safety: reach out to all those who are lost in deep waters. May the strength of your arm and the miracle of incarnation save them.

GK

Orange Juice

And pray in the Spirit on all occasions with all kinds of prayers and requests. With this in mind, be alert and always keep on praying for all God's people.

Ephesians 6:18

You and Me Always, and Forever. . .

The Big Breakfast

A friend of mine has just come back from Wales, where he has been praying with Christians there who want to see God do more in their country. One of the things he said when he came back was, "I used to think that this 'praying without ceasing' thing wasn't really real, but this week I've just begun to touch that."

I was curious, so I asked him what it was like. "Oh, nothing too special," he said as he smiled at me. "Just feeling like God was with me all the time, so it made sense to talk to him about everything."

You may be reading this book while on a silent retreat in an ancient monastery, but I suspect you're more likely to be on a bus, sitting on the loo, or just coming out of unconsciousness as you struggle to get out of bed. If that's you, then don't despair: you can still "stay alert". Prayer *can* be conversations with friends, listening to beautiful music or even watching TV. Just take time every morning to remember that God is with you wherever you go, and imagine he's right next to you through the day. It might start as a discipline, but it can become completely "normal"!

Continental

Prayer is to the spirit what food is to the body: stop eating, and you will eventually die, for sure. But something strange happens on the way: stop eating for long enough, and you lose your appetite. You only get it back when you are actually dying. How hungry for God are you?

Coffee

Plan to pray somewhere new today. Perhaps while you sit on the bus you could pray for the people around you. Perhaps you could sit at your computer and write a prayer on it. Perhaps you could get outside at lunchtime and thank God for the beauty in the world. Praying in new places reminds us that God lives there too.

SH

Orange Juice

For to me, to live is Christ and to die is gain. If I am to go on living in the body, this will mean fruitful labor for me. Yet what shall I choose? I do not know! I am torn between the two: I desire to depart and be with Christ, which is better by far.

Philippians 1:21-23

Torn

The Big Breakfast

How can Paul talk like that? Has he no fear of death? I guess not. For me, I would choose to be alive on planet earth every time. I once saw a little ditty about a gravestone eulogy that said:

Remember, friend, when passing by,
As you are now so once was I.
As I am now soon you will be.
Prepare for death and follow me.

Someone etched this along the bottom:

To follow you I'm not content
Until I know which way you went!

The truth is that, as believers, we know where we are going. That's why we don't need to fear death. The great preacher D.L. Moody said, "Someday you will read in the papers that Moody is dead. Don't believe a word of it. At that moment I shall be more alive than I am now ... I was born in the flesh in 1837; I was born of the Spirit in 1855. That which is born of the flesh may die. That which is born of the Spirit shall live for ever."

Continental

"What no eye has seen, what no ear has heard, and what no human mind has conceived – these things God has prepared for those who love him" (1 Corinthians 2:9). If you were to give Steven Spielberg the brief to make a movie about heaven, then even his brilliantly creative mind could never begin to conceive the presentation God has ready to roll!

Coffee

I remember reading *Peter Pan* as a kid and being filled with hope when he says to his chums, "To die will be an awfully big adventure." You don't need to be afraid.

DB

Orange Juice

Two people owed money to a certain moneylender. One owed him 500 denarii, and the other 50. Neither of them had the money to pay him back, so he forgave the debts of both. Now which of them will love him more?

Luke 7:41-42

Drop the Debt

The Big Breakfast

Everybody should know about it: the campaign to drop the debt. Many developing countries are crippled by the massive interest payments they make every year to the developed countries. They are in trouble, though. They haven't enough revenue to pay the interest, never mind the money they owe. Meanwhile, their country's development doesn't happen. Education, health and industrial development are all held back. The campaign by a number of Christian charities to have the debt dropped, the slate wiped clean, has been quite successful. Governments have taken notice. Some of the debt has been dropped.

Jesus is telling a story here. It has a clear message about dropping debt. He tells the story to challenge the ungenerous heart of Simon the Pharisee, his host at dinner. Simon has watched the actions of a woman who knew she had done wrong, who also knew she had been forgiven and was now responding with gratitude by washing Jesus' feet with her hair. Simon missed this point altogether.

We are often unable to believe that the gift of God's forgiveness to us is a cancelled debt – just like the story; just like the deal with the developing countries. I wonder why.

Continental

Nothing we do can make God love us more. Nothing we do can make him love us less. He made his mind up about us before we were born.

Coffee

Do you sometimes privately wonder if you really need God's forgiveness as much as other people? Ask God to show you your heart.

RS

Orange Juice

For you created my inmost being; you knit me together in my mother's womb ... My frame was not hidden from you ... your eyes saw my unformed body.

Psalm 139:13, 14-16 NIV

The Making of a Man

The Big Breakfast

When Debbie was pregnant with our first son, we went for our 12-week scan at the local hospital. The doctor in the long white coat spread unnecessary amounts of what looked like hair gel on Mum's tum and began the scan. He showed no emotion. The total opposite was true of the doting parents. You could have wedged a pair of coat hangers into our mouths as we watched the images flicker up on to the screen. I could see the head and the little heart beating, the tiny fingers and tiny toes. I felt a tear of joy and wonder trickle down my cheek as I gazed in amazement at this 12-week-old baby who was now fully formed and ready to grow.

"Everything is normal," concluded the white coat.

"No it isn't," I insisted. He shot me a stare. "I have just peered into my wife's stomach and seen my 12-week-old child. That's not normal – it's utterly amazing!"

God didn't blink and you were made. He took time over you, knitting you together inside your mother's womb. He took time out for some quality control and let his own eyes see your body being formed. I even think he allowed a tear of joy to trickle down his holy cheek in amazement and wonder. Make you feel special?

Continental

Answer me this: there are six billion people alive on planet earth right now. How does God keep on managing to make every one so different? I mean, there can't be many more ways of arranging a nose, two eyes and a mouth. Yet he throws away the pattern every time and starts knitting again from scratch.

Coffee

I praise you because I am fearfully and wonderfully made; your works are wonderful, I know that full well.

Psalm 139:14 NIV

DB

Orange Juice

He rescued me from my powerful enemy, from my foes, who were too strong for me.

Psalm 18:17 NIV

The First Emergency Service

The Big Breakfast

There is no one harder to rescue than the person who thinks they are not in trouble. There is no one harder to help than the one who says, "I can handle it". Whatever experience the author of this psalm had been through, he was unafraid to admit his own limitations. The enemies *were* too strong.

How many of us get into difficulty when we underestimate the force of our enemies? Alcohol, drugs, debt, dysfunctional emotions and patterns of behaviour, sexual addictions – these and a thousand other forces can become too strong for us. Like river currents, these things start out in our lives at a strength we can swim against. But momentum builds; the currents grow stronger; we are drawn out of our depth. Before we realize it, we are being carried away.

Without outside help, our situation can only get worse. Rescue, in that moment, turns on our willingness to admit to our need of help. Pride fights against the admission of failure, but that admission may be the first, vital step towards rescue.

Continental

The successful human life is not the life that knows no weakness or failure and needs no help. It is the life that knows when to admit to weakness, when to acknowledge failure, and when to ask for help.

Coffee

God who reaches out to those in need, God who rescues those in trouble, God who gives strength to those whose enemies are strong – reach out to me this day.

GK

Orange Juice

Shortly before dawn Jesus went out to them, walking on the lake ... They were terrified ...

Jesus immediately said to them, "Take courage! It is I. Don't be afraid."

"Lord, if it's you," Peter replied, "tell me to come to you on the water."

Matthew 14:25-28

Carpe Diem

The Big Breakfast

My favourite film of all time is *Dead Poets Society* – it is pure inspiration for the soul. At the start of the film the new teacher, Mr Keating (played by Robin Williams), takes his new class into the great hall to view the trophies and old sepia pictures of Helton boys from an age past. "They are now food for worms, boys," Keating tells the class. "Listen closely as they whisper their legacy to you." As the boys lean in towards the glass cabinets, the teacher whispers these haunting words on their behalf: "*Carpe diem*. Seize the day. Make your lives extraordinary." As an old man, I don't want to look back on my life with nothing but regrets. I want to be a person who made life extraordinary. Who took risks once in a while.

Preachers are so good at knocking Peter for his lack of faith. I have heard them say, "If only he had kept his eyes on Jesus he would never have sunk." The truth is, he is the only person on planet earth, besides Jesus, who has ever walked on water. At least he got out of the boat while the rest missed out on making their lives extraordinary. "Then Peter got down out of the boat, walked on the water and came toward Jesus" (Matthew 14:29).

Continental

A good friend of mine once had the incredible privilege of interviewing Billy Graham in New York. He asked him for some words of wisdom from an older man to a younger. Billy Graham responded by simply saying, "I never knew it would go so quickly. I still feel eighteen years old. Just don't waste a moment of it." Where will the adventure of faith begin for you today?

Coffee

Don't you think that the idea of having to die without having lived is unbearable?

DB

Orange Juice

When Jacob awoke from his sleep, he thought, "Surely the Lord is in this place, and I was not aware of it." He was afraid and said, "How awesome is this place! This is none other than the house of God; this is the gate of heaven."

Genesis 28:16-17 *NIV*

The House

The Big Breakfast

Jacob had cheated big brother Esau, and now he's on the run, like many of us. He doesn't want to have to take responsibility for his actions, so he just goes AWOL. Then what happens? In the middle of nowhere, while he's asleep on a rock, Jacob dreams of heaven opening and stairs coming down and landing right next to him. What does he say? "Oh, this desert must be God's house, and I just didn't notice." Well, that's one way of looking at it. Jacob builds an altar and declares that this particular spot in the wilderness is the "gate of heaven".

According to research, about two out of every five people reading this will have had a similarly dramatic experience of the spiritual dimension in your life. Many of you have never told anyone about it, either because you think people will laugh at you or because you think it doesn't fit in with what you ought to believe. Well, that's what happened to Jacob. He was blown away. Because he hadn't talked to anyone else about his experience, he thought that that particular place was where God lived. Nope. God lives everywhere, but we can all experience him *as if* he lives right here in our living rooms.

Continental

After the philosopher Blaise Pascal had died, a paper dated 23 November 1654 was found in the lining of his coat. Here is an extract from it: "FIRE. God of Abraham, God of Jacob, not of the philosophers and scholars. Certainty. Certainty. Feeling. Joy. Peace."

Coffee

Wherever you are, imagine that you can see what Jacob saw: a staircase leading up to heaven, with angels going up and down on it. Take a minute to hold the image. Now talk to God about how you want him to be present in your life.

SH

Orange Juice

Jesus said to the woman, "Your faith has saved you; go in peace."

Luke 7:50

Spiritual Is Something
We Become

The Big Breakfast

What makes for a good life? TV soaps tell us that sex is the road to all that's good: life begins because of sex; childhood and adolescence are all about discovering it; being an adult is about getting as much of it as you can. So sex must save the world, right?

Well, if it's not sex, what is it? Climbing the corporate ladder? Acquiring a bigger and better car, house, family? Oh, not that either – although you may only admit that quietly, when you're by yourself.

Having a good job is not something to be knocked. They're hard to find, and even harder to keep. Getting on well is okay too, as long as it doesn't demand every second of every day to stay there. And sex, well that's pretty good thing as well, let's be honest.

None of it, though, is enough on its own. We need a relationship with God. Everybody is on a spiritual search these days. Jesus has proved so often that he is the one we're searching for.

Continental

During the 1950s, '60s and '70s, they tried to kill faith in God in many Eastern European countries. They couldn't. Faith is a gift from God.

Coffee

We're all seeking spiritual experience today. Faith in God and Jesus will take us way beyond mere experience and into a relationship. Pass that good news on.

RS

Orange Juice

Do not wear yourself out to get rich; have the wisdom to show restraint.

Proverbs 23:4 NIV

The Antidote

The Big Breakfast

This is going to hurt, but "wounds from a friend" and all that ... Let me tell you a tough truth. Materialism is the biggest challenge to this generation. We've got sucked in bad. The advertisers have convinced us that luxuries are necessities and that we just can't do without them. They have filled our lives with so much stuff that our priorities have drifted off course. It is getting almost impossible to keep up unless you have an endless supply of time and money.

The only antidote to spiralling materialism is giving, and giving extravagantly. Trouble is, our generation is renowned as being the poorest givers ever. Lasting contentment doesn't come from getting more things. John D. Rockefeller was asked how much money a person needs to be truly happy. "Just a little bit more!" he said. Being satisfied means having fewer wants, not "wearing ourselves out to get rich".

A friend of mine managed to break the cycle of buying clothes she didn't really need by holding a twelve-month clothes fast. She saved a heap of wardrobe space and a stack of cash. She got a bigger buzz than shopping by giving a lot of it away to the poor. It sometimes takes drastic measures to get our eyes fixed on Jesus again (Hebrews 12:2).

Continental

"Whoever sows sparingly will also reap sparingly, and whoever sows generously will also reap generously. Each of you should give what you have decided in your heart to give, not reluctantly or under compulsion, for God loves a cheerful giver" (2 Corinthians 9:6-7). Paul's advice to the Corinthian church is as valid now as it was then. What have you cheerfully decided to give this week?

Coffee

Consider this: "Don't wear yourself out trying to get rich; restrain yourself! Riches disappear in the blink of an eye; wealth sprouts wings and flies off into the wild blue yonder" (Proverbs 23:4 MSG).

DB

Orange Juice

They confronted me in the day of my disaster, but the Lord was my support.

Psalm 18:18 NIV

More Than a Bad-Hair Day

The Big Breakfast

When I was mourning the death of my mother, I managed to keep my emotions at bay for several days. I was deeply shocked, but life somehow went on.

A few days after her death, though, I went to get something from the freezer in the garage. I discovered that one of the children had left the freezer door open overnight: it had defrosted, and all the food was ruined. All that was left of its frozenness was a growing puddle on the floor. Somehow, looking at this small-scale disaster, all my inner pain rose to the surface. I collapsed in tears of grief and exhaustion and spent the next 24 hours in bed.

It took a domestic crisis to break my defenses, to force me to face up to my grief. Sometimes it takes a day of disaster to get us to deal with our problems. It is not until we are desperate, with our enemies gloating over us, that we cry for help. But that's where God is. Like the most dramatic of movie plot-lines, it is just when all is lost that all is found.

Continental

Don't be surprised that God allows the day of disaster to overtake you. Very often, it is the very thing you need to force a rescue.

Coffee

Thank you, Father, that you are with us when disaster falls. On the worst days, you mount your rescue plans. It is when we are most lost that you are most able to save us.

GK

Orange Juice
You will know the truth, and the truth will set you free.

John 8:32

Freedom for the Mind

The Big Breakfast
I have had the opportunity to visit Prague a number of times in the last few years, and of all the beautiful things in that most beautiful city, my favourite single thing is a simple inscription in the huge cathedral next to Prague Castle. It reads, "Truth will win". This simple statement was made by the early Protestant martyr Jan Huss, whose statue now dominates the main square of the city. What's great about the inscription is that the cathedral is Roman Catholic, and has been put there not as some perverse statement of victory, but as a sign of unity.

Truth is not nearly as "cool" as freedom. Truth is hard and uncompromising, whereas freedom is big and cuddly and, by definition, wouldn't want to bother you with anything that might change your life. Yet Jesus is saying here that the truth will set us free. How? Well, ask someone who's trying to make a difficult decision, and they'll tell you how much the truth could set them free.

Although I still have many doubts, I am basically sure of Jesus and his message. This sets me free on so many levels: free to get on with my life without having to worry about its meaning all the time; free to make mistakes and know I'm forgiven; free to love, knowing I am loved. The list goes on.

Continental
Meister Eckhart said, "What is truth? Truth is something so noble that if God could turn aside from it, I could keep to the truth and let God go." What do you think?

Coffee
If you have doubts and questions, why not start dealing with them by talking to God about them and resolving to study until you know the truth?

SH

Orange Juice

Blessed is the man who listens to me, watching daily at my doors, waiting at my doorway. For whoever finds me finds life and receives favor from the Lord.

Proverbs 8:34-35 NIV

The Lost Art of Reflection

The Big Breakfast

Reflection – the art of waiting on God – is the lost art of the twenty-first century. A business friend of mine told me how he used to rush out of the house every morning, drive bumper to bumper and arrive at the office just on time. His daily routine sounded frantic. Then one fine summer's day he had a late morning meeting and therefore didn't have quite the same manic rush. He left later, eased off on the accelerator and lifted his head a little. Despite having made the same daily journey for years, he noticed trees and wildlife he had never seen before. He even pulled the car off the road and took time to stop and breathe the fresh air. He thought of his life, his work, his family and his faith. He discovered a moment of quiet reflection that has revolutionized his life. Now it has become a regular practice. Pull over for a moment and let me ask you some questions that will lead you into the wonder of personal reflection.

How is your walk with God today? What books are stimulating your thinking? How are things going with your partner? How are your energy levels? Are you pleased with your physical fitness? Is sexual temptation getting the better of you? When did you last do something just for fun? If Satan was to trip you, how would he do it? Do you like yourself?

Continental

A.W. Tozer writes in *The Pursuit of God*, "It is important that we get still to wait on God. And it is best that we get alone, preferably with our Bible outstretched before us. Then we will draw near to God and begin to hear him speak to us in our hearts."

Coffee

Blessed the man, blessed the woman, who listens to me, awake and ready for me each morning ... as I start my day's work.

Proverbs 8:34-35 MSG

DB

Orange Juice

Hear, O LORD, and answer me, for I am poor and needy.
Guard my life, for I am devoted to you.

Psalm 86:1-2 NIV

Guard My Life

The Big Breakfast

Where do you go when there's trouble in your life? Perhaps
a better question to ask is *who* do you go to? Is it God? "Of
course I go to God," I hear you say. At least, that's the theory.

The truth is, we're not very good at trusting God when
things go wrong. Suddenly he seems very far away, and pretty hard to get close to.
"Was he ever there in the first place?" we begin to ask ourselves. Then those irritating doubts creep in.

We may not question his existence, but we do get mad at him. "Why has he
allowed this to happen to me?" We feel let down. It seems so unfair. You've been
living the Christian life as best you can, so why has this happened?

There may not be a clear reason for your trouble – circumstances that were
beyond your control; someone else's bad decision which left you hurt; being in the
wrong place at the wrong time. In this psalm, David is in deep trouble. God still
figures for him, despite that.

Continental

David's need is raw and desperate when he writes this psalm.
He remains devoted to God nonetheless.

Coffee

When life gets tough, don't be tempted to blame God. This is
Satan's favourite sidetrack.

RS

Orange Juice

He brought me out into a spacious place; he rescued me because he delighted in me.

Psalm 18:19 NIV

Welcome to the Wide Open Country

The Big Breakfast

Marlboro Country is that fictitious part of America where a screen-wide sky is always blue; where cow-hands with chiselled chins are dressed in Gap clothes; where all is space and freedom, and you can't see the cancer wards or hear the coughing.

The persistence and power of the image is evidence of the survival of an ancient idea, familiar to the Hebrew mind – the idea of salvation as a "wide open space". An open landscape spoke to the Hebrews of new opportunities and challenges; of freedom from slavery; of the promise of prosperity and fruitfulness. The same sense of hope and adventure that opened up the American West is present in this abiding image of "a spacious place".

Salvation is not just about buying a ticket to heaven – it is about living an eternal kind of life now. It is a life of new possibilities; a life brimming with potential. For those who have made mistakes in the past, it is a fresh beginning. For those who have never known creative freedom, it is a land of opportunity.

Continental

Salvation is not a turnstile that you pass through: it is a landscape that opens up before you.

Coffee

Wide open is the landscape into which my God has brought me. Wide open is my heart to new beginnings.

GK

Orange Juice

Do you not know that in a race all the runners run, but only one gets the prize? Run in such a way as to get the prize.

1 Corinthians 9:24

Finishing Strong

The Big Breakfast

I went Grand Prix go-karting recently at a circuit not too far away. At the end of a dangerous day's driving, I ended up a dismal eleventh out of 40 other drivers. I still felt like Damon Hill as I sped bravely around the circuit at a top speed of 60 m.p.h. On the way home I realized that real Formula 1 cars reach speeds of 200 m.p.h. I suddenly felt less brave.

One of the greatest drivers of all time was Ayrton Senna who once drove a remarkable race, taking the chequered flag after starting sixteenth on the grid. No one rated his chances of getting on the winner's podium – no one, that is, except Senna himself.

You see, it is not really how you start the race that counts. It's all about finishing. Maybe you've started the race of life well, speeding down the back straight at 200 m.p.h. Or maybe you spun off into the "kitty litter" at the first bend. The question is, will you be there at the chequered flag?

Now is the time to invest in the kind of things that will ensure we'll be there for the long haul.

Earning more money and buying more things won't guarantee we finish this race well. Maybe it's time to buy into some life skills such as peace-making or self-control.

Continental

Are the constant pit stops of life wearing you out at the moment? Remember this: "Though outwardly we are wasting away, yet inwardly we are being renewed day by day. For our light and momentary troubles are achieving for us an eternal glory that far outweighs them all" (2 Corinthians 4:16-17).

Coffee

The author Rudyard Kipling wrote, "If you can fill the unforgiving minute / with sixty seconds' worth of distance run / yours is the Earth and everything that's in it. / And – what is more – you'll be a man, my son!"

DB

Orange Juice

But thanks be to God that, though you used to be slaves to sin, you have come to obey from your heart the pattern of teaching that has now claimed your allegiance. You have been set free from sin and have become slaves to righteousness.

Romans 6:17-18

Freedom for the Soul

The Big Breakfast

Through my church work I know lots of young people who are exploring the world and trying to work out who they are and how they should live. What they want more than anything else is the freedom to do this. What they don't want is me or anyone else telling them how they should live.

I think I could cope with this, if it wasn't for the obvious fact that they are not free at all. Here are some real quotes: "I can't help going out with him." "Everybody else is doing it, so you can't expect me to be different." "It just comes naturally." "It's who I am, so how can it be wrong?"

To me all these people are slaves – slaves to sin and to what the Bible calls "the flesh" – the desires that do sometimes seem to rule us. The kind of freedom that Paul is talking about here is extremely unfashionable in today's world, because somehow we've got the message that the only way to be happy is to indulge every desire we have to the max. Unfortunately, what this has created in our society is a whole class of thrill addicts, who need to take more drugs, have more sex, get more drunk as, each time, the thrill decreases. We are not made to live this way. God wants us to be free to rule over our nature, not to be ruled by it. In this way we become "slaves to righteousness".

Continental

"Sin is a small word with *I* in the middle." In today's world of "greed is good" and "every man for himself", how can you break the mould and live for God and others?

Coffee

Spend some time bringing your own struggles with sin to God. Focus on his forgiveness, and ask him to fill you with his Holy Spirit so you can live for him.

SH

Orange Juice

Guard my life, for I am devoted to you. You are my God; save your servant who trusts in you.

Psalm 86:2 NIV

Confidence in God

The Big Breakfast

Many times in the Psalms we see King David in trouble. We know from reading his life story in 1 and 2 Samuel that his troubles often came through doing what God had asked him to do. Does that seem strange? On other occasions, of course, he got into real bother all by himself. The Bathsheba affair, for example, was entirely his own fault.

Why didn't David give up? Why didn't he tell God to let him off the hook? You can picture it. David had been called by God as a young boy. He had accepted the call. Further down the line, he spent years living as a fugitive, on the run from a mad king. Is that what it means to be called by God? What about that promise of "abundant life"? Where is it now?

David is devoted to God because he is totally convinced about God's commitment to him. That's his secret. His life is clearly under threat. With awesome confidence, David appeals to God. He trusts him.

Continental

Perhaps one reason for David's rock-solid confidence in God can be found in their history. Verse 13 of Psalm 86 allows us to see that God has been there for him before: "For great is your love toward me; you have delivered me from the depths of the grave."

Coffee

Take time to think back over your life with God. Write down all the times when he was there for you. You've got a history with God too.

RS

Orange Juice
I am making a way in the desert and streams in the wasteland.

Isaiah 43:19 NIV

Uncage the Camel

The Big Breakfast
I love this apocryphal story about two camels conversing. One sunny day, little Baby Camel asked big Mummy Camel why camels have such big feet, such long eyelashes and such huge humps. "Well, darling," said Mum wisely, "when we are in the desert we need big feet to walk over the shifting sand. We need long eyelashes to protect our eyes from sandstorms, and big humps to carry water on long journeys."

"So, Mummy," replied the baby camel, "why are we in London Zoo?"

Good question. You see camels were designed to live in the deserts, not in concrete cages. You and I have a faith that is designed to work best in the deserts and wastelands of our world. Not cooped up in the cage of Church. Maybe that's why it goes stale so often.

Where are the wastelands of your world? Is it the local council estate, the shopping centre, the retirement homes, the health clinic? The list is endless. Unless we are prepared to journey to these places, often places where we feel like we don't belong, we will never uncage the gospel and let it loose on a broken world.

Continental
Martin Luther King Jr once said, "A man has not started living until he can rise above the narrow confines of his own existence to the broader concerns of others." Is it time to take your eyes off yourself and start looking to the needs of others?

Coffee
A note was passed around a crowd as they gathered in the capital prior to a revolution to overthrow an evil dictator. It read simply: "If not now, when? If not us, who?"

DB

Orange Juice
Give us today our daily bread.

Matthew 6:11

A Day At a Time

The Big Breakfast
A question much loved by time-management gurus is "How do you eat an elephant?" The answer is "One steak at a time". A similar principle operates in this prayer. How do you tackle the huge mountain of needs and challenges that confronts you when you pray? One day at a time.

Elsewhere Jesus has said, "Each day has enough trouble of its own" (Matthew 6:34), and while there is an emphasis in this petition on *bread,* there is also an emphasis on it being *daily.* This helps us to pray by giving us focus.

By all means talk to God about all the things that you have to talk to him about. By all means look to the future. But when it comes to asking for specific outcomes and answers – ask yourself, What outcomes do I need today? What is there in your day's schedule that cries out for the intervention of God? Keep tomorrow's troubles under lock and key until the dawn releases them. What do you need *today?*

Continental
Don't let the concerns of tomorrow rob you of the joys of today.

Coffee
Creator God, you made a world that functions in days and nights. You fed your people in the desert on bread for one day at a time. Help me to understand the rhythm of the days, and to dedicate my prayers – and my action – to the needs of each new day.

GK

Orange Juice

They devoted themselves to the apostles' teaching and to
fellowship, to the breaking of bread and to prayer.

Acts 2:42

Doing the Business

The Big Breakfast

What's the point of church? Well, I don't think it has to do
with any of the things mentioned in this passage. I think it's to
obey the commands that Jesus gave us when he left us: to
make disciples (Matthew 28:18-20).

The truth is that when the disciples – now called apostles – thought about how
they were going to make disciples, church is what happened. Our job is to bring
people into the Kingdom of God, and church is the best way of doing it. Jesus only
mentioned church twice: once to institute Peter as its leader; and once to give advice
on how to sort out problems. He wasn't that bothered with church in itself, but he
was bothered with teaching people to obey his commands.

Church is about enabling you and your Christian friends to do God's business in
the world more effectively. Sometimes church becomes a self-feeding institution, but
that doesn't mean it's a bad idea. Find me a Christian who can do without teaching,
fellowship, communion and prayer, and I'll eat my Bible. These things are meant to
be done together, so that we can get on with the rest of our lives in the power of
the Holy Spirit.

Continental

"The church is the only co-operative society which exists for
the benefit of its non-members."

Archbishop Temple

Coffee

Think about the most important places where you receive
teaching, fellowship, communion/worship and prayer. How can
you improve these meetings/relationships for the benefit of others
and yourself?

SH

Orange Juice

You are the salt of the earth. But if the salt loses its saltiness, how can it be made salty again?... You are the light of the world ... let your light shine before others, that they may see your good deeds and praise your Father in heaven.

Matthew 5:13-16

Stop the Rot

The Big Breakfast

A friend of mine was asked to pick up an African evangelist from Heathrow Airport and transport him to various venues around the country to preach. He said he had never met such a fearless evangelist. One time, they stopped for lunch at a roadside café and my friend's African guest stood to his feet, quieted the crowd of customers and gave a short gospel message. He even got a rousing round of applause!

I just could never do that. Does that make me a failure in sharing my faith? Absolutely not. Jesus never said, "Go and be salt" or "You must be a light in a dark world". He said, "You *are* salt" and "You *are* light". In other words, you will not be able to help yourself being the preserving salt as you live in a society where values continue to rot away. You can't help lighting up the right path for a generation that stumbles around in the darkness. Doesn't that take the guilt of failed evangelistic attempts away? You see, some are called to preach to stadiums full of people and others to roadside cafés, whereas most are called to rush headlong into our world, enjoy what is good and allow the taste and brightness of our God-filled lives to change what is bad.

Continental

The eminent theologian John Stott once said, "It is time for Christians to stop blaming the meat of society for going rotten when the preserving salt has been taken out."

Coffee

St Francis of Assisi had a similar thought when he told his followers, "Preach the gospel at all times and if necessary, use words."

DB

Orange Juice

You are forgiving and good, O Lord, abounding in love to all who call to you.

Psalm 86:5 NIV

Get Going with God

The Big Breakfast

Have you ever really, really messed up on something? Got it so badly wrong that you want to die with shame? The worst bit is knowing that your own stubbornness got you into this mess. You just had to do it your way.

Then there is our world. How did some of that get so messed up? Try listing the good stuff. Now do the same for the bad stuff. We both know which list will be the longer one! It's really all down to stubborn people who just have to do things their way. Nature and God himself have warned us. Giving God complete control, however, is a bit too scary. Somehow we need to hold on, to keep some of the control for ourselves.

We don't see this kind of holding back from God as sin, do we? As far as we're concerned, sin is killing someone, or sleeping with someone else's wife. But holding back from God is sin too.

Continental

The Psalms are full of verses like today's. God is patiently waiting for us to come to him, to direct things for us.

Coffee

Are you too proud to invite God to lead the charge in your life? Or are you perhaps too stupid? "Lord, I'm sorry" is the place to start. Then get going with God.

RS

Orange Juice

For since the creation of the world God's invisible qualities – his eternal power and divine nature – have been clearly seen, being understood from what has been made.

Romans 1:20

Physical Graffiti

The Big Breakfast

Graffiti artists throughout the world are known for their driving desire – their all-consuming passion – to sign their name in every conceivable place.

Spray-can in hand, they will climb unclimbable walls, hang over death-drop bridges and risk all on electrified train tracks – just to make their mark on the world. There is an artistic motivation, but the primary goal is self-identification. A graffiti artist's "tag" is her or his life. An unsigned work is unthinkable – anonymity defeats the object of the exercise.

For Paul, this same motivation is visible in the works of God. It is not enough to make a good universe – everywhere and in everything, he has signed his work. His tag is everywhere – he can be identified by his work. The creation is not only a masterpiece: it is a signed masterpiece.

Continental

The Invisible Man in the classic story of the same name can only be seen by the clothes he wears. Only when bandages are wrapped around his face can the contours of his features be seen. In the same way, God "clothes" himself in the created world – so that we can see him.

Coffee

To God the Father, who created the world; to God the Son, who redeemed the world; to God the Holy Spirit, who sustains the world; be all praise and glory, now and forever.

GK

Orange Juice
Go! I am sending you out like lambs among wolves.

Luke 10:3

Uncage the Bunny

The Big Breakfast
The biggest mistake I made in my marriage was allowing Debbie to convince me to buy a rabbit. She said we were just going to "pop in for a look" and I ended up walking out with a cute, lop-eared baby bunny that we named Dylan. However, after a couple of years (and the birth of our first son) Dylan started to get neglected. I thought about letting him go in a field near our house, but the vet said Dylan would be dead within a day: "He is a tamed rabbit. He can no longer survive outside his cage."

I think that is exactly what the Church has done with young people. We have sold you a taming faith that means you can no longer survive in the habitat you were created for. We've told you to get converted from your sin but haven't helped you in getting fully converted to the purposes of God. That purpose is not simply to survive in a cage called Church but to thrive in the place we call the real world.

As a church leader, I want to say sorry and to ask you to leave a different legacy to the next generation. Prepare them to live like lambs in a pack of wolves.

Continental
Business guru Charles Handy is one of my favourite authors. He asks this question in *The Age of Paradox*: if we didn't exist, would we recreate ourselves and what would this new creation look like? Ask this of your church community.

Coffee
Martin Luther King Jr once said, "This generation will not be judged for the evil bad people have done but for the appalling silence of the good." Shout this forgotten message out loud to a new generation.

DB

Orange Juice

Some people have got out of the habit of meeting for worship, but we must not do that. We should keep on encouraging each other, especially since you know that the day of the Lord's coming is getting closer.

Hebrews 10:25 CEV

The Bible's Quitters

The Big Breakfast

You may not believe it, but the Bible has the habit of telling us to do something and then admitting that no one's ever achieved it before. Here, right after all those great letters from Paul about how church should be, we have a letter to a church that is failing and falling apart. Seems silly, doesn't it? If you want to convince us that we can do this church thing, why admit that the people who started it didn't succeed?

But that's the great thing about the Bible: it pulls absolutely no punches. There's no way of reading the letter to the Hebrews (we're not sure who wrote it) except as a big kick up the behind to a church on the verge of giving up. Some of the Christians for whom this letter was written had obviously already stopped going to church. Probably the local mall was open on Sunday and there was a great Christians versus Lions match on the TV that afternoon.

Continental

I once had the pleasure of chatting to one of Britain's major church leaders. We were talking about how church was really boring, and he suddenly said, "I don't know what the problem is with 'boring'. Lots of things in life are boring, but we just get on with them." What do you think?

Coffee

If you are a church member, why not do something extra for the good of others rather than yourself? If you don't go to church, how about giving it a try? (If you used to go, how about trying it again?) Talk to God about what you're going to do.

SH

Orange Juice

In the day of my trouble I will call to you, for you will answer me.

Psalm 86:7 NIV

God Will Answer

The Big Breakfast

Heidí Wichlinski, talking a while ago about being engaged to Formula I driver David Coulthard, was philosophical about the danger David is in every time he steps into his custom-built McLaren car. "I try not to think about the danger ... if something goes wrong, well, it's destiny." I guess that's one way to survive. The other David, the one writing this psalm, has opted instead for trusting God at such times.

David had many good reasons for trusting God. He had a long memory, for a start. God had always shown up when he needed him. Remember the David and Goliath story? The young shepherd boy, going out to fight the armour-plated giant. It was a crazy thing to do, but David won. We discover why in I Samuel 17:45 (NIV). David said to Goliath, "I come against you in the name of the Lord Almighty ..." History had taught David to trust God, to go to him when the heat was on.

Another reason for David's rock-solid confidence in God was that he *knew* God – really knew him. When you know somebody properly, trust is easy.

Continental

This sort of talk sounds rather silly today. Nobody believes in God like that any more. Or do they?

Coffee

Whatever is happening in your life today, no matter how tough it is, God will help you sort it out – if you ask him.

RS

Orange Juice

But the fruit of the Spirit is love, joy, peace, patience, kindness, goodness, faithfulness, gentleness and self-control. Against such things there is no law.

Galatians 5:22-23

Get Fruity

The Big Breakfast

I became a Christian in my mid-teens. I had been putting it off for ages because I had a fear that when I got saved I would have to become like some of the people in church. I didn't suit white socks and sandals, and tank tops were definitely not my style! I didn't want to sing in the choir. My understanding of what a Christian looked like was a total misunderstanding. The best description that I've found is the fruit list above – that's what a real believer looks like.

So how can we tell if the spiritual fruit in our lives is growing well? Ask yourself this question: when life bumps into you, what spills out?

I have many heroes in the faith, some dead, some very much alive. One such person brimming with life is an older and wiser man called Joel. I spent four weeks travelling the country with him, watching him and learning from him. He has a very responsible job and when life bumped into him (and boy, did it come crashing in at times) do you know what always spilt out? You got it, love, joy, peace …

See what comes tumbling out of you today as life comes tumbling in.

Continental

How many fruit can you count? No, this is not *Sesame Street.* I want to make a point. Paul says "fruit" (singular) not "fruits" (plural). In the supermarket you can choose to put some fruit in your basket and leave others on the shelf. In God's economy, he wants to develop our whole character.

Coffee

Reread this character list of Paul's. Identify where you feel weak. Make a deliberate choice to take it off the shelf today and ask God to help you work on it.

DB

Orange Juice

Although they claimed to be wise, they became fools and exchanged the glory of the immortal God for images made to look like mortal human beings and birds and animals and reptiles.

Romans 1:22-23

Bone Idol

The Big Breakfast

The battle that runs through the whole of the Old Testament – and is brought here by Paul into the New – is the battle of God versus idols. The worship of the one God, Creator of all, was constantly challenged in Hebrew history by the worship of idols – mini-gods singled out from the creation itself.

This is the irony of God's vulnerability. In his overwhelming desire to come close to us, he has given us created objects of surpassing beauty and majesty – objects that reflect his character, but on a human scale. He gives us things he knows we will like. But we reward him by making those objects themselves our idols. We worship the gift and not the Giver.

Idolatry comes about when anything God has given is made absolute – whether it is animals and birds, or wealth and power. Everything in the creation can be used as a means toward the worship of God, but anything that becomes the end in itself is an idol. When the objects of our lives become the objects of our worship, our grasp on God is diminished.

Continental

To worship is to ascribe worth – to attribute ultimate value. The idols of our culture and lives are those things that we deem ultimately worthwhile – and money, sex and power account for most of them!

Coffee

Worship belongs to you alone, our God. Praise is due to your name only. Where I have fixed my affections on gods that are no gods at all, forgive me, and receive the rightful worship of my heart.

GK

Orange Juice

First, God chose some people to be apostles and prophets and teachers for the church. But he also chose some to work miracles or heal the sick or help others or be leaders or speak different kinds of languages.

1 Corinthians 12:28 CEV

The Kennedy Factor

The Big Breakfast

It is one of the most over-used and misused quotes ever. John F. Kennedy speaks to the American people and says, "Ask not what your country can do for you, but what you can do for your country." Great speech. Only they killed him. Probably not because of that speech, but certainly because he wanted to do things differently.

Imagine a similar revolution in church: people coming together as a community wanting to serve each other and bring their gifts for the enhancement of others' lives. No more, "What do we pay the minister for?" No more, "I got absolutely nothing from that worship time." No more, "I just come to receive, I don't feel called to give anything right now."

Well, the interesting news is that this seems to be pretty much God's plan. Okay, so maybe you might feel (like me) a little intimidated with being an apostle, a prophet or a worker of miracles, but try getting out of being a teacher, a helper, an administrator. If you look through the Bible you'll find there are gifts of making things, of being friendly, of lots of things that we all do. That means, of course, that we have the same responsibility to put our tuppence-worth into the pot as everyone else.

Continental

"No one can have God for a Father who refuses to have the church for a mother."

St Augustine

Coffee

Is there something you could give to your church? It could be a specific gift, or time, or money, or a commitment to pray. Take a minute to think of something that you have, or can do, that would help your church.

SH

Orange Juice

Remove the chains of prisoners who are chained unjustly. Free those who are abused! Share your food with everyone who is hungry; share your home with the poor and homeless ... Then your light will shine like the dawning sun.

Isaiah 58:6-8 CEV

Revival Guaranteed

The Big Breakfast

What a great description of revival! How I long for the day when the light of the gospel rises in the darkness of this godless age and the dim witness of the Church becomes as brilliant as the sunshine in the middle of the day. I want to see that day in this nation before I die.

So how do we get there? More fervent prayer meetings? Wouldn't do any harm. More electric worship services? Sounds appealing. More seeker-sensitive presentations? We need them too.

Hang on. Read the Isaiah verse again, and the answer shines through clearly: the good stuff from heaven comes down when we start spending ourselves on behalf of the hungry and satisfying the needs of the oppressed. One translation suggests we "lavish on the poor the same affection we lavish on ourselves."

The truth is, some often look over the sea to other revivals but wouldn't dream of looking over our street to the lonely pensioner or stressed single mum.

Continental

I know there is a God-given passion in you to be part of a revival generation, and I think I know how you can get there. Hunt out those in need, the hungry and the voiceless, the poor and the disenfranchised. Spend yourself on them and satisfy their needs. Then your light will shine ...

Coffee

"The righteous care about justice for the poor, but the wicked have no such concern" (Proverbs 29:7 NIV). Which are you – righteous or wicked?

DB

Orange Juice
All the nations you have made will come and worship before you, O Lord; they will bring glory to your name.

Psalm 86:9 NIV

Are You Shaky?

The Big Breakfast
There were wars all over the place, and vast numbers of people who didn't believe in God, and natural disasters and political upheavals. We're surrounded by the same kind of situations today. This, then, is a pretty bold statement. "All the nations will worship the Lord!" Has David got his head in the sand?

What David knew, by faith, was that one day everybody would worship God. The thing that troubles me is how little of David's passion we seem to have now. It is as if we believe the hype that "the religion that's true for you isn't necessarily true for me". We Christians apologize for daring to suggest that God is the only true God and other people ought to commit themselves to him! Satan is smart. He knows that he is on to a winner if he can make Christians a little shaky about God's exclusive right to the world's worship.

Continental
The world will one day know that God is the only true and living God. Don't allow yourself to be convinced otherwise.

Coffee
Pray that God will increase your faith in him and your passion for him. The world needs Christians who are consumed with both.

RS

Orange Juice

God gave them over in the sinful desires of their hearts to sexual impurity for the degrading of their bodies with one another.

Romans 1:24

Ideas Have Legs

The Big Breakfast

There is a popular caricature of the believer, and indeed of Paul, in which he begins to salivate with excitement at the judgement of others. His greatest pleasure is to describe the sinfulness of pleasure. A Christian is defined, in this view, as someone who is "haunted by the terrible fear that somebody, somewhere, might be enjoying themselves".

But difficult as today's verse may be, this is a misrepresentation of its meaning. What Paul is saying, in essence, is that "ideas have legs" – that they take you somewhere. What begins as belief flows into behaviour. If you misconstrue the intentions of the Creator, you will misuse the creation, including your own body.

There *is* a degrading side to human behaviour – and to human sexuality. Ask the victim of abuse, or the prostitute forced by poverty and circumstance to sell orgasms to strangers, or the child drawn into the dark web of paedophile exploitation. We don't like to think it of ourselves, but we are capable of the darkest of thoughts and actions.

Continental

There are two dangers in our approach to human sin. The first is to see darkness and degradation in every act – but the second is to pretend that there is no darkness in us at all.

Coffee

Creator God, we do harm to ourselves and to one another when we let the dark side of our nature hold sway. Give us the courage and strength to walk in the light.

GK

Orange Juice

Large crowds were traveling with Jesus, and turning to them he said: "If anyone comes to me and does not hate father and mother, wife and children, brothers and sisters – yes, even life itself – such a person cannot be my disciple."

Luke 14:25-26

Hate Your Mum and Dad

The Big Breakfast

At first reading, I guess that just about counts me out as a disciple. I love my folks, my wife and my kids. I don't hate them. And doesn't the Bible say somewhere we should honour our parents and love our wives and not exasperate our children? What was Jesus getting at here?

The answer is at the start of the verse. Jesus wasn't into hangers-on. He was every marketing man's nightmare, with no interest in big numbers. He wanted to whittle down a large crowd of sightseers. He wanted people who were committed.

I don't believe for one moment that he meant us to treat our closest family with hate. In trying to lose the uncommitted from the crowd, he suggests that his followers must have no higher priority in life than loving him. Debbie is my life and my everything. I am devoted to my two boys and would travel to the ends of the earth for them. Mum and Dad are my two greatest heroes. Yet my devotion to Jesus must always come before them. Tough one, isn't it?

Continental

How do your close personal relationships line up against the Master? Can you honestly say that in a competition he would come first every time? Is Jesus really the number one relationship you have? If not, *you cannot be his disciple.*

Coffee

"My son, give up self and you will find me. Lose the right to choose and the right to own, and you will know nothing but gain. Abundant grace will be heaped upon you the moment you surrender your own will and do not claim it back."

Thomas à Kempis

DB

Orange Juice

"Those who do not carry their cross and follow me cannot be my disciples."

Luke 14:27

Dying to Live

The Big Breakfast

We're still on the subject of being committed Christ-followers. Jesus shaves some more onlookers off the large crowd following him with another outrageous statement. Carrying a cross in his day was a familiar picture of crucifixion and death. Was he really saying his followers had to take their own lives? Don't be daft. To "come with Jesus" means to die to our way of life and live for his. It means sacrificing unhealthy ambition and to "offer your bodies as living sacrifices" (Romans 12:1).

A youth leader of mine from years back became the youngest elder our church had ever seen. The following week, his boss offered him a partnership in the business. It would mean a huge salary, a Jag and a big house in the country. It would also mean giving up all his time to the company. What should he do? He felt so called by God to serve the youth of our church, but the business offer was tempting. This verse from Luke convinced him that to be Christ's disciple he had to give up his own way for God's way. He said no to the boss and yes to the King. Following Christ means the highest level of commitment. We are not called to a Sunday-school picnic but to a bloody battleground.

Continental

The kind of radical devotion this verse demands is rare today. Maybe that's why, in Jesus' day, many of his disciples said, "This is a hard teaching" when they heard it. As a result of it, many withdrew and were not walking with him any more (John 6:60, 66). Have you got what it takes to call yourself a disciple of Jesus today?

Coffee

John Wesley was asked what he would do if tomorrow were his last day on earth. His answer showed the contentment he had with his devotion to God – "Nothing different". Are you content with your walk as you reflect today?

DB

Orange Juice

"Those of you who do not give up everything you have cannot be my disciples."

Luke 14:33

Give It All Away

The Big Breakfast

This is a real toughie. I so wish Jesus had never said it. You see, I love my stuff. I can't image life without my Xbox or my CD player. And where would I be without my beautiful bottle of Issey Myake aftershave or my mobile phone with built-in daily planner? Maybe it is this attitude that so often waters down the intensity of my life with Christ.

This "giving it all up" statement from Jesus must have lost loads from the crowd. It was designed to weed out the spectators from the participators. Get the perspective right, though. I don't think he means that we can't possess anything, but that we mustn't let things possess us. To be a real disciple means to hold stuff loosely.

What do you need to hold a little less tight? What comes between you and your maker? You see, I don't think that all believers automatically become disciples. It's one thing to believe, but it's another to believe enough to let go of relationships that get in the way, ambition that distracts and the stuff that shifts our priorities. The author and pastor Philip Yancey said, "The poor, not the rich, have perseverance for life. Why? Because they have nothing else to hang on to."

Continental

So which one of the words in this verse don't you understand? It's blatantly clear, isn't it? Let go of things and grab on to God. In *The Pursuit of God,* A.W. Tozer said, "There is no doubt that this possessive clinging to things is one of the most harmful habits of life. Because it is so natural it is rarely recognized for the evil that it is."

Coffee

Rudyard Kipling remarked, in an address to university students, "As you go through life, don't seek for fame, or money, or for power, because one day you will meet a man who cares for none of these things, and then you will realize how poor you are."

DB

Orange Juice

Just as a body, though one, has many parts, but all its many parts form one body, so it is with Christ. For we were all baptized by one Spirit so as to form one body.

1 Corinthians 12:12-13

A Biology Lesson

The Big Breakfast

When we're conceived, we start life as one cell. Inside that cell is all the information that tells all future cells what each one is going to be (the DNA). So, one cell finds out that it's going to be a liver cell, while another finds out that it's going to be a skin cell, and so on.

As Christians we are all cells in the body of Christ; we are just given different roles in the body. Yet each cell has all the information needed for every cell in the body. Even if we feel like the corn on the left big toe of the body of Jesus, we have within us the Holy Spirit – God – so that from us a whole body can grow.

Apart from in *The Addams Family*, I've never actually seen a hand alive on its own. That's a fairly important body principle. No matter how wonderful a person you are, you are never going to survive on your own. We live off each other, and there's no point denying it. Just find another member of the body (an individual or a church) who can transmit God's life to you, and hold on for dear life – I mean that literally!

Continental

"The church is one body – you cannot touch a toe without affecting the whole body."

Friedrich Tholuck

Coffee

How can you improve your connectedness to the rest of the body? Listen to God today and see if there is something particular you can do.

SH

Orange Juice

Teach me your way, O Lord, and I will walk in your truth; give me an undivided heart, that I may fear your name.

Psalm 86:11 NIV

Tell Me Your Truth. . .

The Big Breakfast

The psalmist David is pretty clear about one thing. He knows how great God is, and he knows that without God's help he will get it wrong. He needs God to teach him constantly. He needs God to bring him back again and again to the words that are the truth.

I don't hear that word, "truth", used very often these days, at least not in the way David is using it. David is talking about a truth that comes from God. However, the word on the street these days is this: "Tell me your truth and I'll tell you mine." The Manic Street Preachers used that as a title of a song. The Street Preachers aren't on their own. Today everybody seems to believe that things are only true if they feel true.

The Bible is very clear when it tells us to look to God for truth. He alone can help us see it. Here David asks God to teach him. "Reveal the truth to me, Lord."

Continental

What "truth" is David looking for? I imagine he wants to know how God would like things done, and he's ready to follow that.

Coffee

Lord, I have to say it is very hard sometimes to know what's true and what isn't. Help me find your truth, and live by it.

RS

Orange Juice

But you, keep your head in all situations, endure hardship, do the work of an evangelist, discharge all the duties of your ministry.

2 Timothy 4:5

Don't Quit

The Big Breakfast

Sound advice from Paul the apostle to his young apprentice, Timothy. He had been telling him how others were throwing the towel in but that he needed a bit of endurance.

Did you ever see the classic film *Chariots of Fire*? It's a great movie that charts the young Scottish missionary Eric Liddell as he trains for the Olympics. His sister tries to encourage him to hang up his running shoes and go to the Chinese mission field as his father and grandfather did. "Aye, Jen," he says, "I know that God made me to be a missionary and that is what I will be. But he also made me fast, and when I run I feel his pleasure."

You may not be a famous missionary or have a teacher like Paul. You may not fill stadiums with your preaching like Billy Graham or rewrite a nation's history like Martin Luther King Jr, but where do you feel the pleasure of God? Is it in the way you do your job or the way you have been able to share your faith? Do you feel God's pleasure as you serve others, expecting nothing in return? Even if nobody else says thanks, your endurance does not go unnoticed in heaven. Feel his pleasure today.

Continental

Winston Churchill was once asked to speak to the students at Oxford University. As you can imagine, the hall was packed as the great man extinguished his famous cigar and stood to the podium. His most memorable speech ever lasted just four words: "Young people – don't quit!"

Coffee

I know you've thought of giving up, but don't – endure some more.

DB

Orange Juice

They exchanged the truth of God for a lie, and worshiped and served created things rather than the Creator – who is for ever praised. Amen.

Romans 1:25

The Cosmic Ratings War

The Big Breakfast

When competing TV companies seek to assess their relative popularity, they look at two figures: total audience and audience share. They want to know how many TV sets are switched on at a given moment and, of these, how many are tuned to their programmes.

But imagine if TV sets had no off-switch; if they remained on, tuned to *something*, day and night. There would be no neutral sets to discard; audience share would be everything.

This is the picture that Paul paints of worship. Human beings are created for worship, just as we are created for love. There is no off-switch. Worship flows naturally from us to whatever object we make absolute. The screens of our lives are never blank. They broadcast our worship day and night. It is not a matter of *whether* we worship but of *what* we worship.

If you don't serve God, you will serve other gods. In the cosmic ratings war, if you are not tuned in to God's signals, you are watching something else.

Continental

It has been said that those who stop believing in God may set out to believe in nothing, but end up believing in anything.

Coffee

On the screen of my life, let the worship of God be seen day and night. On the screen of my life, let the name of God get all the credit. On the screen of my life, may God and God alone receive my praise.

GK

Orange Juice

Then Peter got down out of the boat, walked on the water and came toward Jesus. But when he saw the wind, he was afraid and, beginning to sink, cried out, "Lord, save me!"

Matthew 14:29-30

Dealing with Doubt

The Big Breakfast

Peter, the guy who ended up as one of the major founders of the Church, is found here *not* walking on water. He is just like us, spectacularly achieving the miraculous and then spectacularly messing up. He had it, but he lost it. Sound familiar? Sometimes I read about great heroes of the Christian faith and I feel terrible. I believe all those bits where they do amazing things, but where they admit to doubts, I seem to brush over them, thinking to myself, "Oh, but they don't have doubts like *I* do". Which is, of course, rubbish. You can't put your trust in God unless there is a chance he might fail you – otherwise it wouldn't be trust. You can't have faith without doubt.

A psychologist once surveyed the congregation of a large, successful church. It was the kind of church where God seemed to be doing amazing things and all the people had their lives sorted out. However, in the privacy of a questionnaire, over 80 per cent admitted to serious doubts. For the vast majority of these people, no one else in the church knew about their struggles, because as they looked out at this wonderful, successful congregation, they imagined that they must be the only one among thousands who didn't get it. You can't help thinking, "If only ..."

Continental

"Faith which does not doubt is dead faith."

Miguel de Unamuno

Coffee

Telling yourself and God the truth can be a hard experience, but you cannot deal with your doubts until you face them head on. Sometimes writing God a letter allows you a comfortable way of expressing things that don't come easily.

SH

Orange Juice

The LORD your God is with you ... He will take great delight in you, he will quiet you with his love, he will rejoice over you with singing.

Zephaniah 3:17 NIV

Your Name Is the Title Track

The Big Breakfast

I thought I'd better read Zephaniah's book just in case I bump into him in heaven. It could be so embarrassing otherwise. Actually, I'm glad I did. It has given me an insight into the character of God that I had never thought about before.

What a great picture of a God who "rejoices over you with singing". He gets up in the morning (figuratively speaking, you understand), throws open the windows of heaven and sings about you. It is your name that he repeats in the chorus. It is your name that features in the refrain. In fact, it is your name that is the title track of the whole album God has written about you which he plays for his pleasure.

If that thought doesn't "quiet you with his love", I don't know what will. If you can indulge me and allow your imagination to be stretched a little, you could almost picture a part of God's character like that of a doting grandfather. He has your picture on his mantelpiece and is always trying to twist the conversation with the angels around to talking about you. He's so proud of you.

So if you hear a heavenly song or some heavenly chatter this morning, it just might be about you.

Continental

The three most awesome words you will ever hear running through your brain and filtering down into the emotional centre of your heart are "God loves you". Let me say it again – "God loves you". He loves you enough never to leave you, even though you may walk away from him. His great delight is in you, right now, as you read this book.

Coffee

I love this line that my friend Mark wrote in a worship song: "My Father, music from your lips puts the beat back into my heart and the joy back into my walk." Rock on!

DB

Orange Juice

Teach me your way, O Lord, and I will walk in your truth; give me an undivided heart, that I may fear your name.

Psalm 86:11 NIV

An Undivided Heart

The Big Breakfast

What is David talking about in the second half of this verse? An "undivided heart"? What in the world is that?

David is clued into himself – that is, he knows he has two sides. One side of him longs for God, really loves him, and knows that God is good, kind and compassionate. This side of him knows that only in God will he discover how to live. David wants to follow that side of himself.

But he has another side too. This is the side that got him into trouble when he saw Bathsheba taking a bath. Just look how far he fell on that one: adultery, lies, deceit, murder. Yes, all of that. David knows himself. He isn't going to be fooled by anyone who tells him he's not a bad guy really!

"Give me an undivided heart." These are the words of someone who really understands God and himself.

Continental

In Proverbs 1:7 (NIV) we are told, "The fear of the Lord is the beginning of knowledge." "Fear" in this context does not mean terror – it means deep respect.

Coffee

Lord, I want to know myself properly, to know when to be happy about myself and when I'm off course. Like David, I want to have a heart that pleases you.

RS

Orange Juice

Shout it aloud, do not hold back. Raise your voice like a trumpet.

Isaiah 58:1 NIV

There's *Every* Need to Shout

The Big Breakfast

The depth of suffering and need in our world is vast. It is easy to become, in the words of the Canadian singer Bruce Cockburn, "paralysed in the face of it all". We stand in the face of an ocean of need and wonder what difference our small splash could possibly make.

For many of us, the paralysis becomes permanent and we sink into inaction, pursuing a Christian faith that has a lot to do with church and singing, and very little to do with the real needs of those who suffer.

But Isaiah, at the very outset of his Manifesto for Revival, offers us hope. Even if you can't *do* very much, you can shout, he says. You have a voice: you can raise it. And every voice, no matter how insignificant, can become in the hands of God a rallying cry. For the Hebrews, a public trumpet call was the equivalent of an air-raid siren – it stopped people in their tracks.

Use your voice, Isaiah says. Change begins when you say what you see.

Continental

Throughout the Bible, there is an emphasis on the power, for good or ill, of words. Here, Isaiah sees words, and our ability to use them, as a powerful weapon we can use on behalf of the poor.

Coffee

God of justice and peace, sometimes you whisper, and sometimes you raise your voice to make me hear. Teach me, in my own life, when it is right to stay silent, and when it is right to shout.

GK

Orange Juice

Who may ascend the hill of the LORD? Who may stand in his holy place? He who has clean hands and a pure heart, who does not lift up his soul to an idol ... such is the generation of those who seek him.

Psalm 24:3-6 NIV

Clean Hands, Pure Heart

The Big Breakfast

Have you ever had one of those moments where the lights just seem to come on for the first time on the really obvious things of life? I had been speaking at a big youth festival and was well into my second week when the band *Delirious?*
arrived. It was a most memorable gig as 5,000 of us squashed into a crowded cowshed to see them perform.

God grabbed my attention through one simple song introduction by Martin Smith: "Who can get up to where God is? Who can stand in his holy place?" He left a pause. My heart leapt inside. That's where I wanted to be. He gave the answer. "Only those of us with clean hands and pure hearts."

That's it! That's why I so often feel in the valley rather than on the mountain top. My hands are dirty. The things I get my hands into are often not pleasing to God. My heart is not clean. I haven't guarded my heart well. I have allowed my eyes to watch, my ears to hear and my mouth to talk about stuff that is just not pure. No wonder I rarely walk up the holy mountain to where my God is.

Continental

The two hallmarks of a God-seeking generation are purity of action and holiness of character. If your eyes are the windows to your heart, what stuff should you be averting your gaze from today? If your hands are the tools of your service, what things should you be letting go of?

Coffee

You'll do best by filling your minds and meditating on things true, noble, reputable, authentic, compelling, gracious — the best, not worst; the beautiful, not the ugly; things to praise, not things to curse.

Philippians 4:8 MSG

DB

Orange Juice

Be merciful to those who doubt.

Jude 22

And the Punishment for Doubt Is . . .

The Big Breakfast

People don't read the book of Jude too often. It is so small that it doesn't seem worthy of consideration. But here's a little gem that lots of Christians need to check out, because, let's face it, our response to Christians who doubt is often less than merciful.

There are a number of common responses: "Oh no, you can't doubt that, because the Bible says it's true." "Oh no, that means that you're going to lose your faith and leave the church." "Oh no, this is happening because there's sin in your life."

Sometimes these statements can be true, but the point is that when people own up to doubt, they don't get mercy, they get "Oh no". This makes it really, really hard to own up to what's actually going on inside us, so that we can end up feeling out on the edge of faith without even wanting to. A friend of mine who is struggling with her faith came to see me with all kinds of weird books that a guy had given her, and I suddenly realized that if I wasn't going to help her work through her outlook on life, there are plenty of others who will.

Continental

"There lives more faith in honest doubt.
Believe me, than in half the creeds."

Alfred, Lord Tennyson

Coffee

Think about how you may have reacted in the past to a fellow Christian who you felt had "let you down". If you were not merciful, repent and resolve to be more like Jesus in dealing with doubt in the future.

SH

Orange Juice

The arrogant are attacking me, O God; a band of ruthless men seeks my life – men without regard for you.

Psalm 86:14 NIV

Über-Celebrity

The Big Breakfast

I read an article in which Victoria Beckham, Posh Spice of the music group Spice Girls, was talking about life as an "über-celebrity". A what? Well, it means being up there in a stratosphere all of your own. Apparently, even Jennifer Aniston and Madonna don't quite make it.

There are many perks, but the downside of having reached these dizzy heights is that everybody – at least in your own country – has an opinion about you. You get hassle on the street and wild stories written about you in the press. Victoria talks at one point about her hatred of a particular TV presenter who, on a weekly basis, "rips us to pieces".

I wonder if David was experiencing this kind of personal attack when he wrote Psalm 86. It is more than likely. David was being hounded by a mad king who was determined to destroy him. There may have been different reasons for the attacks, but they had the same impact on David personally as on Victoria Beckham. We don't know what Victoria does to deal with it. David went to God.

Continental

Is someone or something attacking you right now, pushing you, and your faith, right to the wire? Go to God. Don't keep trying to work it out for yourself.

Coffee

Lord, if I'm honest, I hang on by my fingernails at times like these. Thank you for your strength which stops them from breaking.

RS

Orange Juice

Honor your father and your mother, so that you may live long in the land the Lord your God is giving you.

Exodus 20:12 NIV

Bringing Up Your Parents

The Big Breakfast

Mark Twain once said something like, "When I was fourteen my father was so stupid I could hardly bear him. But by the time I was twenty-one I was so amazed at how much he had learned in seven years." Often it is only in hindsight that we can give our folks the honour and respect for the influence they have had on our lives. While they are far from perfect, they deserve our gratitude. I love my mum and dad dearly, but I was thirty years old before I really told them how grateful I am for them. I wrote them a letter trying to express it. The reply from my dad is a treasured memory that I carry with me wherever I go. Here's an extract: "Well son, what a wonderful letter to receive, reading it certainly brought tears to our eyes ... I must say we have often wondered what you thought of us as parents ... I think back to those summer holidays, we did have some fun didn't we, but then I always had fun with you."

What have you always wanted to say to honour your folks? Say it soon, before it's too late.

Continental

This commandment is the only one with a promise attached. If we treat our parents with honour and respect we will live a long life. Find a way today to be creative in your affection for your folks.

Coffee

Billy Graham once said that "nobody ever said on their death bed that they wished they'd spent more time at the office". If you still can, plan this week to change your schedule and pick up the phone, write or even call round to see your parents.

DB

Orange Juice

You cannot fast as you do today and expect your voice to be heard on high.

Isaiah 58:4 NIV

The Fast Show

The Big Breakfast

Isaiah faced a generation that knew all about religious observance. Like the Pharisees in Jesus' day, they knew how to put on a show. Praying, singing, fasting and public displays of humility were all in their lexicon of spiritual performance.

Unlike other generations in the history of Israel, they were not slow to admit their need of God. They knew they stood in need of the renewing presence of God. It was the behavioural dimension of faith that they were less sure of. Reducing Judaism to rituals and public actions, they continued, outside the sphere of public religion, to flaunt God's laws. In the way they did business, in the way they dealt with conflicts and differences of opinion, in the way they treated slaves and workers, they paid no heed to the laws of God.

Religion they knew. Private morality they understood. But public justice was a foreign language to them. It is not difficult to see how many of us – in part or in full – fit much the same profile today.

Continental

Prayer without practice is pretence; worship without works is wasted. The call of God is to obedience – in every sphere of life.

Coffee

God of Isaiah and of Jesus, you send prophets to call your people back to faith. Raise up prophets in our generation – and when they come, give us the courage to listen.

GK

Orange Juice

Jesus...said to Thomas, "Put your finger here; see my hands. Reach out your hand and put it into my side. Stop doubting and believe."

John 20:26-27

The Power of Touch

The Big Breakfast

It's not fair, is it? There are only a few people who have had the privilege of having their doubts completely blown out of the water by meeting the living God. The echo of that encounter with the risen Jesus is what powers the church to this day: those guys really saw him! And that started the biggest movement the human race has ever seen.

I have quite a few friends who became what I call "semi-retired Christians" in their twenties. It was too hard to believe, or too hard to do, so they just "toned down" all the difficult bits. Today many of them seem nostalgic for a time when they once had a reason to live.

Without the chance of putting a hand in Jesus' side, it's hard to say to such people, "Stop doubting and believe," but I think there are times when that is the right response. Doubt can make your life turn to ice, freezing every decision and every way forward. Sometimes you need to jump out in faith and step onto what looks like thin ice ... then you'll know if your doubts are well founded. If God is real, he can cope with the odd challenge!

Continental

"Faith is the daring of the soul to go farther than it can see."

William Clarke

Coffee

Spend a little bit of time in quiet, thinking about big decisions you have to make and/or scary things you have to do. Can you agree with God to take a leap of faith? What would that mean for you in the situation you are thinking of?

SH

Orange Juice
Everyone who wants to live a godly life in Christ Jesus will be persecuted.

2 Timothy 3:12

The Genuine Article

The Big Breakfast
Sometimes the best encouragement to one's soul is to hear it how it truly is. So here goes: the truth is if you love Jesus you will be persecuted. If "to live a godly life" is your pursuit then pain along the path is a certainty. For some it is no more than a loss of pride, but for others it can mean the loss of life.

The true story is told of a priest in communist Russia who one Sabbath was leading the service of the weary faithful when the ancient building began to echo with the sound of kalashnikov rifles loading up. The meeting had been disturbed by a group of militiamen and their angry-sounding leader. He told the crowd that any Christian left in the building would be shot in two minutes. Some hurried out. Others remained, holding firm to what they believed. Eventually the militia leader told the trembling few that he wasn't going to shoot anyone today; he needed to hear about Jesus and he wanted to make sure he heard it from the "genuine article".

Persecution at any level will serve as a good test to our commitment. Be honest: are you really the "genuine article" to the people closest to you?

Continental
I think the most painful persecution comes from your own kind. Why does the Army of Christ enjoy shooting itself in the foot, stabbing itself in the back and tearing itself apart in civil war? Don't provoke persecution, but expect it. Don't fight each other, but support each other in life's daily battles.

Coffee
One of the few Greek words I know is *martorea* – the Greek word for witness. You will know something of the pain of being a "martyr" as you witness to a broken world, but you're in great company.

DB

Orange Juice

Give me a sign of your goodness, that my enemies may see it and be put to shame, for you, O Lord, have helped me and comforted me.

Psalm 86:17 NIV

The Sign of Leo

The Big Breakfast

The psalm is written by David – the guy who was so sure God wouldn't let him down that he took on a giant with nothing but a slingshot and some stones. What has happened to his confidence? Why is he asking God for a sign?

Actually, the sign isn't for David's benefit at all. It is for others. It is for the people who don't believe in God, to let them see who God is. The thing is, these "signs" are there all the time, even today.

Tony Blair, the British Prime Minister, became a father for the fourth time not so long ago. This was the first baby to be born to a serving Prime Minister in Britain for 150 years. The safe arrival of baby Leo was a sign of God's goodness, just as it is with the safe arrival of every newborn baby. God is there, and has been there all along. It is a sign of his goodness.

We're back to faith again. The signs get missed because God has been pushed out of the picture. In their spiritual search, people are looking in other directions these days. God is good, though. He keeps on demonstrating his love, even when we are not looking.

Continental

You don't acquire trust and confidence in God overnight. It often takes us to hit some hard spots before our vision clears and we see him as he really is.

Coffee

Pray for your friends today, that these wonderful "signs" of God all around them might open their eyes to him, so that they see him as he really is.

RS

Orange Juice
Is not this the kind of fasting I have chosen: to loose the chains of injustice and untie the cords of the yoke, to set the oppressed free and break every yoke?

Isaiah 58:6 NIV

Fast Forward

The Big Breakfast
In contrast to the outwardly impressive fasts of the religious Hebrews, Isaiah paints a radical picture of a different kind of fasting. Like an expert surgeon, he takes a scalpel to the world-view of his peers. He forges a dynamic link that is entirely new to them – between the "spiritual" and the behavioural dimensions of faith.

"It is an act of prayer," he says, "to obey. It is an act of worship to seek justice." Worship that pleases God is not about words and music and religious observance – it is about lives of obedience that bring the will of God to the earth. The liberation of the oppressed is a celebration of the God of Israel. Feeding the hungry is feasting on God. Loving my neighbour is an act of worship.

Isaiah goes on to outline the areas in which action is required. Spiritual disciplines are tough and take years to master, and so will lifestyle change! This is not an easier way, but a better way – and it is God's way.

Continental
Fasting is easy to understand, but hard to do. Justice is exactly the same. We find it easy to understand and explain the need for justice, but harder by far to deliver it.

Coffee
Teach us, Creator God, to offer the obedience of our daily lives and the liberation of the poor as acts of sacrifice and praise.

GK

Orange Juice

I will build my church, and the gates of death will not overcome it.

Matthew 16:18

God's Theatre on Earth

The Big Breakfast

Jesus' gritty determination seemed to rub off on the early Church. It is almost as if you need some attitude to follow Christ. There is a sense in which God loves angry young people. Take the big boys of the Bible. What have Moses, David and Paul got in common? Well, for one, they were all murderers. Moses killed a man, David slept with another man's wife, then bumped him off to cover his tracks, and Paul was a serial killer. Yet God took their passions and shaped them for good, not bad. They were not content to be merely spectators; they had to be at the heart of the action.

The truth of Jesus' words was plain to see for the early Church. He would build his church. It all starts with 120 in the upper room. Peter then preaches the first sermon of the new Church and 3,000 get added. Acts 2:47 says God added people daily (that's at least 365 a year!). In the end Luke gives up counting and says, "thousands of Jews have believed". Are you a season-ticket spectator in the stands or do you regularly make the team on the field? Maybe it's time for a change. Maybe it's time to nail your colours to the mast.

Continental

Did you know that there are more churches in the UK than all the supermarkets of the big chains put together? It is obvious that the Church is present in nearly every community. It is also obvious that just being there is not enough. It will take action on our part to see Jesus "build his church" in our nation – wherever we live.

Coffee

Pop icon Boy George wrote of a trip to church that bored him silly: "The Church badly needs a facelift because it's God's theatre on earth and he should be packing them in." His conclusion is eye-opening, isn't it?

DB

Orange Juice

Then your light will break forth like the dawn, and your healing will quickly appear; then your righteousness will go before you, and the glory of the Lord will be your rear guard.

Isaiah 58:8 NIV

Recipe for Revival!

The Big Breakfast

There are surprisingly few biblical passages that speak of the type of experience that the contemporary Church might call *revival*. Isaiah 58 is one of the few. It captures something of the hunger, the longing for God's blessing. It offers compelling and intriguing pictures of what that blessing might mean. And it offers a reliable, tried-and-tested, God-backed route *into* that blessing.

The surprising fact, for those who associate revival more with increased prayer, is that the key given here is *obedience,* not prayer. These people had prayed and fasted. They even had organized nationwide days of repentance and supplication. When it came to asking God for revival, they were up there with the best of us. But they were ignoring the poor. Their words were many – their actions few. And it wasn't enough.

Perhaps there are times when God's switchboard is so jammed with the cries of the poor that our petty calls for blessing don't get through.

Continental

When we cry for God to act – when we long for his blessing – are these times when action, not supplication, is the key?

Coffee

"Many are the words we speak; many are the songs we sing; many kinds of offering – now to live the life!"

worship leader Matt Redman

GK

Orange Juice

Those who say, "I know him," but do not do what he commands are liars, and the truth is not in them.

1 John 2:4

Living a Lie?

The Big Breakfast

I have often heard it said that young people today don't know how to worship. Rubbish! Just one look at the bedroom wall of most teenagers will show you how well they worship pop stars, fashion icons and sporting heroes alike. We all need heroes to follow and role models to emulate – it's how we were made.

When I was twelve, Johan Cruyff was captain of Holland in football's World Cup finals. His amazing footwork and goal-scoring talent made me want to be more like him. I rushed out and bought an orange football shirt, parted my hair to the left and copied his moves from the TV. I knew he was the greatest footballer in the world and I wanted to play like him.

You see, what I believed about Cruyff affected the way I behaved in the game. The same has to be true about God. What we really believe about God affects the way we live in the game of life. The calibre of our belief is measured by the quality of our behaviour. I don't want to live a lie. I want my everyday life to match up to my beliefs. I want to take God seriously and for others to see this lived out before them.

Continental

If you want to do a little self-test on your walk with God, first ask yourself if you behave in a way that shows your beliefs. Then ask someone else to see if your mouth matches your actions. This kind of pruning may be painful, but it is the only way to grow good fruit.

Coffee

Would you buy hair-restorer from a bald man? Of course not. His appearance undermines the product. Would your friends buy into Jesus? Only if your appearance matches up to your words. Take a look in the mirror today.

DB

Orange Juice

When the builders had finished laying the foundation of the temple, the priests put on their robes and blew trumpets in honor of the Lord ... They praised the Lord and gave thanks ... singing: "The Lord is good! His faithful love for Israel will last forever."

Ezra 3:10-11 CEV

Foundations

The Big Breakfast

Ezra and Nehemiah are not the best-known books in the Bible, by a long way. However, I think these two books have a lot to say to us in the West. They describe a situation in which a small group of people faithful to God (the Jews returning from exile in Babylon) is trying to re-establish their religion in their homeland. It is not the most exciting story ever – lots of building, basically – but it is about the hard slog that many of us feel as we try to sort out being a Christian in what is often called a post-Christian environment.

Here, early on in the book of Ezra, the first few people have returned and have built the foundation of a new temple for God. Even though the temple isn't even near finished, they take the opportunity to get all their fancy gear on and praise God.

This is not always something I do – praising God when things aren't sorted out yet. God has to answer *all* my prayers before he gets any thanks from me! But reading this passage, I feel that maybe our worship today has lost something. It seems like these guys were desperate to worship God and did so at the earliest opportunity. Hmm ... how often do I feel like that?

Continental

The famous Westminster Confession asks the question, "What is the chief end of man?" The answer is: "To glorify God and enjoy him forever."

Coffee

Praise God! If you can't find the words, just use the phrase in today's passage – "His faithful love for Israel will last for ever" – replacing "Israel" with "me" or "us".

SH

Orange Juice

"Love the Lord your God with all your heart and with all your soul and with all your strength and with all your mind"; and, "Love your neighbor as yourself."

Luke 10:27

Heart Surgery

The Big Breakfast

Have you ever tried to lose weight? Most of us girls have. I know guys are weight-watchers too, but it is a girly thing to talk about it! It is a real grind. Unless you're one of those naturally disciplined people, you'll lose a few pounds, put them on again, then lose them again. Maybe for something special you might stick with the low-fat routine for long enough to make a real difference.

Loving God with all our heart is a good deal more important than losing weight. In fact, it is the essence of what being a Christian is all about. Yet on our own, by our own effort, to love God like this is impossible. We may reckon we love God like this, when something good happens, but unfortunately we get cold again very quickly. We need a bit of spiritual heart surgery to be able to give God the love he's really longing for. When we invite Jesus to journey with us, to stop us in our tracks and deal with the me-centred stuff, then this kind of love for God and our neighbour can grow.

Continental

The order Jesus gives us – of loving God and then our neighbour – is important. Our inner spirituality, the heart stuff, will show itself in how we treat others.

Coffee

Who is your neighbour? Your neighbour is anyone you meet. When we let God perform heart surgery on us, we find we care for that neighbour deeply.

RS

Orange Juice

A bruised reed he will not break, and a smoldering wick he will not snuff out.

Isaiah 42:3 NIV

Breaking Point

The Big Breakfast

It doesn't take a prophet to tell you that life can so often be a bruising experience. Girls I have fallen head-over-heels in love with have unceremoniously dumped me. I have had friends murder my character with unwise words. I have wept till it hurts at the loss of loved ones, been unemployed, been kicked out of a church, failed all my exams and made the most stupid decisions possible.

Maybe you've had similar experiences. You once knew what it was to stand strong and tall, but now you are bent double and bruised by the pain of life. Maybe you still feel that way today. The memories of previous traumas, and the tumours that still eat away at your soul, cause you to hang your head and let your shoulders drop.

If you feel at breaking point, you can be sure that even when others fail you or your own stupid lifestyle choices let you down, Jesus won't break you. He will only build you up again. His voice will be one of concern and care, not condemnation. His love will not end in hurt but in healing.

Why run away from that kind of support? Why leave him out in the cold when he wants to welcome us back into the warm?

Continental

It seems to me that the older you get the easier it is to let the flame of faith smolder away. Do you remember being proud of a faith that burnt bright? They called you a fanatic and you didn't care. What was it that caused the flame to become a flickering light? Take Paul's advice and begin again to "fan into flame the gift of God, which is in you".

Coffee

Think about *The Message's* new spin on this verse, which says of Jesus: "He won't walk over anyone's feelings, he won't push you into a corner."

DB

Orange Juice

If you spend yourselves in behalf of the hungry and satisfy the needs of the oppressed, then your light will rise in the darkness, and your night will become like the noonday.

Isaiah 58:10 NIV

Reversal of Fortune

The Big Breakfast

Fridge doors used to be there for paintings brought home from play-school and for scribbled shopping-lists. Not any more. It is now possible to buy themed collections of magnetic words from which to fashion all manner of creative writing – from love-letters and poetry to household messages: "Your dinner's in the dog."

Imagine that you had such a word-set made up of the language of 21st-century advertising. From the slogans bombarding us each day, you might construct a common message: "Spend all you have on yourself, until *your* needs are satisfied."

Now imagine that Isaiah comes to call. You leave him alone in the kitchen for a few moments, and before you know it he has messed with the words to turn the message round. With a subtle change of word order, he has switched the polarity on consumer culture: "Don't spend *on* yourself, but spend *yourself*. And don't stop spending until the needs of the oppressed are met." It is with such simple words that revolutions are constructed.

Continental

What would the impact be if you started to keep track of your spending of yourself as closely as you track your spending *on* yourself?

Coffee

Dear God, I enjoy spending. I take pleasure in the anticipation of buying something for myself. It is one of the things that most satisfies me. Help me, selfless God, to spend myself with equal joy.

GK

Orange Juice

After this I looked and there before me was a great multitude
that no one could count, from every nation, tribe, people and
language, standing before the throne in front of the Lamb ...
And they cried out in a loud voice: "Salvation belongs to our
God, who sits on the throne, and to the Lamb."

Revelation 7:9-10

Jesus, Come On!

The Big Breakfast

There's this guy I know called Caleb who, whenever I meet
him or hear of him, is always shouting, "Come on!" He has a
specially designed T-shirt which proclaims, "Freedom, come
on!" But his favourite "come on" is "Jesus, come on!" You can't
really argue with that – it's how the Bible ends, in the last few verses of Revelation,
only most translations put it more politely: "Come, Lord Jesus." But since I met Caleb,
I prefer his version.

I can't wait to see what John saw. I guess it's what most of us hope for: all kinds
of people – all races, nations, classes, you name it – worshipping God together. I
realize that to some this will sound like hell: all those people who are *not like* me in
heaven, everyone equal. But those people, if they make it, will have to enjoy it or try
the other place.

Maybe that's the Devil's strategy ... get us all to hate each other now so we won't
be able to enjoy heaven when we get there? But he's gonna lose. We're going to
meet Jesus face to face and look into his eyes and finally know what love is. I can't
wait for the party; Jesus, come on!

Continental

We should give God the same place in our hearts that he holds
in the universe.

Coffee

Remember all that Jesus has done for you – you might want to
write things down – and thank him, in whatever way seems right.

SH

Orange Juice

We … glory in our sufferings, because we know that suffering produces perseverance; perseverance, character; and character, hope. And hope does not put us to shame.

Romans 5:3-5

Fat Sheep Survive

The Big Breakfast

How daft can you get? Who ever heard of being glad about suffering? Where can you find the good in the bad? How can hard times be something to be thankful for?

I once stayed with a Lebanese family in Beirut. Before the civil war my host had worked in finance and had travelled regularly on business to the Scottish Highlands. I asked him how life in the city of Beirut differed from that in the Scottish hills. "Easy," he said. "It's the sheep!" He explained that his overriding memory of the craggy Scottish hillsides was of how fat the sheep were compared to the skinny, lop-eared versions that populate the parched hills of his country. "Put a sheep from Beirut on a mountainside near the lochs and it would be dead by the next morning," he said. And he was right. The harsh Scottish winters had somehow toughened the sheep for survival.

We rejoice in life's storms because each one produces the perseverance to weather the next one as the very character of Jesus is pressed into us. Spending your days merely roaming the sun-drenched hillsides of life and choosing to escape the dark clouds will eventually lead to ruin at the first sight of a storm.

Continental

Do you know how a precious and rare pearl is formed in an oyster? I am told that it's the constant grinding and irritation of tiny grains of sand that get inside its shell. Instead of rejecting it, the oyster encases it in layers of beauty to form a pearl. Will you let your life today grind you down or will you allow it to produce beauty in your character?

Coffee

C.S. Lewis once wrote, "God whispers in our conscience, speaks in our silence and shouts in our sufferings. It is his megaphone to rouse a deaf world."

DB

Orange Juice

A man was going down from Jerusalem to Jericho, when he fell into the hands of robbers. They stripped him of his clothes, beat him and went away, leaving him half dead. A priest happened to be going down the same road, and when he saw the man, he passed by on the other side. So too, a Levite, when he came to the place and saw him, passed by on the other side.

Luke 10:30-32

Too Busy

The Big Breakfast

An American psychologist, fascinated by the story of the Good Samaritan, once did a research project among theological students at Princeton College in New Jersey. He asked four students, known to be popular among their peers and of general good nature, to prepare a sermon on the Good Samaritan. They each had to give their sermon at a set place and time. The psychologist then arranged for four other students to pretend to be ill or injured at some point close to the venue where the sermons were to be given. Every one of the theological students rushed past the sick student without stopping. They all said they had an important sermon to give and hadn't time to help. Even the psychologist was shocked.

In the story Jesus told, the Levite, another religious man, also passed by the beaten man. Was he too busy? Perhaps he thought he was. It is also possible that he was a copycat. The priest hadn't stopped, so why should he? The Jericho road was very straight, and the Levite would have seen the priest. He knew he hadn't stopped.

Continental

There are always good reasons for not doing the right thing. At least we can convince ourselves in this way. The question is, what would Jesus have done?

Coffee

Lord Jesus, help me to be influenced and guided by your values and standards in everything I do.

RS

Orange Juice

The Samaritan went to him, poured olive oil and wine on his wounds and bandaged them.

Luke 10:34 NCV

Hidden Meanings

The Big Breakfast

I'm going to Kenya this summer with 10 young people. None of us has been there before, so we decided that a fun way to find out a little about Africa was to spend an evening watching the movie *Out of Africa*. Now, I love this movie. I have watched it two or three times, so I was blown away when I realized I'd missed one of the main twists of the plot. How could I not have seen it before?

The thing was, it was slipped in very subtly. It was just one brief scene that had to be put together with another much later on in the movie.

There are a few subtle twists in this story of Jesus too. Oil and wine were often used to clean wounds. They were also used in worship services as symbols of God's love. In the Old Testament God is seen putting a bandage on the wounds of his people. The twist that Jesus put into his plot would have been a big shock to the people listening to him. God is represented in his story by a Samaritan, a person who was hated.

Continental

God will surprise us all the time. He loves and reaches out to those we hate in the same way that he reaches out to us.

Coffee

The values of the kingdom will always be shocking to us. It is what we do with them that matters to God.

RS

Orange Juice

Then he put the hurt man on his own donkey and took him to an inn where he cared for him.

Luke 10:34 NCV

Walking Beside the Donkey

The Big Breakfast

Some stories have so many twists to them that it is hard to keep up. The Samaritan put the wounded man on his donkey in order to take him to safety. That was the obvious thing to do, considering that they were in a dangerous place, with robbers hiding in the hills above them. What is not so obvious to us, reading the story all these years later, is that the Samaritan's actions were another real shock to the people listening to the story being told by Jesus. By putting the man on his donkey, the Samaritan was giving up his place to a stranger. By doing this, he changed from being a wealthy merchant (most likely to have been his profession) to being a servant. In Middle Eastern culture, the only person to walk beside an animal while another person was riding on it was a servant or slave. Even today, it would be pretty difficult to get a travel guide to ride with you. They insist on leading the donkey. It is all about respect.

Continental

Throughout the Bible we find many pictures like this one, showing people who give up their rights or position to serve others. Most significant of these is Jesus himself.

Coffee

Lord Jesus, it is pretty clear that one of the big things about being a Christian is putting other people first. I'm not very good at that. Please help me.

RS

Orange Juice

But first, you must start respecting the Sabbath as a joyful day of worship. You must stop doing and saying whatever you please on this special day.

Isaiah 58:13 CEV

Just Another Manic Sunday?

The Big Breakfast

Isaiah 58 is the prototypical Freedom Song. It speaks of liberation for the oppressed, of abundance for the poor, of new life for the masses. It is as close as the Bible gets to flying a Red Flag and hitting the streets for a revolution.

So it is incongruous, to the twenty-first-century mind, that the chapter ends on the Sabbath. Sabbath observance, to us, is about legalism – about a view of religion that is anything but liberating.

But Isaiah knows what it is about. God's Law, exemplified in the rules of the Sabbath, is all about freedom. It is the Sabbath that tells the employer that he cannot own his workers' bodies and souls – nor, for that matter, his slaves, animals or land. No matter how caught up we become in our get-rich schemes, there is a time when God says "Enough!" and we must take our hands off.

Every part of the creation – from atoms to empires – must be allowed rest and recovery. Our exploitation of the earth is limited by design. God's cry of "Time out!" is also a cry of freedom.

Continental

Sabbath-rest is good news for the poor; it is the powerful who are constrained and limited by it.

Coffee

God of Sabbath-rest, teach me today what it means to rest in you. Grant to all those who are wearied by labour and struggle the rest that you alone can provide.

GK

Orange Juice

But while he was still a long way off, his father saw him and was filled with compassion for him; he ran to his son, threw his arms around him and kissed him.

Luke 15:20

Remind You of Anybody?

The Big Breakfast

I was so sure that the flight I was on was going to be my last. It was with an airline I'd never heard of, on a plane that looked as if it had become obsolete about the time the Beatles broke up. I held my breath as the thing lumbered slowly down the runway and up into the Middle Eastern sky. I was travelling with an Arab Christian friend to Jordan, where he was to be reunited with the family he hadn't seen for a few weeks.

We eventually touched down – three times – and bundled hurriedly out of the plane, through baggage reclaim and towards the exit. My friend must have been excited about seeing his wife and two young boys again but he never showed it. "I'll take the bags," I offered. "You run on ahead."

He dropped his case and turned to me sternly. "Arab fathers never run." In that moment, the weight of what the prodigal son's father did came crashing into me. He broke with all tradition and did what no father with dignity would ever do – he ran and ran, working up a sweat in the sun. He dispensed with a formal handshake and threw his arms around his boy publicly. He even cut short the lad's well-prepared repentance speech with the order to prepare a banquet. Remind you of anybody?

Continental

When my eldest son was a baby, he once covered every available space on his face, hands and body with rapidly melting chocolate ice cream. Then he began to choke. I didn't hesitate – I didn't stop to clean him up, I gave no thought to my own appearance. I just lifted him up, cleared the blockage and held him tight, with all his mess pressed against my clean white shirt. Remind you of anybody?

Coffee

"If you, O Lord, kept record of sins, O Lord, who could stand? But with you there is forgiveness" (Psalm 130:3-4 NIV). Reminds me of the Master. Worship him.

DB

Orange Juice

His master replied, "Well done, good and faithful servant! You have been faithful with a few things; I will put you in charge of many things. Come and share your master's happiness!"

Matthew 25:23

Tomorrow Is the Next Today

The Big Breakfast

You may know this story: a rich boss goes away for a while and hands out his resources to three of his most trusted workers to use as they see fit for the good of their employer. One of them buries the money – a talent (a unit of weight and currency) – and is sent away into "outer darkness". But the other two invest their talents and come back to their returning boss with the interest. He is over-the-top happy: seemingly not because he's made money, but more because the two have been faithful with what he has given them.

This story is undoubtedly a picture of what it is going to be like when we meet God. He's going to say to us, "Well, I put you in the twenty-first century, one of the most affluent periods in world history, with world-wide communication and travel, and I gave you the gospel to share with people and my Spirit to help you. How did you do?" How are we going to answer? "Well, Lord, I thought your good news was so special that I buried it in the church and kept it safe." Uh-uh.

This is one of a number of stories in the Bible that tell us that the end of the world is going to involve us meeting God and telling him what we've done with our life. So how do you feel about that?

Continental

"God has not called me to be successful, he has called me to be faithful."

Mother Teresa of Calcutta

Coffee

What "talents" has God given you? Take a moment to thank him for all the good things in your life, and think about how you can use all you have for God.

SH

Orange Juice

O Lord, our Lord, how majestic is your name in all the earth!... When I consider your heavens, the work of your fingers ... what is man that you are mindful of him?

Psalm 8:1, 3-4 NIV

Puddle Walks

The Big Breakfast

I've had such fun today. I've learnt to recapture the wonder of life from my 18-month-old son, Nathan. My wife is out of town visiting her family and so I've had our two boys all to myself. The sun was warm despite an early-morning downpour. We decided on a walk around the grounds of Upton House, a stately home not far from where we live.

For Nathan it was a day of firsts, each new discovery accompanied with jubilant squeals of delight. First it was the feel of running his little hands over a damp, beautifully mown lawn. Then his brother presented him with a trapped butterfly that tickled his smiling face as it flew to freedom. Moment by moment his little eyes grew wider with a joy-overload as he splashed through the puddles, caught his reflection in the clear water of a pond and then tottered off down a stony path with his hands clasped behind his back like a patrolling headmaster.

He and his brother fell into a contented sleep on the way home, leaving me to ponder how I could recapture that childlike innocence. I felt as if I had lost the wonder of life. How much more dynamic would my worship be if I "considered God's heavens, the work of his fingers" more often?

Continental

The next time I go to worship I may just squeal in wonder at those beautiful God moments and then splash about in the puddles of the Father's love that our church community demonstrates so well.

Coffee

Affirm with me: "Ah, Sovereign LORD, you have made the heavens and the earth by your great power and outstretched arm. Nothing is too hard for you" (Jeremiah 32:17 NIV).

DB

Orange Juice

Now the tax collectors and "sinners" were all gathering around to hear him. But the Pharisees and the teachers of the law muttered, "This man welcomes sinners and eats with them."

Luke 15:1-2

The Welcome Wagon

The Big Breakfast

Christian tradition paints the Pharisees as the pantomime baddies of the Gospel narratives. Wherever Jesus went, we imagine, cries of "They're behind you!" would alert him to a slapstick gaggle of Pharisees, out to trip him up.

We see these men as small-minded, mean-spirited, selfish – the conspiratorial enemies of Christ. The truth is less comic, and more complex. Pharisees were committed, consistent, single-minded. Their focus was on the things of God, and their willingness to apply their faith to the tiniest detail of daily life was extraordinary. The zeal that consumed them was zeal for Israel's God.

What set them at loggerheads with Jesus, and vice versa, was this: they had forgotten the character of the God on whom they focused so much zeal. Desire for God had hardened into the dogma by which desire was quenched. The search for truth became a system by which truth was suppressed.

Church history shows us just how easy it is for those who believe to become those who suppress belief – for followers to become Pharisees.

Continental

Unlike the Pharisees, the tax collectors and "sinners" gathered to hear Jesus. What was it about Jesus that made him so attractive to ordinary people?

Coffee

Reflect on your meal-times of recent weeks – how often have you been willing to break bread with "the wrong sort of people"?

GK

Orange Juice

And they sang a new song, saying: "You are worthy to take the scroll and to open its seals, because you were slain, and with your blood you purchased for God members of every tribe and language and people and nation."

Revelation 5:9

The Moment

The Big Breakfast

Maybe you're feeling a bit unsure of what you're going to say when you meet God on the so-called "Day of Judgement". Well, I have good news for you: God has already prepared a script for you. In the book of Revelation, God shows John, the writer, a scroll that has the names of everyone who can enter into God's new world, but the scroll can be opened only by someone who is worthy. John ends up in tears because no one can be found who is worthy to open the scroll which will allow people to come into their inheritance. Then the above happens.

Here, on the biggest scale possible, is the good news about Jesus: his death opens up the gate of heaven and lets us in. Without Jesus' sacrifice for us, our resurrection on the last day would be a pretty unpleasant affair. God would look at us and say, "Well, you're not worthy to be with me forever. Is anyone willing to stand up for this person and say they're okay?" And then there would be an eternal silence.

Jesus' death was not just an historic event: it changed history *forever!*

Continental

Glory be to Jesus
Who in bitter pains
Poured for me the life-blood
From his sacred veins.

traditional Italian hymn

Coffee

Imagine Jesus taking you to the front of a large queue of people trying to get into an event or nightclub. The bouncers are saying to everyone, "Your name's not down, you're not coming in". Then, as you approach the entrance, the bouncers say, "Who do you think you ... oh, you're with Jesus. Fine, come in." How do you feel?

SH

Orange Juice

Even there your hand will guide me, your right hand will hold me fast.

Psalm 139:10 NIV

Signposts

The Big Breakfast

How do we know God is always guiding us? Isn't it all down to a bit of luck, good or bad?

Maybe Joseph in the Old Testament can help. He had jealous brothers, and a stupid father who was no doubt responsible for causing the brothers to be jealous. Joseph himself had an arrogant side. He boasted a lot. He was also a silly dreamer. He saw things in his dreams that he would have kept to himself if he'd had any wit at all. But no, Big Mouth tells his brothers that they will one day bow down to him as a king. Imagine it. They weren't happy. So Joseph was sold as a slave. His brothers reckoned that was the last of him.

Years later, however, Joseph turned up again, and guess what? The brothers bowed down to him because of his powerful position. Read all about it in Genesis chapters 37 to 46. It is an amazing story. The main thing to notice is that God was there all along. He was in charge of things; he was watching out for Joseph and guiding what happened.

Continental

The signposts along the way include circumstances that come together in an unexpected way, a helpful word from a friend and a disappointment that later you can see was a good thing.

Coffee

The fact that God is guiding us doesn't mean that we stop thinking for ourselves. He works with us to guide us by or through the decisions we make.

RS

Orange Juice

Then Jesus told them this parable: "Suppose one of you has a hundred sheep and loses one of them."

Luke 15:3-4

Alien Nation

The Big Breakfast

In our day, a shepherd might be tempted to respond to Jesus' question with a shrugged "fair enough". A one per cent loss on the initial investment is not the end of the world – it is probably better to keep the 99 safe than to risk all searching for the one that was stupid enough to get lost. Why not just accept that this is "the survival of the fittest"? That's without even beginning to think of insurance.

We have so immunized ourselves against loss that the odd sheep dead or dying really doesn't matter. How else can we tolerate the loss of six million lives each year to starvation; the recruitment of over 80 million children worldwide into the slavery of child labour; the death of 40,000 children every hour from preventable diseases?

By contrast, God's view of loss is extravagant and outrageous – he will go to the ends of the earth to prevent the suffering of just one human being. There is no loss adjustment in the kingdom of heaven – just the extravagance of a 99-to-1-risk-taking God.

Continental

How would your life change if you took on a godly intolerance of the lostness that you witness every day?

Coffee

Alienation ... is an ache in the deepest part of you, a longing which nothing in the world ever quite touches ... the sense of being lost comes like a fragment of a song ... Finding the way is all about coming home.

Mike Riddell (Godzone, Lion, 1992)

GK

Orange Juice

Praise be to the God and Father of our Lord Jesus Christ, who has blessed us in the heavenly realms with every *spiritual blessing* in Christ.

Ephesians 1:3 (emphasis added)

Joys-R-Us!

The Big Breakfast

One Saturday, a few Christmases ago, I trudged wearily through the winter snow to the megastore Toys-R-Us. I'd gone with a good friend, his seven-year-old son, Jonathon, and a huge crowd. Jonathon's dad said he could have anything he wanted from the store as long as it cost no more than the five pounds. The boy ran off like a hungry lion, devouring every sparkly new toy he could feast his eyes on. He soon came back and tried to bargain for a higher allowance, but to no avail. The imposed limit meant it took him hours to decide. Eventually he decided on a little £4.99 working model of C3PO from the *Star Wars* films, the closest thing to the £5 limit. Value for money!

The "spiritual blessings" that Paul was describing are like our heavenly Father taking his kids to his megastore of good things, but unlike an earthly father he says, "All this, every good thing you can see, it's all yours because of Jesus." No limits here, no sale items or returns, just pure spiritual blessings from the heavenly realms.

Continental

Paul wrote of these spiritual blessings from a prison cell. I spent today in a prison with a prison officer from our church. There was no hope there, only chains of sadness. Yet even Paul's chains couldn't stop him from getting excited about his blessings. Don't be a whinger today – change your perspective and watch your chains drop off!

Coffee

Stop right now, before the rest of this day unfolds, and thank God for his heavenly blessings. The list seems endless. Undeserved grace, eternal life, freedom from guilt, healing from pain, a new purpose to life, sweet, sweet forgiveness ...

DB

Orange Juice

Then I heard the voice of the Lord saying, "Whom shall I send? And who will go for us?"

And I said, "Here am I. Send me!"

Isaiah 6:8 NIV

Missionary Required: Enquire Within

The Big Breakfast

Okay, so Isaiah gets called. That's fine – he was Isaiah, not me. I'm just normal. I've not been called to Outer Mongolia or even Inner London. Isaiah was special: that's obvious because ... well, because he did what he was told, for a start. And, he trusted God, which makes him almost unique in my experience. Me, I'd require any request from God to be signed in triplicate before I took any notice.

I'm not the world-changing type. I just want to sit in the corner reading my copy of *Esquire/Elle/Good Housekeeping/fill in your favourite here* and bother nobody. I've done it for years and I expect that this state of affairs will continue until the day when the Lord takes me from this terrible old world and into his glory.

I do hear this voice sometimes, asking, "Whom shall I send?" But I just tell the voice to try Tony down the road. I once heard him pray out loud, so I imagine he must be the missionary type.

Anyway, I'm not perfect. I know that all the people God used in the Bible were perfect, like David, Samson, Peter and all the saints – well, Jesus definitely – so God can't use me. Am I safe yet?

No, you're not, so stop trying and give in.

Continental

Nobody in the Bible, when given a job by God, ever said, "Fine, that's easy".

Coffee

How does God want to use you? Are there things that he has already asked you to do that you need to go back to? Make room for listening to God today.

SH

Orange Juice

"... But when this son of yours who has squandered your property with prostitutes comes home, you kill the fattened calf for him!"

"My son," the father said. "... this brother of yours was dead and is alive again; he was lost and is found."

Luke 15:30-31

Watch Your Language

The Big Breakfast

The brother's anger manifests itself in grammar. The servant tells him, "Your brother has come," but when he speaks to his father, his brother is "this son of *yours*". Language betrays the depth of feeling.

It is the father who has been wronged and rejected – and yet it is the older brother who keeps the offence alive. He really has no grievance against his brother – but he uses the younger son's irresponsibility as a vehicle for his own frustrations. His response is to present his father with a choice – "It's you and me or you and him."

But the father will have none of it. *His* language is the language of reconciliation – "*We* had to celebrate because *this brother of yours* is alive again."

How often do we try to maintain a relationship with our Father whilst breaking a relationship with a brother or sister? God's desire is for reconciliation – not only between child and parent, but amongst children too.

Continental

Love is like a television picture – there's no point in having the vertical hold adjusted if the horizontal hold is out of control.

Coffee

As you speak to God, be aware that when you pray using such words as "this son of yours", he will often reply in terms of "this brother of yours".

GK

Orange Juice

Before the world was created, God had Christ choose us to live with him and to be his holy and innocent and loving people. God was kind and decided that Christ would choose us to be God's own adopted children.

Ephesians 1:4-5 CEV

From Orphan to Heir

The Big Breakfast

Here Paul captures the dynamite truth of the gospel that exploded into a Bethlehem cattle shed two thousand years ago. Let me quote these verses again from the *Bloomin' Obvious Bible* (Colour Pictures Edition):

You got picked before God ever flung up a star into the night sky or rolled out a mountain range. With no other motivation but sheer, gratuitous love he picked you out among many orphaned souls to eat at his table; not as a visitor or a temporary guest but as a son or a daughter. He did it because he wanted to and because adopting you meant that nothing else in the history of the universe he had created could ever give him so much pleasure. Not even England beating Germany on penalties.

He is really glad to have chosen you. Despite your tantrums and selfish choices, despite your blatant rebellion, he is still proud of you. He still thinks you were worth every drop of blood that spilt from the body of his only son so that today you can call yourself his heir and adopted child.

Continental

My friends Chris and Ruby were childless for fifteen years. Just yesterday they flew back from Manila with their newly adopted daughter, Michelle. You should have seen the unstoppable joy on their faces. Remember today your heavenly Father's joy the day he picked you up from a foreign land and brought you home.

Coffee

When God created Adam and Eve, his intention was to populate his planet with "holy, innocent and loving people" (Ephesians 1:4). I still firmly believe that is his intention today. So as God's precious child, take a look at yourself again in the same way that he looks at you – holy and innocent.

DB

Orange Juice
Watch out! Be on your guard against all kinds of greed; life does not consist in an abundance of possessions.

Luke 12:15

Who Wants to Be a Millionaire?

The Big Breakfast
The pressure is huge. Should he take what he's got and run, or risk it all, go for the next question and become a millionaire? Chris Tarrant can't help him. He must get the question absolutely right first time. What a lonely moment. What does it matter, though? It's just another game show. It will be somebody else tomorrow.

Game shows, the National Lottery, scratch cards – they're in your face every day. What has this done to us? I reckon it has probably turned us into fun-loving but rather misguided people. The message of the game show and the lottery is that money makes you happy. The more you have, the better things will be for you. So go on, take the risk, go for the next question, get the million.

Jesus must be so sad as he watches all this. He knows that the more we have, the more we want. "Watch out!" he says. "Be on your guard against all kinds of greed." Your life shouldn't be measured by, or depend on, what you own. The trouble is, we're continually being told just the opposite.

Continental
Jesus would be happier with what Tony Campolo once said: "The prize is not what you get, it is what you become."

Coffee
Ask Jesus to help you see the things in your life that subtly draw you to the "must have" mind-set. Then determine to live the kingdom life.

RS

Orange Juice

I saw the Holy City, the new Jerusalem, coming down out of heaven from God.

Revelation 21:2

So What's Heaven Like?

The Big Breakfast

This verse is from the end of Revelation. Sometimes I skip all the dragons and other creatures in this book because I want to rush to the end to see what God has shown us about what life in the new creation is going to be like. The news is: it's a big city.

That's right: no sign of any people with wings and white dresses. Now I don't know about you, but if someone asked me to picture God's perfect future for creation, I wouldn't pick a city. No way. Dirty. Smelly. Crime-ridden. No trees. And so on.

There's another thing about this city, this new Jerusalem. There's no temple, no church. I'd always imagined that life with God would be like being at church all the time. I confess to worrying about getting bored singing Christian songs forever. Funnily enough, God's idea of perfect creation seems to have more similarities with his first effort than we had imagined. We won't need a church because wherever we go, God will be with us. Beyond that, our job will be to be a good citizen of this new Jerusalem.

Continental

Look! Look! God has moved into the neighborhood, making his home with men and women! They're his people, he's their God ... Look! I'm making everything new!

Revelation 21:3-5 MSG

Coffee

Try to imagine this new Jerusalem. What would it be like to walk through a big city and know that God was with you wherever you went? Allow that sense of God's presence to lead you to worship him.

SH

Orange Juice

When you go without eating, don't try to look gloomy as those show-offs do ... I can assure you that they already have their reward. Instead, comb your hair and wash your face. Then others won't know that you are going without eating. But your Father sees what is done in private, and he will reward you.

Matthew 6:16-18 CEV

Holy Arrogance

The Big Breakfast

I know. You woke up this morning desperate for caffeine, opened this book for a word of encouragement, and what you got was "go without eating". What possible benefits can going without food really have?

Well, if it was a practice good enough for Jesus, it must therefore be worthy of some consideration. Matthew records: "After Jesus had gone without eating for forty days and nights, he was very hungry." Understatement of the decade or what? Most of us would struggle to let even a day go past without at least a bagel or a burger passing our lips.

I also believe that fasting is a kind of holy arrogance. It is saying to God that you are serious about an issue. So serious, in fact, that you're prepared to go without physical sustenance as you pray and that you won't accept no for an answer. What are you so desperate to catch God's attention with that you will add fasting to your petitioning? Whatever it is, the promise is clear. The Father will reward you as you fast and pray. Is it a day's meals you need to sacrifice, a week's TV or a month's shopping for the latest labels? You choose ...

Continental

If fasting were an option for the Christian, Jesus would have said "*if* you fast". If fasting were a command, he would have said "you *must* fast". However, it was his assumption that real followers would fast, so he says "*when* you fast". Can he make the same assumption of you?

Coffee

The Methodist preacher William Bramhall said, "The reason why Methodists in general do not live in this salvation is there is too much sleep, too much meat and drink, too little fasting and self-denial, too much preaching and hearing and too little self-examination and prayer." Where will you stand?

DB

Orange Juice

The chief priests accused him of many things. So again Pilate asked him, "Aren't you going to answer? See how many things they are accusing you of."

But Jesus still made no reply, and Pilate was amazed.

Mark 15:3-5

You Say It Best When You Say Nothing At All

The Big Breakfast

For the most part, Jesus is remembered for the things he said. There are certain moments, though, which have significance not for what was said but for what was not said.

Standing before Pilate, it is not the eloquence of Christ that speaks volumes but his silence. It is not that Jesus is afraid of verbal conflict, or that he has no answer for his accusers. On other occasions, he has engaged in lengthy and complex debate with these very men. He is silent because a greater purpose is at work.

The powerlessness to which he surrenders himself is also wordlessness – he will not use the weapon of his tongue in his own defence, nor allow himself the satisfaction of a well-aimed verbal missile. In his silence is a personal power by which even Pilate is confounded.

Months earlier, Christ's disciples had said to him, "You have the words of eternal life". On this occasion they might equally have said, "You have the silence of eternal life".

Continental

Religions of the East and ancient Christianity alike make creative use of silence in prayer. What might its recovery mean for your personal spiritual walk?

Coffee

Why not commit yourself to finding a few moments of silence today, to explore the richness of prayer without words?

GK

Orange Juice

Then Jesus told this story: "There was a rich man who had some land, which grew a good crop. He thought to himself, 'What will I do? I have no place to keep all my crops . . . I will tear down my barns and build bigger ones.'"

Luke 12:16-18 NCV

How Are You Using It?

The Big Breakfast

She's worth somewhere in the region of £22 million and she's only 25 years old. Mel B, Scary Spice, has done okay, don't you think? She is one of the most successful pop stars around today. Talking recently about having money, she said a few things worth noting. For example, she doesn't think of herself as rich, but as someone who can help her family and friends.

In the verse above, Jesus has just warned the people listening to him about becoming greedy. Don't make the mistake of measuring your life by wealth, he says. He goes on to tell a story about a wealthy farmer. This is obviously an important point he's making. His story is repeating the warning he has just made. He's painting a picture of how some people behave. When they have it good and make more money than they need, they just spend it on themselves or save it for themselves. Building a bigger barn isn't a good idea. It's not God's idea. Wealth comes to us as a gift and we must use it wisely.

Continental

You may not think you're rich. Nonetheless, whatever you have is a gift from God. How are you using it?

Coffee

Lord Jesus, it is so easy to think of what I have as only for my own use and pleasure. I'm sorry.

RS

Orange Juice
A happy heart makes the face cheerful, but heartache crushes the spirit.

Proverbs 15:13 NIV

Sacred Laughter

The Big Breakfast
I drove home today from what proved to be a very difficult and intense meeting. My mind was racing with words both said and unsaid. I could almost feel my heart aching in my chest. My spirit had been dragged down, if not a little crushed. God knew that I needed to crack a smile on my face and get a clearer perspective. I am sure God invented laughter as one of life's little shock absorbers. I switched on the radio. It was a satirical news show. I laughed like a hyena all the way to my front door.

I can see a whole bunch of humour in the Bible – not least Jesus telling the apocryphal tale of Mr and Mrs Raven building a barn (Matthew 6:26) or the almost Pythonesque picture of fat camels squeezing through the eye of a needle (Mark 10:25)! And how about the comic irony of Joseph teaching the Creator of the world how to hold a hammer? The sad thing is, so many Christians have had their humour gland surgically removed. We really are boring people to hell. Don't run from the lighter moments of life. Embrace them tightly and discover a God of life and laughter right at their centre.

Continental
American pastor and author Charles Swindoll said of laughter, "I think it is often just as sacred to laugh as it is to pray or preach or witness." I agree with him. I mean, when cheese gets its picture taken, what does it say?

Coffee
Queen Victoria is famed for saying, "We are not amused". Is that true of you? Here's one that might check out how rusty your smile has become.

Q: How can you spot a Christian fish?
A: It's got a car stuck to its backside!

DB

Orange Juice

Your sacrifices mean nothing to me. I am sick of your offerings of rams and choice cattle; I don't like the blood of bulls or lambs or goats. Who asked you to bring all this when you come to worship me? Stay out of my temple!

Isaiah 1:11-12 CEV

The Bad News First

The Big Breakfast

Welcome to Isaiah, one of the most dense, beautiful, mysterious and misused books in the Bible. From the bits you normally hear in church, you would think that Isaiah was a book about Jesus, but in fact Isaiah is about one of the most turbulent times in the history of God's people. It covers the time of the decline and fall of the great kingdom of Israel. The political situation, as Israel broke into two and ultimately destroyed itself, was as awful as it could be, but then it got worse. Isaiah deals with the coming invasion of Judah and her exile in Babylon.

And there is no polite introduction: here we are in chapter 1, and God is saying some hard stuff to his people: "Are you sure it was me who wanted you to worship me like this? Are you convinced that all your religious ceremonies are the kind of worship that I desire? Well, I'm not. You have created a religious system that provides you with a cheap form of grace that gets you out of taking responsibility for your lives and gets you out of having to confront *me*. Yes, I hope you remember what this is all about: you humans coming to terms with me, your God. It's not about your selfish needs and wants – leave those to me – it's about the glory of the Creator and how you are going to deal with *that*."

Continental

Tradition is the living faith of dead people; traditionalism is the dead faith of living people.

anonymous

Coffee

Are we seeking God or seeking to salve our consciences? Ask God to show you anything in your own life that has become a way of showing yourself and others that you are okay, and not real worship.

SH

Orange Juice
The Lord is my shepherd, I shall not be in want.

Psalm 23:1 NIV

Up Close and Personal

The Big Breakfast
Great poet and songwriter as he was, even David had to write 22 psalms before he had a hit! So the Broadway joke goes.

The truth is, for many people, Psalm 23 is the only psalm – possibly the only fragment of the Bible – that they know. Its moving words and strong images have written themselves into the very heart of our culture and history – from the lifeboats of the *Titanic* to the mourners at countless funerals each day.

The miracle of this poem of worship is captured in its first five words. "The LORD" is *Yahweh* – a Hebrew name meaning "HE IS", derived from Moses' encounter with the "I AM" of the burning bush. HE IS universal and unnameable, above all and over all. He cannot be pinned down to time and place. The world cannot contain him and words cannot describe him. Yet HE IS my shepherd – intimate, earthy, humble, near at hand.

If David knew anything, he knew that it took humility to be a shepherd. The God who is "up there and unapproachable" is the same God who is up close and personal.

Continental
The God who made the world of which I am so small a part has chosen to be part of my small world.

Coffee
God my shepherd, thank you for choosing to live in my world. May any distance between us be dissolved. May I know you, up close and personal, today.

GK

Orange Juice
Be still, and know that I am God.

Psalm 46:10 NIV

Relax ...

The Big Breakfast
I am a big fan of noise and frantic activity. I grew up in "loud London", where I spent my days in the hustle and bustle of an inner-city school playground and my evenings either playing football, watching football or listening to music welded on 10. I love noise. Or should that read, "I LOVE NOISE"?

If truth were told, the thought of "being still" frightens me to death. Is this really the only way to know God?

The Hebrew word here (*raphah*) means "relax". Now that I can do. One commentator suggests it means to cease striving. So the way to know God is to relax, to cease striving, to slow down.

When did you last do that? When did you last drive under the speed limit, not rush your supper, switch off your mobile phone for a day or read a book in a piping hot bath? If we don't do these kinds of things we run the risk of falling deeper into the tyranny of the busy and continually struggling with stress.

Worse still, we run the risk of not knowing God. You have my permission to find a space to relax today. Then you will know that he really is your God.

Continental
I dug this out of an old book I was given. It is a few lines written by an old friar near the end of his life. "If I had my life to live over again ... I would relax, I would limber up, I would be sillier than I have been this trip ... I would ride on more merry-go-rounds. I'd pick more daisies."

Coffee
Join in Augustine's prayer of old: "O Lord, you have made us for yourself, and our heart is restless until it finds rest in you."

DB

Orange Juice

I'll say to myself, "You have plenty of grain laid up for many years. Take life easy; eat, drink and be merry."
But God said to him, "You fool! This very night your life will be demanded from you."

Luke 12:19-20

Eat, Drink and Be Merry – Not

The Big Breakfast

There's a lot of it around these days. "Have a good time. Enjoy yourself. Go on, why not? There isn't much else to get excited about!" Despite the fact that our times are so technologically advanced, nobody seems to be very hopeful about the future. In fact, "future" is a scary word. It is best not to think about it. Live it up now.

The good news is that the future doesn't need to be scary. Walking with Jesus and getting onto his wavelength puts a whole new colour on things. He has a much better deal to offer. There are a few guidelines that are important, though.

He warns us not to get tempted to go down the "eat, drink and be merry" route. Our lives should be more than that – God expects more of us. Don't think you can do what you like and it won't matter. If you're following Jesus, it does matter. It matters a great deal.

Continental

The rich man in the story made one big mistake: he left God out of the picture. He thought he was in charge. Not so.

Coffee

Lord Jesus, all I have is a gift from you. Help me to think more about the surplus you allow me to have, and then use it properly.

RS

Orange Juice

Come, all you who are thirsty, come to the waters; and you who have no money, come, buy and eat!

Isaiah 55:1 NIV

A *Very* Special Offer

The Big Breakfast

Marx had a point: he described religion (he was talking mainly about Christianity), as "the opium of the masses", because poor people who should have been more angry about their lot were kept happy by faith.

It's a toughie, because over the years rich Christians *have* told poor Christians not to moan about being poor and just to carry on being happy and paying their taxes. The favourite English hymn, "All Things Bright and Beautiful", contains a verse which goes, "The rich man in his castle,/ The poor man at his gate,/ God made them rich and poor ..." Well, you get the idea. However, Christians all over the world have fought for political, social and economic freedom for themselves and their brothers and sisters.

This beautiful passage challenges God's people to change their attitude towards material possessions. But we know, even from elsewhere in Isaiah, that God cares about everyone having enough to eat and drink. God's not telling us to go live in a shed in the woods and eat nuts and berries, but he is reminding us that all that stuff we work for is, in ultimate terms, pretty useless.

Continental

But put God's work first, and these things will be yours as well.

Luke 12:31 CEV

Coffee

Read Isaiah 55:1 to yourself a couple of times, picking out a phrase or two to really think on. Meditate on the words and let God speak to you.

SH

Orange Juice

When [the disciples] landed, they saw a fire of burning coals there with fish on it, and some bread ... Jesus said to them, "Come and have breakfast."

John 21:9, 12 NIV

Breakfast with God's Son

The Big Breakfast

My favourite time of day to meet with people is over breakfast. I love the smell of fresh toast and coffee, mixed with warm conversation, while watching the sun crack open the sky on a brand new day. I have breakfasted with family, good friends, politicians, colleagues, reporters, actors, footballers, even a tramp on Marylebone Station in London. But can you imagine breakfasting with the world's creator? What would you say to him? What might he say to you? Who would pick up the tab?

The disciples were gripped with disappointment. Their Messiah had died and with him their hopes and their dreams. They had gone back to their old way of life – fishing. And on their first trip out they caught nothing. Then the stranger's advice from the lakeside hauls them a huge bounty. Suddenly they are full of beans and scrambling ashore to find a Saviour who is very much alive and frying up fish for breakfast. His invitation to them still stands for us today and tomorrow and the days after that: "Come and have breakfast with me." Worth getting up for, eh?

Continental

Breakfast with God. Not just a clever book title but a definite daily reality. No matter that your life is frantic and full of failure or fear, he still wants to cook breakfast and lay a place for you at the table. Tell him what's on your mind and ask for his companionship today. Pass the butter please...

Coffee

I find it quite ironic that this story tells of a carpenter shouting instructions from the shore to a bunch of fishermen. Listen for the advice from heaven today, but remember that it often comes from the most unlikely of sources.

DB

Orange Juice

He makes me lie down in green pastures, he leads me beside quiet waters.

Psalm 23:2 *NIV*

Pasture Eyes

The Big Breakfast

Sheep, down through the ages, have had a bad press. We think of them as stubborn and stupid. We picture them straying into danger, wandering off mountainsides. But there is one area in which the average sheep is, I confess, brighter than I am. It is this: sheep know what's good for them. The shepherd leads the sheep to food and water, and the sheep know what to do. My experience of human behaviour, including my own, is less positive.

How often do we resist the God who leads us to food, shelter, refreshment and rest? How many of our difficulties result from our stubborn refusal to accept these good gifts? What God intends as refreshment, we shirk as duty. What he offers as rest, we misinterpret as restriction. Failing to see, or to trust, the good pastures to which he is leading us, we invent an endless list of other "needs" and press blindly for their fulfilment. We need eyes to see the perfect provision he has made for us in the place in which we stand.

Continental

When you look around at the place God has brought you to, do you begin to see the safe pastures and quiet waters you need?

Coffee

When we claim to have foresight, second sight and insight, but in reality even our first sight is short, Father, open our eyes.

GK

Orange Juice
He remembers his covenant forever, the word he commanded, for a thousand generations.

Psalm 105:8 NIV

The Hat

The Big Breakfast
When I was 16, I was a rock star, travelling the country with my guitar slung around my neck, performing at this gig and that. My mates were really jealous – all those famous people, being famous myself. When the recording deal fell through, I woke up. I was only a rock star in my dreams.

I actually was a singer. I even made a recording, and I did make it onto a few stages. On one memorable occasion I was singing at a religious meeting. A friend of mine had asked me to come as he was preaching. At the end a man in a grey suit thanked us. His words about me went something like this: "Our wee friend was good, but we wish she'd worn a hat." It beats me what wearing a hat had to do with being a rock star!

It's funny how I remember that remark. Our memories can make us laugh. They can make us cry, too. We may even block them out. God has a great memory. He remembers the promises he has made to us, and he keeps them.

Continental
Good memories are a blessing. Bad memories are a curse. They can leave us wishing we were dead. God remembers his promises. He has promised us the best, which includes the healing of memories.

Coffee
Are you hurting today because of a bad memory? God is a wonderful Father with a long memory, and he's waiting for the opportunity to heal that hurt.

RS

Orange Juice

The Lord gave and the Lord has taken away; may the name of the LORD be praised.

Job 1:21 NIV

What Spills Out?

The Big Breakfast

Why was Job praising the name of the Lord? He was a very wealthy man who had lost his servants and his many cattle in a dramatic raid and firestorm. He had been blessed with ten kids, and they had all died in a freak tornado storm (Job 1:13-19). He had lost the lot, and gained some rather nasty boils into the bargain that even Clearasil couldn't shift (Job 2:7).

What was his reaction? Did he sign up to the "why me?" brigade? Not Job. He came to God empty-handed and vulnerable. Naked, in fact – totally dependent on him. Then he began to praise his name.

At first glance this paints a picture to me of Job as some kind of spiritual superman. I could never be like that. But Job was a person just like you and me – yet it was said of him that he was "blameless and upright; he feared God and shunned evil" (Job 1:1 NIV). It proves to me that this kind of attitude of the soul can be attained. I can demonstrate my trust in God right at the heart of chaos and calamity.

What spills out of you when the pain of life really starts to bump in?

Continental

If complaining were an Olympic sport, I am sure some of us would be gold medallists. For many, moaning has become a regular pastime. Whether it is our local politician or our local preacher, we spend more time complaining about them rather than worshipping our God.

Coffee

Paul's advice to the church in Philippi was to "do *everything* without grumbling or arguing" (Philippians 2:14, emphasis added). Get the drift? Everything. Yep, everything.

DB

Orange Juice

The Spirit of the Sovereign Lord is on me, because the Lord has anointed me to preach good news to the poor. He has sent me to bind up the brokenhearted, to proclaim freedom for the captives and release from darkness for the prisoners.

Isaiah 61:1 NIV

The Jesus Manifesto

The Big Breakfast

I love this passage. I have a really vivid image in my head of that moment in Luke chapter 4 where Jesus reads it out, and as the villagers sit in silence waiting for Jesus to comment on the meaning of the text, he says simply, "What you have just heard me read has come true today" (verse 21). Drama! It is another of these passages which had a special meaning at the exact time when it was written as well as the meaning given to it by Jesus. One of the special things about this passage is the fact that, in the middle of all this stuff about the servant, the same person is "anointed", something which implies a king and/or priest. So, the servant is also a king ... Now, who could that be ...?

A bit like an anagram on a TV quiz – some people just seem to "get it" while others can stare and stare without ever working out the secret of the riddle. Those people who heard Jesus reading this passage just turned to each other and asked, "Isn't this old Joseph's boy?" Well, wouldn't you, if the man who made your chairs suddenly claimed to be the Messiah?

If you've got a Bible to hand, you might want to read a bit more of the chapter, because it's heady stuff. Our God is a God who changes things and who wants to see us involved in changing things.

Continental

Sometimes we think God is a spiritual being who isn't concerned about our physical selves; sometimes we think of him as a kind of social and political agenda. He's both. Thank you, God.

Coffee

This passage is a vision of freedom. Jesus identified this passage with his early proclamation of the gospel. Do you feel like you are living a gospel of freedom? How can you begin to live more in the way of Jesus?

SH

Orange Juice

Even though I walk through the valley of the shadow of death,
I will fear no evil.

Psalm 23:4 NIV

Shadow Boxing

The Big Breakfast

The language at this point in this familiar psalm is very specific – not "the valley of death" but "the valley of the *shadow* of death". The physical image is of a ravine or mountain pass so deep and steep that the sun rarely hits its floor: to walk through it is to pass into shadow.

For sheep, this is a place not of danger but of fear. It is not what might happen to them that holds them back from walking this way, but what they imagine might happen. In real terms, the sheep are in more danger drinking from the quiet waters – where lions and bears are known to prowl; where their defences are down; where the shepherd is most likely to nap! But shadows have a habit of worsening fear. And sheep, like people, will hold back from shadows as much as from real dangers.

The shepherd knows that this route is both necessary and safe – and he is on his guard to keep it so. But the sheep, if they are to follow, must face their fears.

Continental

What are you most afraid of? The passages of your life that are, for you, places of shadow are the places where God most wants to walk with you.

Coffee

Father, I am driven and controlled by fear, and by fear of fear. Deliver me, so that I may walk every path you call me to in obedience, trust and joy.

GK

Orange Juice

The Lord explained: "Jeremiah, I am the Lord God. I rule the world, and I can do anything!"

Jeremiah 32:26-27 CEV

Mission Possible

The Big Breakfast

Put your finger in this page, close your eyes for a minute and think about the things that just seem impossible right now.

Now imagine you are about 14 years old. Your boyfriend, Joe, is due round any moment, and a heavenly presence fills your room. The angelic being has got an important message: "God on high has decreed that he wants to borrow your womb for his son. When he is born, give him the name Jesus." You are naturally a little shocked at the news. Especially since you have never, you know … So how can this be? Besides, what will your folks say? And Joe, he'll go nuts. You put this to the angel with a strong sense of urgency. Don't fret, comes the reply, "nothing is impossible with God" (Luke 1:37 NIV).

So answer the question. Is anything too difficult for God? Absolutely not! If he can encase himself in a set of bones, travel through time and space and then spend nine months in the womb of a teenage virgin called Mary, he can make possible your impossible. I have no idea what that is for you right now, but I do know one thing: nothing, and absolutely nothing, is impossible for God.

Continental

My friend Jeff used to work with tough-nosed London street kids. He sometimes worried about the day ahead as he walked from his home to the youth centre next to the Courage brewery. One morning he noticed the neon brewery sign flickering. It read "Take Courage", as he pondered a God who said that nothing was impossible for him.

Coffee

"'No chance at all,' Jesus said, 'if you think you can pull it off by yourself. Every chance in the world if you trust God to do it'" (Luke 18:27 MSG). Get yourself out of the driving seat and let him take the wheel today.

DB

Orange Juice

Isaac brought her into the tent of his mother Sarah, and he married Rebekah. So she became his wife, and he loved her.

Genesis 24:67 NIV

Read All About It

The Big Breakfast

Ally McBeal – now there's a girl who's unlucky in love; or just plain stupid. Billy, Larry, Victor, the list goes on, and I'm missing out a few. There are a lot of people on that show who are a bit messed up by past relationships.

Now Isaac and Rebekah, that is a wonderful love story. Read all about it in Genesis 24. The Bible has a whole collection of great love stories. The story of Ruth and Boaz is another one. They had a different way of finding their mates in Bible times. I'm not sure how well I would have coped if my dad had made all the decisions for me! On the other hand, when I look at the mess a lot of us get ourselves into, maybe it wouldn't be so bad.

We make a lot of mistakes in love, and yet we all want to be loved, to have that special relationship. God wants to help us in this part of our lives too.

Continental

It is sad to see that these days advice on how to find a boyfriend or girlfriend all seems to come from horoscopes in popular magazines. I'd give that advice a big miss.

Coffee

God is very interested in all of your life. *All* of it. Give him a chance to help you in this important area. He wants to help you avoid messing up.

RS

Orange Juice

See, the LORD is coming with fire, and his chariots are like a whirlwind; he will bring down his anger with fury, and his rebuke with flames of fire.

Isaiah 66:15 NIV

He'll Be Coming Round the Mountain . . .

The Big Breakfast

"He'll be coming round the mountain when he comes ... He'll be wearing pink pyjamas when he comes ..." Except here we have the original quote and it actually says, "He'll be flaming fires of anger when he comes," which adds a little twist to things, don't you think?

There's this annoying thing about God: unfortunately for us, God never conforms to what we want him to be, so while the idea of God as a consuming fire is not exactly *en vogue*, here it is in the Bible.

God gets angry. His anger burns against sin, and many people are gonna get burned. There's no way around this. Even St Paul – a proper saint, no less – said that a good person will get to heaven "like someone escaping from flames" (1 Corinthians 3:15). We're going to arrive at the Pearly Gates rather warm, and with a faint smell of smoke about us. Like a survivor of a car crash, we will meet God filled with the adrenaline rush of miraculous life, the blood coursing through our veins suddenly audible, and beautiful, and wonderful.

Continental

Many people, most notably Sigmund Freud, have criticized Christians for "making God in their own image" – taking only the parts of God they like. In what ways might you be doing this?

Coffee

Pick up a newspaper or watch the TV news today. What do you think God is angry about?

SH

Orange Juice

You do not even know what will happen tomorrow. What is your life? You are a mist that appears for a little while and then vanishes.

James 4:14

Fragile Life

The Big Breakfast

Life is more fragile than we think. I'm reminded of a tense train journey from Banbury to London Marylebone. On the previous day in Paddington, just a few miles from my destination, two commuter trains collided at high speed, killing over 30 people and creating one of Britain's worst rail disasters.

The businessman who sat opposite me was reading a newspaper. The headline was simple and filled the front page: "Commuters die on their way to work". Nobody who had boarded that train to London would have dreamt it to be their last journey. It made my journey particularly strained. I gazed around to see a train carriage full of people all reading the same newspaper headlines. It seemed that one of the drivers had jumped a red light, with horrific consequences. We all travelled in an eerie silence.

James catches the mood well when he describes you and me as "mist that appears for a little while". Take time to pause and thank God for giving you this day. For many it will be their last; for many today was never afforded to them. But for you, God has given you another day to live. Life is precious. Learn not to waste a moment.

Continental

An old youth leader of mine used a spool of cotton thread to explain how our lives now compare with eternal life. He asked me to hold an end of cotton between my thumb and forefinger. He then unravelled the rest of the reel around the room. It took him an age. Compared with life beyond the grave, he said, our lives now are as short as the bit between my fingers.

Coffee

"Lord, I don't take this day for granted. I won't wish it to end until I've managed to thank you for it over and over again." Pray that prayer again over lunch, over supper, and before your head hits the pillow tonight. Be thankful!

DB

Orange Juice

You prepare a table before me in the presence of my enemies. You anoint my head with oil; my cup overflows.

Psalm 23:5 NIV

Sleeping with the Enemy

The Big Breakfast

Even in its time and context, this is a bizarre image. The prayer and longing of Israel was always that they might be granted "rest from our enemies on every side". The sign of peace was the absence of enemies. The feast took place far from the battlefield.

But David, since his youth as a shepherd, has become a shrewd military commander. He knows well that the absence of enemies is not always the sign of peace. True victory is to triumph in the presence of one's enemies. David wants his enemies where he can see them – where he knows, once and for all, that they are no threat to him, and where they can see him.

The anointing with oil is a sign of God's vindication. The overflowing cup is the measure of his provision. God's answer to the spiritual battles you face is not to take you away from your enemies to the false peace that pretends they are not there. It is to overwhelm you, in the very presence of your foe, with the anointing and abundance of his mercy.

Continental

There are times when God delivers us *from* our troubles – more often, though, he delivers us *in* our troubles.

Coffee

My instinct, Lord God, is to run from battle. I don't like confrontation and I would rather have no enemies at all. Thank you that your plan is not flight but victory.

GK

Orange Juice

Create in me a pure heart, O God, and renew a steadfast spirit within me.

Psalm 51:10 NIV

Rules Are Good

he Big Breakfast

Christina Aguilera and Britney Spears are battling it out. Who really is the "Teen Queen of Pop"? For the two girls who started out as friends in the show *The Mickey Mouse Club* (1992), the question now being asked is which of them is the "real babe". So we must judge them on their bodies, their best physical assets and, yes, whether or not they're virgins.

We live in a sex-saturated society. We can't get through a single day without somebody somewhere telling us how great sex is. God has a lot to say about sex. He thinks it's great – after all, he invented it. But he has given us a few guidelines, "directions for use" if you like. When we ignore these, we get into a lot of bother. King David discovered this. He took another man's wife to bed with him. He may have enjoyed it, but it eventually drove him to murder her husband in order to cover up what he'd done wrong.

In this psalm he's asking God to give him a pure heart. He realizes that things got out of hand because his heart and his desires were all screwed up.

Continental

A few years ago, the Baptist Church in America began a campaign called "Proud to be Pure". Teenagers signed a pledge not to have sex until they got married. *More* magazine wrote it off as nonsense. What do you think?

Coffee

God knows that our sexual drive is a strong one that can take us over. He wants to help us control it. Ask him to help you.

RS

Orange Juice

Anyone who will not receive the kingdom of God like a little child will never enter it.

Mark 10:15

Jump from the Top Step

The Big Breakfast

I think some nursery rhymes should be banned. Have you thought about the words to some of them? Remember this line from "Goosey Goosey Gander"? "And if you see an old man standing unawares, grab him by the left leg and pull him down the stairs." And we wonder why we live in such a violent society today!

I am convinced that our faith needs to become less childish and more childlike. There is a distinct difference. We need that simple naive acceptance of God's love for us mixed with our total trust in him. My two-year-old will launch himself off the stairs into my arms, never thinking that I could possibly drop him. I am his father and, in his eyes, his daddy will always catch him without fail. Simple childlike faith.

If only I could recapture some of that same reckless abandonment to my heavenly Father. Why is it that I hold back so much and so often? I miss out on the adventure and thrill of diving into the arms of my Creator and squealing with delight as he holds me close.

Continental

Remember the tale about the emperor who had no clothes? It took a little scruffy lad to be uninhibited enough to say what everyone was thinking. Can you start to dismantle some of that grown-up safety net that so often gets wrapped around your view of God and the Church? Because unless you do *you cannot get into God's kingdom.*

Coffee

The writer Randall Jarrell is quoted as saying, "One of the most obvious facts about grown-ups, to a child, is that they have forgotten what it is like to be a child." Lose the confusion and accept again today that your perfect Father in heaven loves you, his very special child. Dive once more into his open arms.

DB

Orange Juice

Here there is no Greek or Jew, circumcised or uncircumcised, barbarian, Scythian, slave or free, but Christ is all, and is in all.

Colossians 3:11

Politics and Religion?

The Big Breakfast

There are some things that Christians don't talk about, like the fact that in every Western country ethnic minorities end up with their own churches. Or the fact that Christianity is now a Southern Hemisphere religion, with white people in a minority. Or the fact that not so long ago, in South Africa and parts of the United States, racism was taught as a "biblical" principle.

Well, we know the reasons for that, and we don't need to dig them up. But we do need to think Christianly about issues of race. By the middle of the century, those from a European ethnic background will be in a minority in the USA, so we gotta get wise sooner or later.

So we must start from the baseline. And the baseline isn't just that we are all made equal (I defy anyone to show me how God has made one person to be of lesser worth in his sight than another): the "here" that Paul is talking about in this verse is the Church – God's universal Church throughout the world. There is no such thing as a black church, a white church, an Asian church – there is only God's Church, where these differences disappear. It makes John Lennon's song "Imagine" seem a little unambitious really, doesn't it?

Continental

When the missionaries arrived in Africa the Africans had the land and the missionaries had the Bible. They taught us to pray with our eyes closed. When we opened them they had the land and we had the Bible.

Jomo Kenyatta

Coffee

Start these few days by searching your own heart. Is there any prejudice that you need to repent of?

SH

Orange Juice

Surely goodness and love will follow me all the days of my life.

Psalm 23:6 NIV

Wakey Wakey!

The Big Breakfast

Picture yourself on a cross-Channel ferry, watching the land you have left behind recede in the distance. Across the water, stretching almost to the horizon, you will see the fading trail, the wake, of the boat on which you stand. As the huge propellers plough through the sea, they churn up the water to leave this frothing, white-topped pattern behind them.

This image is something like the picture given in this psalm. The Hebrew shepherd would always lead from the front, not from behind. Ancient shepherding was an entirely different proposition from the dog-aided cajoling of today.

But as we follow the shepherd and forge ahead, what comes behind us? For David, the miracle of God's shepherding will be seen in the goodness and mercy that follow him. In each place that he goes, on each path of righteousness on which he is led, he will leave behind the pattern of goodness and mercy. The presence of God will not only mark his life – it will also mark the places where he has been.

Continental

As you pass through your workplace, your home, your community – what do you leave in your wake?

Coffee

I am conscious, Father, that wherever I go, I leave a mark. Strengthen me, renew me, change me, so that goodness and mercy follow in my wake.

GK

Orange Juice

Then the righteous will answer him, "Lord, when did we see you hungry and feed you, or thirsty and give you something to drink?" ... The King will reply, "Truly I tell you, whatever you did for one of the least of these brothers and sisters of mine, you did for me."

Matthew 25:37, 40

The Normal Christian Life

The Big Breakfast

From reading this story that Jesus tells about separating the sheep and the goats, it is clear that we need to think carefully about the criteria for finding favour with the Almighty. The story tells of a time when Jesus will separate people "as a shepherd separates the sheep from the goats" (Matthew 25:32). The favourable ones are not necessarily the successful church leaders or clever Bible scholars. They are not the greatest preachers or most poetic songwriters. They are not even the people who feel it their "Christian duty" to do a weekly soup run or organize a jumble sale for worthy causes.

The righteous people, the ones who miss out on eternal punishment and find eternal life (Matthew 25:46) are the ones who feed the hungry without thinking about it. They welcome strangers quite naturally. They see the poor and naked and don't think twice about buying them the best set of clothes available. They even willingly take time out to visit the drug-pusher, the prostitute or the thief living behind bars.

When did your faith last get close enough to the poor to smell their need and hear the silent cry of their inner souls? You say you love them, but have they ever heard you say it? Have they ever seen it in action?

Continental

Authentic followers of Christ assume that cleaning up the vomit of the user, cradling the diseased and dying or sacrificing what they have for those who have little is a natural, expected part of their daily lives. They would live this way without even thinking about it. They don't need a preacher to motivate them to live this way. You would hear them say, "Surely that's the way every Christian lives, isn't it?" Is it?

Coffee

We must grasp this. Feeding hungry faces is as much worship as singing praise songs, if not more. Why? Because in both you will see the face of Jesus gazing back at you.

DB

Orange Juice

The Lord is close to the brokenhearted and saves those who are crushed in spirit.

Psalm 34:18 NIV

Broken Pieces

The Big Breakfast

There must be a million love songs about broken hearts. I'm sure you can easily think of one. Maybe you'd rather not because right now your own heart hurts too much. Or perhaps you have a vivid memory of a time when it did. It's pretty much impossible to get through all that relationship stuff without taking an arrow in the heart.

God is great at rebuilding relationships. His whole purpose with us is restoring that which is broken between him and us – which we broke in the first place. I reckon God knows all about a broken heart.

There's a great line in the film *City of Angels:* "He gave those bozos down there the greatest gift in the universe – free will." So he did. That freedom can allow us to be very selfish, especially when it comes to relationships. We forget that another person is involved. We get caught up with ourselves and what we want.

If your heart is broken, God knows what that's like. He's very close to you, even if it doesn't feel like it.

Continental

I remember well the first real broken heart I had. I cried and cried, and felt I would die from the pain. One of my close friends hugged me for a long time.

Coffee

If your heart is breaking and you think you'll suffocate from the pain, just know that God's great arms are hugging you very tightly.

RS

Orange Juice

The Lord bless you and keep you; the Lord make his face shine upon you and be gracious to you; the Lord turn his face toward you and give you peace.

Numbers 6:24-26 NIV

Shalom

The Big Breakfast

This prayer is the closest we have to a "Lord's Prayer" of the Old Testament: it's what God tells Aaron (the first Israelite priest) to say as a blessing over the people. It introduces us to a big word in the Old Testament: peace. The Hebrew word is *shalom,* and you will often hear Jewish people greet each other by wishing peace on each other using this ancient word. Likewise, Muslims bless each other with the Arabic *salaam.*

Unfortunately, like our woolly word "love", "peace" doesn't really cover the full meaning of *shalom,* which is much, much more than an absence of war or noise. *Shalom* is a big, fat word, encompassing all the desires and aspirations of God's people in the Old Testament. *Shalom* encompasses what we are looking for when we pray, "Your kingdom come, your will be done on earth as it is in heaven."

In different places in the Bible *shalom* can mean "completeness", "security", even "prosperity" (if you have time, have a look at Jeremiah 29:7). So don't underestimate it: this word has all the power of God's first covenant in it. If you're looking for God's plan for how people, communities and nations should live together, *shalom* is your word. It pulls together all the major themes of the Old Testament: God's people, God's justice and God's purpose.

Continental

The English word "peace" brings to mind restfulness and tranquillity, but the Hebrew word *shalom* recognizes that such a state does not come about by accident; neither is it a place you escape to. *Shalom* is truth, justice and righteousness ruling in our world: to get there, we won't have much time for snoozing!

Coffee

Why not pray this blessing for yourself and for others around you today?

SH

Orange Juice

As the deer pants for streams of water, so my soul pants for you, O God.

Psalm 42:1 NIV

Check Your Pants

The Big Breakfast

A few years back, I preached in an old Pentecostal church. Just before I spoke, the worship band led people in a series of worship songs, the final one being the old classic, "As the deer *pants* for water so my soul longs after you". The worship leader paused midway through this song to encourage us all to speak out our prayers. One elderly lady's prayer left me doubled over with pain as I attempted to hold the tears of laughter back, "O Lord," she said, "some of us only have short *pants* tonight, others I know have only long *pants* ... yet for me, Lord, I honestly don't have any *pants* at all." I just managed to pull myself together in time.*

The psalmist's words from centuries past ring loud today with this question. How thirsty are you to know God today? How parched is your palate and how chapped are your lips? Was opening the pages of this book a real chore today or are you serious about taking in another long, cool, thirst-quenching drink from his Spirit? If you look into your soul this morning, what is it you really thirst after?

*For all you Stateside – *pants* in the UK means *underwear*.

Continental

Where do you go to drink from God? Whether it is alone with this book or in a small group of like-minded believers or church on a Sunday, make sure you drink often – certainly more than once a week. If you are thirsty, you stop to drink at least once a day. If you don't, you just dry up.

Coffee

You can hear the desperate heart cry of the writer in the verse that follows. "My soul thirsts for God, for the living God. When can I go and meet with God?" Have that same passion to find God today and every day.

DB

Orange Juice
The Son is the image of the invisible God.

Colossians 1:15

Portrait of the Artist

The Big Breakfast

The Bible speaks of the image of God being found in three places. In Genesis, women and men are described as "made in the image of God". In Romans 2, the invisible qualities of God are said to be "made visible" in what he has made – the Creator is seen in his creation.

But nowhere is the language of the Bible as specific and strong as here in Colossians. Jesus is not just *a* picture of God, he is not just somewhere to look to see something of God revealed – he is the exact likeness, the "icon" of the invisible God. If God had a passport, Jesus would be the picture in it. If you talked to God via Web Cam, Jesus would be the face you would see.

You can learn a lot about Vincent van Gogh from his pictures. The character of the artist comes through in his work. But it is only in a self-portrait that his physical likeness is seen. Jesus is God's self-portrait – his ultimate and final effort to let the world see what he is like.

Continental

Consider the creation. Meditate on the likeness of God in your fellow women and men. But for the whole picture, take the time to study Jesus.

Coffee

In the wonder of all that you have made, *Father, show yourself to me.* In the beauty of your creatures, women and men, *Father, show yourself to me.* In your Son Jesus, the perfect likeness of the eternal God, *Father, let me see you as you are.*

GK

Orange Juice

The ground of a certain rich man yielded an abundant harvest. He thought to himself, "What shall I do? I have no place to store my crops." Then he said, "This is what I'll do. I will tear down my barns and build bigger ones ..."

But God said to him, "You fool! This very night your life will be demanded from you. Then who will get what you have prepared for yourself?"   *Luke 12:16-18, 20*

The Barn Man

The Big Breakfast

God's thundering response must have been a huge shock. This man was going to die. It really wasn't important that he had barns full of good stuff.

I don't know about you, but I've read this story many times and I always think the barn man was a total fool. He was selfish too, really selfish. It's strange, however, that I never seem to see *myself* as being the barn man. I can somehow read the story and get all judgemental about the rich man – but the thing is, if I'm open to Jesus, if I'm listening to the point he's making, I should see that he's got *me* in mind! My barns are very full too. Jesus says, "You fool".

Is Jesus making a virtue out of poverty? Should we only keep enough to buy the essentials and give the rest of our money away? I don't imagine that's quite the point Jesus has in mind. It's much more likely that he's emphasizing the importance of the attitudes in our hearts, which will determine how we behave towards God and others.

Continental

There are two investments this foolish man could have made. Firstly, he could have given time to family and friends. Secondly, he could have trusted God, not himself, and lived out of that trust rather than following selfish ambition.

Coffee

Lord Jesus, it is so easy to be blind to my own selfishness. Help me to see what's really going on with me. Help me to change.

RS

Orange Juice

The Lord appeared to Solomon during the night in a dream, and God said, "Ask for whatever you want me to give you."

1 Kings 3:5 NIV

Homer Simpson and the Almighty

The Big Breakfast

One of my favourite theologians is Homer Simpson. In one *Simpsons* episode he decides to give up on church, and that night the Almighty himself comes to visit in a dream. I wonder if sometimes we underestimate the power of God speaking to us in dreams. It is a very biblical occurrence. Imagine you, like Solomon, had a heavenly dream where God, sounding a bit like the legendary genie of the lamp, offers you a chance to ask him for anything you wish. What would your answer be?

Solomon's answer is incredible. He asks God: "Give your servant a discerning heart ... to distinguish between right and wrong" (1 Kings 3:9). God's response is equally spectacular: "Since you have asked for this and not for long life or wealth for yourself ... I will do what you have asked ... there will never have been anyone like you, nor will there ever be" (1 Kings 3:11-12).

As God is always reckless in his affection for his children, he goes on to promise Solomon, "Moreover, I will give you what you have not asked for – both riches and honor" (1 Kings 3:13).

Continental

So how do we get wisdom? Is it reserved for the spiritual elite or can we all share in its benefit? The book of James tells us that the start of the process is simple. "If any of you lacks wisdom, you should ask God, who gives generously to all without finding fault, and it will be given to you" (James 1:5).

Coffee

Feel the urgency of this proverb, and let it stir your soul into action: "Wisdom is supreme; therefore get wisdom. Though it cost all you have, get understanding" (Proverbs 4:7 NIV).

DB

Orange Juice

For to us a child is born, to us a son is given, and the government will be on his shoulders. And he will be called Wonderful Counselor, Mighty God, Everlasting Father, Prince of Peace.

Isaiah 9:6 NIV

Hope for the Future

The Big Breakfast

If you have ever been to a Christmas carol service (and most of us have at one time or another), you've probably heard this prophecy about the coming Messiah (it means "anointed one"). It is quoted in Handel's *Messiah,* full of pomp and with a very jaunty tune. But, of course, later in Isaiah we are reminded that "He was wounded and crushed because of our sins; by taking our punishment, he made us completely well" (Isaiah 53:5 CEV).

Jesus was a bringer of *shalom,* of the kingdom of God. He came to institute a time of good news, freedom, healing, pardon and God's favour (see Luke 4:18-19). There is a great sense of joy in the words of the prophet: he is full of hope that God is going to do something new and dramatic to bring about peace. And later on, while speaking about God's servant Israel, he is also prophesying about the cost Jesus would pay to begin the in-breaking of peace into our world.

Take yourself back to that carol service. Imagine you're hearing these words for the first time as you wait for your country to be invaded. The dream of God intervening and changing history is so attractive as to be almost unbelievable ... Will you believe it?

Continental

Just think on these words for a minute: "By taking our punishment, he made us completely well."

Coffee

Jesus, thank you for all that you did for me in living and dying and rising again. I love you and worship you.

SH

Orange Juice
The Son is ... the firstborn over all creation.

Colossians 1:15

First Things First

The Big Breakfast
The firstborn son held a very privileged place in both Hebrew and Roman mythologies. He was the heir; the true successor to the father. Under the father, he held a place of authority in the family. In a patriarchal culture, he carried immense responsibility, and enjoyed privileges to match.

Paul uses this image to try and capture the uniqueness of Jesus. Jesus is the "son and heir" of the created order – one with us, and yet above us. He is the one destined to lead the universe.

But there is more here. The firstborn also had a role in the Hebrew sacrificial system. It was the first fruits that were given back to God in the tithe. The sacrificial lamb was a firstborn lamb.

Just as God asks us to give the first and best to him, so he offers his first and best in sacrifice for us. Jesus is uniquely placed to rule the universe, and uniquely qualified to give himself for its redemption. The measure of the stature of Christ is a measure of the generosity of God.

Continental
As the "firstborn Son", Jesus is not only the privileged ruler of the universe – he is also our big brother. In one person, the ultimate authority and the ultimate intimacy come together.

Coffee
Blessed are you, Lord Jesus Christ: King of the universe, yet born of the Virgin Mary.

GK

Orange Juice

They gave as much as they were able, and even beyond their ability.

2 Corinthians 8:3

Stop Praying

The Big Breakfast

We forgot the collection baskets in church last Sunday so we had to use a pot from the kitchen. The collection was a noisy affair!

I used to preach quite regularly in a Pentecostal church. The first time I witnessed their style of collection, it amazed me. The entire congregation lined up in front of the pastor with their offerings and they were quite at liberty to put notes in and take change out. Sometimes the pastor would call for people to line up again if he felt the bag was too empty.

It doesn't matter how you give to God as long as you give as much as you are able, and beyond. Be honest with yourself. Do you give regularly? If the answer is no, then start. It's a biblical command and not an option for the authentic follower of Christ. Now take some time to figure out how much you are able to give. Finally, don't give the figure you have just written down or thought of – give more. Don't fool yourself about needing to pray about it first. The best way to start is by being generous in the giving of your time, possessions and finances. Then and only then will your spirit become generous. It seems to me that when we give *even more* the adventure really begins.

Continental

Archbishop Temple once said, "The last place that gets converted on a man is his pocket." How easy it is to talk a good game when it comes to our commitment to God. How much harder it is to demonstrate it with our actions.

Coffee

"All the believers were one in heart and mind. No one claimed that any of their possessions was their own, but they shared everything they had ... there were no needy persons among them" (Acts 4:32, 34). Is this true of your church?

DB

Orange Juice

"For I know the plans I have for you," declares the Lord, "plans to prosper you and not to harm you, plans to give you hope and a future."

Jeremiah 29:11 NIV

A Man Called David

The Big Breakfast

My friend David told me a marvellous story recently. He had been for a job interview the day before. When he got home, his eight-year-old son overheard him telling his wife how he'd got on. Jonathan came running into the kitchen and said, "Daddy, does God have plans? Did God plan that the man who was interviewing you for that job would know that a man called David would come for the interview, and would he know that God wants a man called David to get that job?" What about that for insight from an eight-year-old?

Does God have plans? He certainly does. He has terrific plans – big plans about the future of this planet and the people living on it; plans for whole nations of people, from every ethnic and cultural background; plans that the sun will keep shining and the rain will keep falling so all those people can grow food to feed themselves. The biggest deal of all is that he has plans for us as individuals, plans that are good, very good indeed.

Continental

You might ask, "What about all those times when the rain didn't come, or came too much and too often? What about the innocent victims of war or terrorism? Were those part of God's plan?" What do you think?

Coffee

God's plans are always good, but we need to work in partnership with him, not against him. We need to follow the way he tells us to live, not ignore him.

RS

Orange Juice

I will make a covenant of peace with them; it will be an everlasting covenant. I will establish them and increase their numbers, and I will put my sanctuary among them forever. My dwelling place will be with them; I will be their God, and they will be my people.

Ezekiel 37:26-27 NIV

The Real Deal

The Big Breakfast

For me, the phrase, "My dwelling place will be with them: I will be their God" is at the centre of what it means to have peace. It is something that you find all over the Bible, this idea that at the heart of God's plans is the simple desire for relationship.

Sometimes God has been pictured as having no feelings, or even as being incapable of feeling, yet this hunger to be with his people seems to be more than just a picture of God. Ultimately words are only a grasping after God, but a "covenant of peace" can signal for us a whole area of God's character. When you think of peace in future, think big!

What would it mean for you to make a *covenant* – a binding agreement – of peace with God? God has already outlined his side of the deal: it will be forever, it will result in multiplication, and God will live with you. What's your side of the deal?

Continental

"You will never find peace and happiness until you are ready to commit yourself to something worth dying for."

Jean-Paul Sartre

Coffee

What is one thing you will pray for and one thing you want to change about your circumstances in order to honour God's covenant of peace?

SH

Orange Juice

He came to that which was his own, but his own did not receive him.

John 1:11

Speechless

The Big Breakfast

I can recall three moments in life that really left me speechless. The first was when I was only eight years old and my dad took me to my first professional football match. I can't remember too much about the game, only the feeling of being speechless as I walked through the turnstile and up into the electric atmosphere of a roaring crowd waiting for the game to begin.

The second event that left me in that same speechless state came a few summers back. A good friend bought me a ticket to see the British Formula 1 Grand Prix at Silverstone. It was the roar of the engines this time that took my breath away and gave me a memory to treasure forever.

The third was when I read this verse for the first time and realized the magnitude of what God did to rescue me. The thought of God coming to his own creation, the people he made, his sons and daughters, with the answer to this life and hope for the next – and we chose not to receive him, but to string him up.

It steals your breath to think of a God who picked up his kids in his arms, went to kiss them with his love, and all they did was to wriggle free and run off.

Continental

It would break my heart to have my three boys turn their backs on me. It would crush me beyond hope to have them slam the door on my affection and leave me out in the cold. It literally broke the Father's heart when we murdered his Son.

Coffee

What of us who have received him? "Yet to all who did receive him, to those who believed in his name, he gave the right to become children of God" (John 1:12).

DB

Orange Juice

For in [Jesus] all things were created: things in heaven and on earth, visible and invisible, whether thrones or powers or rulers or authorities; all things have been created through him and for him.

Colossians 1:16

Christ in Creation

The Big Breakfast

In all truth there is great paradox. The contradictions in the Bible are not the end of faith, but its beginning.

This Jesus, born of a teenage mother in the blood and sweat and straw of an impoverished stable, is the same Jesus who was there when the composition of blood, and the make-up of sweat, and the genetic code of straw were all decided.

Immense is the love of the Father for the creation; more immense still is the love of the Father for the Son. Before the world came into being, there was this passion, this exchange of love between Father and Son. Jesus is both the expression and the object of the Father's love. He is the Creator, and the reason for creating. Faith in Christ begins not at Calvary but in Eden.

Continental

At every stage of salvation history, Jesus is at the centre of God's action. In creation, it is through Jesus that the world is made. In the Fall, it is in Jesus that God enters into his broken world. In redemption, it is in Christ that all things find fulfillment.

Coffee

Christ the Creator, I praise you for the world that you have made. Christ Incarnate, I welcome you as brother and friend. Christ the Redeemer, I honour you as King of a universe made new.

GK

Orange Juice

We have around us many people whose lives tell us what faith means.

Hebrews 2:1a NCV

Story Time

The Big Breakfast

One of the things we do well in Ireland, where I live, is tell stories about one another. When they're told with a bit of Irish "blarney" thrown in, they can sound like bestsellers! The great thing about these stories is that you get to hear about people's lives – the fun stuff, the rough stuff, the good and bad stuff.

I reckon that God wants us to get into telling stories. That way we get to hear the great things other Christians have done and how they've handled their lives. This verse in Hebrews is trying to tell us how much we need one another. Being a Christian isn't supposed to be worked out all by ourselves. If we look at other followers of Jesus, we will learn from them. In fact, by looking at their lives, we will get some help in understanding about faith, and that's a tough one to understand sometimes.

Continental

There are a whole load of famous people who would fit the bill here – Mother Teresa, Martin Luther King Jr . . . Think today of someone you know personally, whose life helps you to understand faith better.

Coffee

Lord Jesus, thank you for the people who have lived great, faithful lives. Help me to learn from them.

RS

Orange Juice
You have filled Jerusalem with your teaching.

Acts 5:28

What's Your Bhag?

The Big Breakfast
I love reading business and leadership books. My favourite book of the moment is *Built to Last* by James Collins and Jerry Porras. A good friend gave it to me, and I simply couldn't put it down. One chapter is entitled "BHAGs – Big Hairy Audacious Goals". It suggests that people who make their lives count always have goals that are *big, hairy and audacious.*

It made me question what my goals were for the task God has given me. Were they big enough? It came to me like a bolt out of the blue when I read what the high priest said to the early church leaders in Jerusalem. He commanded them to stop preaching about Jesus because they had filled Jerusalem with their teaching. A quarter of a million people lived in the city, and everyone knew what the Church stood for – parents, newspaper editors, business gurus, prostitutes, drug addicts, alcoholics, homosexuals, schoolchildren, nurses, shopkeepers. Even those from other faiths knew. I realized that hardly anyone in my town knows why we exist as a community of believers. My BHAG is to change that in the next five years. What's the passion that drives you?

Continental
My goal is that all the 16,000 homes in my town and its 40,000 inhabitants will know about the kingdom of God because of what our church teaches. Sure it is big, if not a touch audacious. You could even class it hairy! But it's a dream that creates a passion in me that often keeps me awake at night.

Coffee

In 1960 American President John F. Kennedy presented his BHAG: "within the next decade to place a man on the moon and bring him back again". He died in 1963, but his dream came true in 1969. Big dreams don't depend on those who dreamt them in the first place. Tell someone your dreams today, before they fade away.

DB

Orange Juice

Whatever you do, work at it with all your heart, as working for the Lord, not for human masters, since you know that you will receive an inheritance from the Lord as a reward. It is the Lord Christ you are serving.

Colossians 3:23-24

The Light Side

The Big Breakfast

I once had a really surreal weekend listening to two different Christian speakers at two different events. Amazingly, both were talking about work. Less surprising was the fact that they didn't agree. The first speaker said that because God wants us to be happy and fulfilled, we should look for a new job if we are unhappy in our present one. We just need to find a place where we can be fruitful. The other speaker said that leaving a job without God's permission is an act of unfaithfulness to God, and that we should do everything in our power to make our job work.

The second speaker spoke from this passage particularly, and I guess I can see where he was coming from. In our society, there are lots of jobs that just need doing, like stacking shelves and answering phone calls (or doing schoolwork – that's your main job when you're a student), and they are never going to be particularly exciting.

Sometimes we have to let go of our desire for money and prestige, and focus on pleasing God (and our employer) by working hard where we are. Who knows, if you work "as for the Lord", you'll probably shine and get a promotion!

Continental

"A dairymaid can milk cows to the glory of God."

Martin Luther

Coffee

What can you do today that will be for God?

SH

Orange Juice

He is before all things, and in him all things hold together.

Colossians 1:17

Every Breath You Take

The Big Breakfast

Jesus spans the past, present and future of the created order. In him, the verb "created" loses its captivity to the past historic tense. It is true to say that Jesus creat*ed* everything, but it is also true that he goes on creat*ing* – holding everything together moment by moment.

To speak of God as Creator is not to describe a job he once held for six days several aeons ago; it is to speak of an ongoing dynamic relationship between the eternal God and the universe he has made.

It took science 20 centuries to catch up with this idea. Since Einstein physicists have been engaged in the search for the "theory of everything" – the unifying principle by which the whole universe exists. Jesus is that principle – through a moment-by-moment decision of his will and love, he holds everything together.

Black holes can't bounce without Jesus. The stars can't shimmer without Jesus. Particles can't party without Jesus. You can't breathe without Jesus.

Continental

The act of creation is a 24 hours a day, 7 days a week, 52 weeks of the year ongoing declaration of God's love.

Coffee

As a star abides in the light of God, as the planets abide in the patterns set out for them, as the dust of the earth abides in the love of the One who formed it, may I abide in Christ this day.

GK

Orange Juice

See what great love the Father has *lavished* on us, that we should be called children of God! And that is what we are!

1 John 3:1 (emphasis added)

It's Spread Thickly

The Big Breakfast

"Lavished". What a great word – so opulent that it should stand alone.

How great is the love the Father has LAVISHED upon us.

It is such a big word. It's the kind of word that should be taken for lunch to the Ritz Hotel, dressed in an Italian suit and entertained at the opera in Vienna. You can't even say the word without raising the tone of your voice along with accompanying hand gestures. God is no cheap lover. He has lavished his love and affection on you.

Let me explain it another way. My mum and dad are very different, especially when it comes to breakfast-table habits. My dad spreads the butter carefully across the surface of the toast, ensuring every corner is covered. He then measures the jam out precisely before spreading it evenly on top of the butter. My mum is different – the creative type. She dollops on the butter, pushes it around the toast a little, then spoons out a lavish portion of jam. Yum! I always preferred it when my mum lavished breakfast on me as a kid.

Continental

How much do you think God loves you today? This verse says that his love doesn't dribble out like a leaky tap. It pours out from heaven like the water cascading over Niagara Falls. His love for you is "spread thickly". Make sure you take a bite at the start of the day today.

Coffee

"We're never left feeling shortchanged. Quite the contrary – we can't round up enough containers to hold everything God generously pours into our lives through the Holy Spirit!" (Romans 5:5 MSG). Let your heart worship this outrageously generous Saviour.

DB

Orange Juice

Let us look only to Jesus, the One who began our faith and who makes it perfect.

Hebrews 12:2 NCV

Celebs

The Big Breakfast

When I was a kid I used to go to my Gran's for part of the summer holidays. She always bought Rice Krispies for breakfast. The back of the cereal box always had a puzzle or game on it. We needed something to do on those rainy days! I remember once the back of the box had the boys from Liverpool on it – Paul, John, George and Ringo. (Yes, it was a long time ago!) They were everywhere in those days.

We still live in a celebrity-obsessed culture. How many of those gossip magazines are out there now, telling us who has just married whom, or who has split up from whom, and all the other stuff that's going on in their lives? We're fascinated by it. We're also addicted to it. We want to know all about these people. Do we secretly think they have inside knowledge on how to sort things out? Whether we like it or not, we look up to our celebs. They're our mentors.

Continental

Celebrities are human too. They'll get some things right and other things wrong, just like us. If you want to look up to someone, look up to Jesus.

Coffee

Jesus is much more than a great mentor. He's right in there with us, working things out so that our lives and our faith grow.

RS

Orange Juice

We must honour our God by the way we live, so the Gentiles can't find fault with us ... Now give back the fields, vineyards, olive orchards, and houses you have taken and also the interest you have been paid.

Nehemiah 5:9, 11 CEV

Justice in Action

The Big Breakfast

Judah was famine-stricken, and in order to buy food from outside the country the people needed money. They mortgaged their property to the few rich Jews that there were and ended up in trouble because of the huge interest that was being exacted. Nehemiah was having none of this. "We've just got all these people out of slavery, and you want to make them slaves again," he says. The nobles agree and give the money back.

Then, after the first example of debt cancellation, comes the first example of "fair trade". Well, not quite, to be honest, but it's close! The governor of Judah was entitled to live on the choicest foods that were available to him, all "paid for" by tribute, which meant that all the people had to give him their best produce as a form of taxation. Nehemiah records that he and all his family refused this food so that the people who had grown it could eat it and benefit from the fruits of their labours. They agreed to pay for their own food so that everyone got a fair deal.

Sometimes people see these campaigns for social justice as modern inventions. Those people need to read their Bibles a bit more.

Continental

Borrowing money and shopping are both deeply spiritual and moral activities. They are both very easy to do. How can you shop and spend more justly?

Coffee

Does God want you to intervene in a social issue of which you are aware? Spend some time listening to him.

SH

Orange Juice

When he saw the crowds, he had compassion on them, because they were harassed and helpless, like sheep without a shepherd.

Matthew 9:36

Relentless Pursuit of the Lost

The Big Breakfast

We need to recapture a sense of how God feels about "the lost". One of the most eventful routines in our family life is the weekly trip to the supermarket. It takes all our efforts to fill the trolley with goods while hanging on to two kids. One day we lost our four-year-old son, Matthew. A chocolate bar in the shape of a light sabre had caught his eye and we got a couple of aisles ahead of him. When we noticed we were an offspring short, what do you think we did?

You couldn't imagine us saying to the manager, "We come in most Mondays, so if you find him we'll pick him up then." No. Debbie bellowed his name while I ran up and down the aisles, shoving people out of the way. Eventually we found him, embraced him fondly, then berated him!

If a shepherd lost one of his sheep, he would engage in that same passionate pursuit. That is what God thinks about those who don't know him. So why is it that the Church lets "the lost" slip so easily by, without even a simple word of hope?

Continental

In Britain, 1,500 people join the Church every week, but the bad news is that 1,600 die each week. The even more depressing news is that around 80,000 people leave the Church each year. Whatever country we live in, lost people matter to God, so they must start to matter to us.

Coffee

"Show your power, O Lord." There are two lines from this song that always stir my heart: "We ask not for riches but look to the cross./ And for our inheritance give us the lost." Maybe it is time to stop asking God for *riches* and to start asking for *the lost* people in your world to become your inheritance.

DB

Orange Juice

You are the salt of the earth. But if the salt loses its saltiness, how can it be made salty again?

Matthew 5:13

Pass the Salt

The Big Breakfast

To the Jew, salt was rock-salt – essentially a mixture of sodium chloride and rock dust. Pure salt as we know it was unavailable, and the purity and quality of the mixture varied – hence the possibility of "salt" without "saltiness".

The rocky dust in your hand might look like salt, but it is powerless – in the Greek, "dull" or "moronic". It has no edge or taste. It will neither preserve the freshness of food nor enhance its flavour.

Such is the fate of humankind without the wisdom of God. We may look like the bosses of creation, but we will lack the insight, the creativity, the dynamism to bring the best out of all that God has made. We will neither preserve the goodness of the earth, nor add flavour to its fruits. The cosmos will go on without the vital spark that God intended us to bring.

What can bring that spark back? Jesus doesn't answer the question, but leaves it hanging. This is the need he has come to meet. This is the mission of Christ.

Continental

What gifts and insights has God given you for the benefit of his cosmos? When it comes to using them, are you salty, or dull?

Coffee

"Your God is too small," J.B. Phillips once wrote. Ask God to give you a glimpse of the sheer breadth of his purposes for the creation.

GK

Orange Juice
By helping each other with your troubles, you truly obey the law of Christ.

Galatians 6:2 NCV

A Little Help from My Friends

The Big Breakfast
"A Little Help from My Friends" is a great song. The Beatles had loads of them. Even after all these years, we're still singing the lines.

One of the best things about being part of the Christian family is all those good friends we can make, people who are there for us. Part of their job as Christians is to be there for us, just as it's part of our job to be there for them.

To be a Christian is to belong to an amazing club that has members all over the world. And there's more: everyone in that club is there for you. They're there to help when you're in trouble. But you need to let them know when you're in trouble. There was a really sad story in our local news recently. A young girl killed herself because she couldn't take the bullying at school any more. Nobody actually knew she was being bullied until it was too late. Why didn't she tell someone?

Continental
We keep things to ourselves because we're afraid or ashamed, or because we reckon we can work it out for ourselves. Sharing is better.

Coffee
Talking about some of the really deep things that concern you takes courage and trust. Give a Christian friend the benefit of the doubt and tell them what's bothering you.

RS

Orange Juice

My soul finds rest in [waits in silence for] God alone.

Psalm 62:1 NIV

Waiting Room?

The Big Breakfast

Being an activist, my frequent prayer is the well-loved plea, "Lord, give me patience, but could you hurry up about it, please?"

Do you ever ponder the really big questions in life? I still can't find an answer to what you have to plant to grow seedless grapes. But I do know this: we have developed the seedless variety because we have lost the ancient art of patience. Life is too frantic to pick out the pips, even though the ones with seeds are so much juicier!

For me, I would much rather do anything than wait, even if it's the wrong thing. Breakfasting with God can't be hurried. A bowl of muesli with the Messiah must never be rushed. How could we begin to think that a quick "Morning, Lord" as we stuff a piece of toast in our mouths and rush headlong into the day could ever become the staple diet of the authentic follower of Christ?

Where does your soul find the rest it craves? Maybe it's in music, maybe it's in sport, or maybe it's in a summer's walk in the woods with friends. Wherever it may be, spend it with God, not running on ahead but waiting with him. You can't run and wait both at the same time.

Continental

My theological anorak buddies tell me that the word "silence" here is best translated "a quiet whisper". What a great picture. We whisper our affection to God in a crowded world so that only he can hear, just as lovers whisper to each other in a restaurant. What will you whisper to him today?

Coffee

In verse 5 of the psalm, David turns his declaration into a command to himself. "Find rest, O my soul, in (wait in silence for) God alone." Get tough with your own inner life. Pursue patience.

DB

Orange Juice

Ezra opened the book. All the people could see him because he was standing above them; and as he opened it, the people all stood up. Ezra praised the Lord, the great God; and all the people lifted their hands and responded, "Amen! Amen!" Then they bowed down and worshiped the Lord with their faces to the ground.

Nehemiah 8:5-6 NIV

The Big Book

The Big Breakfast

Books, eh? Who needs 'em nowadays, what with radio, TV, computers, mobile phones and all the rest? What funny things they are, bits of paper stuck together with words on them. I get my news on my super-light-fits-in-my-pocket home multimedia washing machine.

Books. Apparently we live in a "non-book culture". Oh dear, you're so out of fashion reading this, then, aren't you! Put it down right away, you can't possibly learn anything from it!

The Book. How would you start a big party? A book reading? Well, perhaps not. Here is old man Ezra at the beginning of the city of Jerusalem's celebrations of the completion of the city wall. I'm sure that if there had been fireworks and the Spice Girls they would have been there too, but this bit would always have come first: a book reading.

And what a book. Ezra reads the Law, the Pentateuch, the first five books of the Bible! And as he opens the book (well, scroll, probably) what's the people's response? They praise God!

Continental

A famous guy once said, "When one has tired of London, one has tired of life." I think Ezra and Nehemiah would have echoed Psalm 119 and said, "When one has tired of the Scriptures, one has tired of God."

Coffee

If you have a favourite Bible verse, read it through and remember how much joy you have received through reading the Scriptures. If you are finding the Bible dull and dry at the moment, pray that God will inject some passion into the next time you pick up a Bible.

SH

Orange Juice

You are the light of the world. A city on a hill cannot be hidden.

Matthew 5:14

Give Us a Light!

The Big Breakfast

The image is of a city at night. From a thousand lamps and torches, light collects to blaze out across the valley. Jesus does not say that a city *should* not be hidden but that it *cannot*. The message to humanity is clear – for good or ill, what you do will be visible in the world.

God has given to the human race the capacity to make a difference in the cosmos – in intelligence and gifting, in talent and skill. Whatever we do with that capacity, it will make a difference, and the difference will be seen. Like the Great Wall of China, which, they say, is clearly visible from space, we make our mark on the world. And what a mark we have made – in ozone depletion; in mass starvation; in the destruction of thousands of species per day and deforestation at one acre per second.

We understand in individual lives that what is sown is later reaped – but the city on a hill is a picture of the corporate dimension. In the same way, Jesus is saying, "Your sins will not be hidden." The impact of humanity, for good or ill, will blaze out across the universe.

Continental

If you were asked to summarize the human record as stewards of creation, what words would you use?

Coffee

"If you want to understand the Creator, seek to understand created things."

Columbanus

GK

Orange Juice
When you are angry, do not sin, and be sure to stop being angry before the end of the day. Don't give the Devil a chance to defeat you.

Ephesians 4:26-27 NCV

Go On . . . Get Mad!

The Big Breakfast
You have my full permission to blow your stack once in a while – at the right time and for the right reasons, of course. Paul clearly says, "*when* you are angry do not sin", so don't let anyone ever tell you that anger is wrong. It is a God-given emotion. Even Jesus got angry, especially with religious nutters (Matthew 23). The key is that in our anger we must not sin and we must resolve it "before the end of the day".

I have been trying to think about the times recently when I got justifiably angry and when anger got the better of me. I remembered a struggling gay friend who got thrown out of his church and felt kicked in the teeth by God. That got me angry. I also recalled a heated dispute in a crowded car park because somebody "stole my place". That time anger got me.

Think back over your journey this past week. When did you let anger get you? Maybe even now it is still eating away at you inside. Do you need to make a phone call to resolve it? Do it before the day is out, and you will stamp on the Devil's foot that has been wedged in the door of your soul.

Continental
Sure, Jesus yelled at a few priests. He even lost his rag in the temple courts one day, but it was also recorded that "All spoke well of him and were amazed at the gracious words that came from his lips" (Luke 4:22). Get the balance?

Coffee
The seventeenth-century clergyman Thomas Fuller once wrote, "Anger is one of the sinews of the soul". If we learn to harness its power from within, it is less likely to do damage from without.

DB

Orange Juice

He said to them, "When you pray, say: 'Father, may your name always be kept holy.'"

Luke 11:2 NCV

It's How You Do It

The Big Breakfast

What is the word you hear used most often? It's probably God's name. I often wonder why things turned out like that. Why don't we hear people say, "Oh my Buddha!" or "For Mother Nature's sake!" It's strange that we laugh at that idea. I don't know why God's name has become an easy swear-word, but I do know that God doesn't like it. In fact, it upsets him a great deal.

The big question is, why don't we Christians do something about it? We listen to the misuse of God's name every day, but we rarely challenge it. I know: it would seem prudish, or far too religious, or perhaps an invasion into other people's rights and space. I guess it's how we do things that's important. I agree that we have no right to tell other people how to speak or what language they can use. We do have a right, however, to defend the reputation and dignity of our Lord. This is a political incorrectness well worth fighting for.

Continental

There is much about God, and about being a Christian, that's treated as irrelevant today. There's nothing irrelevant about God, and the way we use his name does matter.

Coffee

Lord Jesus, I have to say that I've become far too familiar with the misuse of your name. Help me to defend your reputation in wise ways.

RS

Orange Juice

He said to them: "You are well aware that it is against our law for a Jew to associate with Gentiles or visit them. But God has shown me that I should not call anyone impure or unclean."

Acts 10:28

The Weirdest Vision

The Big Breakfast

This is one of my favourite stories in the Bible, which I consider to contain one of the greatest miracles in the Bible.

Peter is staying at a friend's house, waiting for his dinner to be served. He's starving! Going out onto the roof of the house, he has a vision of all the wee beasties that are forbidden him by the Old Testament law. God then tells him that he should eat all of it. It's almost impossible to explain how shocking this message from God is: because nearly every taboo has been broken and we are so unshockable, the only modern equivalent I can think of would be for God to ask a parent to invite the local child abuser to babysit.

But Peter gets the message: in matters to do with what is acceptable to God, God decides, not us. As the vision ends and Peter goes downstairs to eat, he finds that a messenger has arrived from a Roman called Cornelius, who wants Peter to visit him. Instead of saying, "Ugh, nasty Gentile, I'm not going," he learns the message from the vision and goes to see Cornelius. This is his opening speech, and it's impressive. Peter was willing to reject hundreds of years of Jewish culture because God was showing him that he was doing something new.

Continental

God is a God who breaks down boundaries. What boundaries are there between you and your church and the people who live around you? Are there some people you are unwilling to accept, or, more likely, people who just don't fit in? What does this message say to us today?

Coffee

Pray for someone you know who is very different from you. Pray that God will bless them and that he will show you how to share God with them.

SH

Orange Juice

Many of the Samaritans from that town believed in him because of the woman's testimony.

John 4:39

Who Would You Choose?

The Big Breakfast

Okay. You've got the job. God asks you to find a top evangelist to tell the message of his love to your entire town, so you start by short-listing some potential candidates:

- Your minister – too busy preparing his Sunday sermon
- Billy Graham – far too famous
- Your old religion teacher – too busy sewing patches on his elbows

At that moment, a woman from the local council estate wanders in, carrying some heavy shopping and an equally burdensome reputation for men she isn't married to.

"She's the one I want."

"Sorry, Lord?" you cry.

"Melanie. She's the one I want. The one I really, really want."

"But, Lord, she's not one of us. Do you know how many men she's been with? She's not even a Christian."

Jesus chose such an evangelist. Don't ever think God can't use the unusable to bring entire towns face to face with himself.

Continental

When I first read this story of Jesus and the Samaritan woman it taught me a lot about how to share my faith (John 4). Tired and thirsty, Jesus met her in the midday sunshine at the local drinking well and asked her to help him get a drink. Maybe "Can you help me?" really is better than "Can I preach to you?"

Coffee

Sometimes our fear stops us speaking about God. "What if I say the wrong thing?" Take heart. This woman's first words to the town were: "Come and see a man who ..." You can hear the response, "Oh boy ... not another one!"

DB

Orange Juice

Neither do people light a lamp and put it under a bowl.

Matthew 5:15

Lighting Fires

The Big Breakfast

Until the harnessing of electrical power, there was no light without fire and no fire without light. In the time of Christ, to speak of light was to speak of fire.

Oil lamps – a clay reservoir of oil with a wick to give a single, fragile flame – were the main source of light in every household. Olive groves were significant in part because they provided the oil used for light: they were the power stations of their day.

The instinct to put the light under a bucket is not as senseless as it might appear. A single draught or gust of wind could snuff out the flame in an instant. Under a bowl, it could be protected from such a fate – but its light would be wasted.

The choice is stark. To be valuable, the light must be vulnerable – over-protect it, and it loses its purpose. Take the risk, Jesus is saying. Use your gifts; expose your light to the potentially harsh winds of criticism, rejection and failure. Without risk, there is no light.

Continental

Olive-oil lamps give out, with their light, fragrance and a measure of warmth. To hide your light is to deprive human culture of the fragrance of God, and of the measure of warmth that you might bring.

Coffee

"Lord, grant me ... that my lamp may feel thy kindling touch and know no quenching; may burn for me and for others may give light."

Columbanus

GK

Orange Juice

He said to them, "When you pray, say: ' . . . Give us each day our daily bread.'"

Luke 11:2-3

Have You Ever Been Really Hungry?

The Big Breakfast

Have you ever been *really* hungry? I mean so hungry that you might pass out because your blood sugar level is so low? For most of us, this kind of hunger usually means that, while we may have missed breakfast or lunch, we can be sure that we'll get some dinner in the next hour or two. We don't have to stop and think about where our dinner will come from. It will be there for us every day, and that's just part of life. Aren't we fortunate?

For other people, the source of the next bite of food is not a given. Our societies are still very divided between the haves and the have-nots, and for many that means their daily bread can also be a have-not.

I once read an article by a relief worker in the Sudan, who was helping people caught in a terrible famine. He told the story of a woman he saw gathering scraps from a rubbish heap. Before she or her children ate the meagre meal, she bowed her head and thanked God for the food.

Continental

Our food and everything else that keeps us alive is a gift from God. Remind yourself of this every day.

Coffee

Lord Jesus, forgive me for taking the daily food I eat for granted. Thank you for giving me what I need and more. Teach me to share.

RS

Orange Juice

Nothing is as wonderful as knowing Christ Jesus my Lord. I have given up everything else and count it all as rubbish. All I want is Christ and to know that I belong to him.

Philippians 3:8-9 CEV

Toilet Talk

The Big Breakfast

It seems to me that the Bible translators must have been suit-wearing, middle-class academics who never really came to grips with the language of the market-place. The Brethren gland within me understands their caution in using the word "rubbish", but if you read this verse in the Authorised Version, it comes nearer the mark: "I count it all dung."

Now we're getting to the bottom of what Paul is trying to say. Now we see the priorities in his life. Let's revisit this verse again in the Bloomin' Obvious Bible (Colour Pictures Edition):

There ain't no competition here. What's the point in trying to keep up with the Joneses when the warehouse of heaven's best is bulging at the seams for me? Walking in step with the Master has meant ditching all the shiny stuff that slows me down. I reckon all those glittery bits are a pile of poo compared to a fresh delivery of Jesus to my soul and to my feet.

Excuse me, but when you see all that stuff for the crap it really is (not my words but the apostle Paul's), your Christ quota will go through the roof and following him becomes less duty and more joy.

Continental

Do you consider your career a loss compared to the greatness of knowing Christ? Do you consider your home, your bank balance, your wardrobe, your car or your new DVD player in the same way? Tell me how exotic holidays can ever match up to basking in the brilliance of God's undeserved grace for you.

Coffee

This verse . . . a little bit strong? Feel offended? I think Paul's audience would have felt the same. I also think that they would have got the point. Have you?

DB

Orange Juice

How beautiful on the mountains are the feet of those who
bring good news, who proclaim peace, who bring good tidings,
who proclaim salvation, who say to Zion, "Your God reigns!"

Isaiah 52:7 NIV

Kill the Messenger?

The Big Breakfast

Being a messenger can be a nasty job. The practice of killing
the bringer of bad news dates all the way back to biblical times
(see 2 Samuel 1:15). Kings would sit in their castles waiting for
someone to come over the hill: Have we won our battle?
Who has been killed? No wonder the Bible talks about how wonderful the messenger is when he brings good news!

Just a few weeks ago I heard that I'm going to be a dad. Then, last week, I heard
it was going to be twins! That was really good news, but boy, does it mean my life
is going to change! News has that effect on you: if it didn't signal that something new
and different was happening, it wouldn't be news.

Christians are the people of the gospel, the good news. One of the interesting
things about Christianity is that if you ask ten people why they became Christians,
you'll probably get ten different answers. That's okay: God is good news to all of us!

Continental

Are we a good-news people to our world or a bad-news
people?

Coffee

Think of three words that sum up what has been good news to
you about being a Christian. If you have a pen handy, why not
write them down in the space here.

SH

Orange Juice

"Do not think that I have come to abolish the Law or the Prophets; I have not come to abolish them but to fulfill them."

Matthew 5:17

I Fought the Law...

The Big Breakfast

The annual Darwin Awards are given to those who promote evolution by removing themselves from the global gene pool in the least intelligent and most spectacular fashion.

The recipients in 1999 included a terrorist who sent a letter bomb to an enemy, helpfully including a return address. When the postal service was unable to deliver the package, they returned it to him. He promptly forgot what it was, opened it and was instantly killed.

These words of Jesus are a letter bomb addressed to the Jewish leaders. On the surface, it seems innocuous to talk of fulfilling rather than abolishing the Law, but inside this package is the explosive truth that the Law alone is not enough. The Law stands in need of fulfillment because it is incomplete. It is not the full revelation of the nature and character of God.

The Old Testament scriptures were the sacred, untouchable, unchangeable core of the Hebrew faith. Jesus, with the audacity of a man who is either morally twisted, terminally insane or telling the truth, calls time on the partial revelation and drops the bombshell: the full picture of God is now here.

Continental

It is often hard, when we have boxed and labelled God in systems that we control and understand, to recognize and welcome fresh revelation.

Coffee

What are the structures that Jesus the revolutionary might demolish in your life? Make an honest inventory – and invite him to bring fulfilment.

GK

Orange Juice

Mary ... sat at the Lord's feet listening to what he said. But Martha was distracted by all the preparations that had to be made.

Luke 10:39-40

Ignore the Rodent

The Big Breakfast

Pussycat, Pussycat, where have you been?
I've been up to London to visit the Queen!
Pussycat, Pussycat, what did you there?
I frightened a little mouse under her chair!

How often are God's subjects guilty of holding an audience with the King and getting distracted by something under his throne? Sure, they are often legitimate distractions. When will God answer my prayers about a partner? How can I invite the entire office to Bible study? Is that a new wig on my minister or is he just combing his hair forward?

Jesus and the crew drop in for tea and someone's got to cut the crusts off the cucumber samies. Mary waits and Martha works. She gets all steamed up about it. It's not that Martha was wrong to get busy, it was her attitude that let her down. "Tell Mary to help me!" was her demand to Jesus.

I love the warmth and graciousness of Jesus' response. "Martha, Martha, you are worried and upset about many things, but few things are needed – or indeed only one. Mary has chosen what is better." Don't miss out on what is best.

Continental

What are you worried about today? What's making you upset? I am sure they're all good, legitimate things. But don't let them distract you. Trade them in for a few minutes at the feet of Jesus. Rest your arms on his knees, gaze up into his eyes and listen to his conversation. Feeling better?

Coffee

Disciple, Disciple, where've ya bin?
I've been to church to see the King!
Disciple, Disciple, what did you there?
I turned up late and mumbled a prayer!

DB

Orange Juice
He said to them, "When you pray, say: ' . . . Forgive us our sins . . .'"

Luke 11:2, 4

What a Strange Word!

The Big Breakfast
I recently heard a very well-known pop singer tell young people that if something felt right, it must be okay for them and they should go ahead and do it. "Sin," she said, "is a strange word anyway! Sin isn't a word we use any more. Have you noticed? In fact, it's almost like it belongs to some foreign language." I guess that for some it *is* a foreign language. We don't talk any more about things being a sin, which means "wrong". According to many people, things are neither right nor wrong: there is only choice. You choose the thing that's good for you. We've removed that word "sin" from our dictionary.

The Bible makes a lot of things very clear. One of them is that right and wrong are not decided by us. Sin means doing wrong, and we need to ask God to forgive us when we sin.

Continental
God's ideas of right and wrong will never reach their sell-by date, because our best interest is always at the heart of them.

Coffee
Lord Jesus, help me to listen to you about what is right and wrong, and not to the popular ideas all around me.

RS

Orange Juice

"I promise to be with you and keep you safe, so don't be afraid."

Jeremiah 1:8 CEV

You're Not Alone

The Big Breakfast

The other day I took my mum to see an evangelistic comedy magician. It sounds terrible, doesn't it? Actually, he was really good. Anyway, at the end of the evening my mum explains why she doesn't want to go to church, and I know that I'm supposed to say something wise and spiritual at this point. Instead, my mouth goes dry and my tongue sticks to the roof of my mouth.

You see, my mum knows everything about me. She knows what a hypocrite I am, that I always took so long with the washing up that she would give up on me and do it herself, that my bedroom door had "Do not enter: health hazard" stickers on it for a reason. How can I tell her how to sort her life out when mine still seems to be in a mess? I just felt so alone.

God lets us know that his work is a partnership. I would never advise anyone to serve God alone (Jesus never sent anyone out on their own), but if it happens, God promises to be closer than a friend, closer than a mother, closer than breathing.

Continental

I will not leave you as orphans; I will come to you.

John 14:18

Coffee

Try this simple exercise as a form of prayer: imagine yourself in a situation in which you are scared to acknowledge you are a Christian. Now imagine Jesus is standing right next to you. Pray that you can be aware of Jesus with you wherever you go.

SH

Orange Juice

And God raised us up with Christ and seated us with him in the heavenly realms ... in order that ... he might show the *incomparable riches of his grace*, expressed in his kindness to us in Christ Jesus.

Ephesians 2:6-7 (emphasis added)

Amazing Grace

The Big Breakfast

This "grace" word is often used in church, in the Bible and in Graham Kendrick choruses. So it must be either an easy word to rhyme or a very important word. But what does it mean? And what are "the incomparable riches of his grace"?

Philip Yancey recorded a true story that appeared in a Boston newspaper some years ago. A young woman had grown up poor and homeless but later found a good job and became engaged to a high-flying businessman. The couple confirmed the Hyatt Hotel for their reception. However, the man soon got cold feet and walked out on her. She had to cancel the hotel booking but stood to lose a great deal of money if she did. A thought came to her: "Why don't I have this party anyway?" She set about inviting all the homeless she once knew to join her. So on that night, at a five-star hotel in Boston, those who normally scavenged cold pizza from rubbish skips ate the finest foods from hand-painted plates.

This is outrageous grace at its sweetest. It means us not getting what we deserve. In fact, it means us getting what we definitely don't deserve.

Continental

How do we get saved, then? By sitting in the front pew for 30 years? By regularly supporting "what's-his-name" on the mission field? By reading more books, listening to more sermons, or attending more prayer meetings? Or is it simply by the incomparable riches of his grace expressed in his kindness to us in Christ? Ask the thief on the cross!

Coffee

Allow the realization of this undeserved grace to crash into your soul more often, and you will walk more humbly, speak more gently and judge less harshly.

DB

Orange Juice

Paul then stood up in the meeting of the Areopagus and said: "People of Athens! I see that in every way you are very religious."

Acts 17:22

A Mars a Day

The Big Breakfast

Paul's visit to Mars Hill (Areopagus) has become something of a rallying-point for Christian cultural engagement. We know by this stage that Paul is the great Apostle and church-planter. He has demonstrated the keenest religious mind of his generation. But here he goes further – grasping philosophies less akin to his own experience; quoting poets known to the Greeks.

His arguments begin not with his experience but with theirs. Before speaking, he has taken time to walk the city. He has observed and absorbed the lifestyles of these intellectual seekers. Inwardly, he has registered disgust at the idolatry of the city, but outwardly, this is the very point at which he establishes rapport.

Paul's approach is clear – far from emphasizing how different Christians are from their pagan neighbours, he builds a platform of common experience. "We all ask the same questions," he is in effect saying. "Now here are the answers I have found."

Without common ground there can be no contact, and without contact there can be no conversation.

Continental

For Paul, evangelism is as much about making connections as it is about making converts.

Coffee

Creator God, you are the one in whom we live and move and have our being. Many are those who worship you without knowing your name. Make connections, we pray, that you might be worshipped, by name, throughout the earth.

GK

Orange Juice

Therefore, if you are offering your gift at the altar and there remember that the brother or sister has something against you, leave your gift there in front of the altar. First go and be reconciled to that person; then come and offer your gift.

Matthew 5:23-24

Deal with the Bad Stuff

The Big Breakfast

A friend of mine upset me once. I told another friend about it and got the whole thing off my chest. Quite a few months later, the person who had upset me called and asked if we could meet for a coffee. I was happy to meet. I'd forgotten all about the incident. The first words my friend said to me, even before the coffee was poured, were, "I'm here to ask for your forgiveness". I was stunned. I'll never forget the impact of those words.

My friend understood something very important. It is impossible to worship God properly if we have anger in our hearts towards another person. In Matthew chapter 5, Jesus is telling his followers about the things that matter a whole lot to God. One thing God cares about a great deal is what's in our hearts, especially how we feel about other people and the attitudes that control how we feel. "Deal with the bad stuff," Jesus says. Unless you do, you can't worship God properly.

Continental

Ray Davey, who was a POW during the Second World War, said, "If the Church has nothing to say about reconciliation, then the Church has nothing to say!"

Coffee

Lord Jesus, you call us to live by the values of your kingdom in everything we do. Give me the desire and the will to do it.

RS

Orange Juice

The Lord God formed the man from the dust of the ground and breathed into his nostrils the breath of life, and the man became a living being.

Genesis 2:7 NIV

A Walking Miracle

The Big Breakfast

A grand piano has 240 strings by which the world's finest concert pianist can produce a soul-churning melody. But the human ear that enables an audience to hear these sounds consists of 240,000 strings.

A TV camera has 60,000 photoelectric elements, which can capture any image. But the human eye, which functions unceasingly in any weather for around 70 years and has automatic focus, contains more than 137,000,000 elements.

A top-of-the-range, industrial IBM computer can handle the equivalent of one neurone of information at a time. But your brain has as many as 200 communicating pathways meeting in a single nerve cell or neurone. This means that in your brain there are 10,000 million neurones, each one serving as a mini microcomputer.

The psalmist grasped something of this when he wrote of how fearfully and wonderfully made he was (Psalm 139:14). Take time to reflect, to stop and think. You are a walking miracle, a full-page colour advert to your Master's creativity and power. You may not feel like it today, but you are the pinnacle of his creation and he is proud of you.

Continental

I would go as far as to say that it is heresy for so many of our churches to be the dullest places on planet earth. What has happened to our creativity? You were made in the image of a creative God, the architect, designer and builder of this astonishing human frame of yours.

Coffee

My Father, breathe again your life and your creativity into my soul and let me live once more. Let me dance as once I did, let me work, let me sing, let me play and let me pause again to praise your most holy of names. Amen.

DB

Orange Juice

After John was put in prison, Jesus went into Galilee, proclaiming the good news of God. "The time has come," he said. "The kingdom of God has come near. Repent and believe the good news!"

Mark 1:14-15

News of the Kingdom

The Big Breakfast

Jesus talks a lot about the kingdom of God. Nobody ever knew exactly what he was talking about, but that was all part of the plan. Often when we think of the kingdom, we think of heaven as a place in the future, but here Jesus says that the Kingdom is near ("upon you" is the best translation). The news that we have is that God is breaking into this world, that he's not some far-off, distant God who has just made the world and then gone for a smoke. Jesus himself is a sign that God is close: God was willing to become like us in order to get the message across. Now that is good news!

But then we get this word "repent", which literally means "turn around". The news about God's in-breaking Kingdom means that things have got to change: not just for the power-brokers, as Jesus has already said, but for all of us. Things can never be the same again. Once God calls us, we need to respond. He doesn't ask us to be perfect, but he does ask us to turn around and face him. If we move, we move towards him, and the closer we get to him, the more our lives are shown up in the light. We have to decide whether we want all that stuff to be shown up.

Continental

"If you have behaved badly, repent ... On no account brood over your wrongdoing. Rolling in the muck is not the best way of getting clean."

Aldous Huxley

Coffee

If Jesus came to visit you tomorrow, what would you want to do to get ready? Talk to God about it.

SH

Orange Juice

From one man he made all the nations, that they should inhabit the whole earth; and he marked out their appointed times in history and the boundaries of their lands.

Acts 17:26

We Are a Skin Kaleidoscope

The Big Breakfast

Identity is a powerful force. Gangs will fight for it; races struggle for it; nations go to war for it. There is something at the very heart of the human experience that looks for a sense of belonging, of *home*.

The God of whom Paul speaks in Acts 17 does not love humanity in some generic, blurred sense – he sees the detail. God is aware of your nationality. He knows your culture and speaks your language. In bald terms, "He knows where you live." And he loves diversity. His kingdom is a kaleidoscope, a glorious salad-bowl with ingredients from every tribe and tongue tossed together.

Paul has challenged the people of his day to surrender their local gods and to worship the God of the universe. But the miracle of the Incarnation is that a universal God becomes a local God. God wants you to know him as the keeper of the cosmos – the Lord of all – but he also wants to move into your neighbourhood.

Continental

"Think globally, act locally" is a slogan coined by the Green lobby and used by many organizations. It is also, according to Paul, God's strategy.

Coffee

"Those who have ears. Those who have cares. Those who have fears. Those who have tears. Let them hear ... and see ... and feel ... and breathe."

Mike Riddell, alt.spirit@metro.m3

GK

Orange Juice

If a brother or sister sins, go and point out the fault, just between the two of you alone ... But if they will not listen, take one or two others along.

Matthew 18:15-16

The Three-Point Plan

The Big Breakfast

I've done it. I've discovered the way to stop nations fighting, political parties accusing each other of scandal, close friends falling out with each other and churches splitting. We simply do what Jesus told his disciples to do in these verses. I've lived through the untruths that have caused a church to split and believers to ignore each other in the street. I've suffered at the hands of gossips. I'm sure you have too.

So here is his three-point plan. First, *go* ... It is your responsibility to make the first move and not to let it fester away, even if you don't think it's your fault! Second, *go and point out* to that person. Not to anyone else, but to that person. Don't tell anyone else before you tell them. In theory they are doing the same thing and you will meet in the middle to work it out *just between the two of you.* So you must keep it private. Third, if it is a real tough one to resolve, *take along one or two others.* Your aim must be to find a resolution, not to pick a fight. When Tony Blair became Prime Minister of Britain, he said, "Enough of talking – it is time now to act." When will you act on this principle?

Continental

Jesus goes on to say that "if they listen to you, you have won them over". Some of my deepest friendships are with people I have had to confront or people who have had to do the same with me. Some of my saddest memories are of people who chose to work up their anger rather than work out their differences.

Coffee

You may have seen the Second World War security posters that read "Careless talk costs lives" or "Loose lips sink ships". Maybe our churches would be safer places to be if that hung on our walls rather than next week's coffee schedule. Watch your talk carefully today.

DB

Orange Juice

Therefore confess your sins to each other and pray for each other so that you may be healed.

James 5:16

Telling All

The Big Breakfast

One of the in things right now is "telling all" – confessing something you did to a friend as a joke, but he didn't know it was you; or some awkward situation in which you found yourself, that makes you go red just thinking about it. I've noticed that some of the teen magazines around now are getting into the tell-all habit in a big way.

I've no idea if the folks in the magazines feel healed. There *is* a place for confessing things. We need to start by telling God and asking him to forgive us. But we sometimes need to tell a buddy – a good buddy, someone who cares about us and who wants good things for us. Telling all like this can really help to sort a bad situation out. It allows us to see our mess more clearly and, if the buddy is a good one, he or she will help us face our mess and say sorry. That way we can find healing.

Continental

Get into a partnership with a friend where you can both talk honestly about your struggles and failures as Christians. It will really help you beat the bad stuff.

Coffee

Ask God to show you which of your friends could be this kind of buddy to you.

RS

Orange Juice

The Spirit of the Lord is on me, because he has anointed me to proclaim good news to the poor. He has sent me to proclaim freedom for the prisoners and recovery of sight for the blind, to release the oppressed.

Luke 4:18

The Good News Manifesto

The Big Breakfast

This is the moment when Jesus brought both good and bad news to the people of Israel. Good news: God's salvation is available to everyone, no matter who they are. Bad news: that means that those who claim to hand out God's grace on his behalf are now out of a job.

This is the key to the good news of Jesus: whatever God has for us, it's up for grabs to anyone who wants it. This is revolutionary stuff: Jesus' good news was for all the people who couldn't get into the temple in Jerusalem – the poor couldn't afford a sacrifice, those with disabilities were considered unclean and the prisoners ... well, they speak for themselves. Thank you, Jesus!

Continental

Good news for the poor: what does that mean for the rich?

Coffee

What are the things that make you a prisoner or a poor or blind person? Say to yourself, "If I turn to him, nothing can keep me from God, nothing can keep God from me."

SH

Orange Juice

The sheep know their shepherd's voice. He calls each of them by name and leads them out. When he has led out all his sheep, he walks in front of them, and they all follow, *because they know his voice.*

John 10:3-4 cᴇᴠ (emphasis added)

Voice Mail

The Big Breakfast

My father-in-law, Ken, realized one of his life's ambitions when he left a jet-setting business in London and moved to the country. It was here that he and his wife began looking after sheep. I loved those crisp Christmas holiday mornings when we would wrap up warm and head off down the lane to count the sheep. Me in my scarf and bobble-hat and Ken looking the part in his Barbour jacket, flat cap and green farmers' wellies. When he yelled, "Sheep!" the flock would come running, and he would feed them sheep nuts, count them and pull any missing ones out of the hedgerows.

I looked after those sheep one summer, and even though I wore Ken's coat and hat, called them by the same name and offered them the same sheep nuts, they would always run away! Sometimes we wonder what God thinks about our life choices. Why does he seem to keep so quiet? Is that really his voice guiding me? Confusion rapidly sets in. Sheep know the shepherd's voice. No matter how it is dressed up, they always recognize the genuine article. Are you walking close enough to the Master today so that you can clearly distinguish his voice from a stranger's? His tone is filled with encouragement, discipline, grace and hope.

Continental

Fascinating Sheep Fact No. 223: When a sheep rolls over on to its back it can't get itself upright again. Many die like this, easy picking for a hungry fox. The only way it can get back on its feet is for someone to grab its coat and turn it over.

Coffee

Who do you know today who may have taken a tumble and could do with a call to put them back on their feet? Take some time to make that call.

DB

Orange Juice
May God be gracious to us and bless us and make his face shine upon us.

Psalm 67:1 NIV

Us and Them

The Big Breakfast
Sometimes the smallest words we know are the most dangerous. The word *us* is a good example.

We are driven to form an "us" around ourselves – to love and be loved, to belong. My most valued relationships are those that take me from being "me" to being "us". "Us" is one of the warmest words we use, and without it we are lost and alone.

But the danger is that our "us" produces a "them". For every friend, there is an enemy – real or imagined. For every insider there is an outsider. The prayer, "May God bless us ..." is silently echoed with the response, "but not them". When this happens, the word "us" becomes one of the coldest in our lexicon. Ask a black South African how it felt to hear the "God Bless Us" of the white regime during the years of apartheid.

The challenge is to learn that the "us" we pray for can be *all of us*. Wherever we put a boundary marker, God's love flows beyond it – he longs to bless us *and* them.

Continental
If the "us" of our prayers is not "all of us", then it shouldn't be any of us at all.

Coffee
Forgive us, Father, that the *us* of our lives has been exclusive. Forgive us that we have sought your blessings on us alone. Bring us, we pray, to an *us* that truly is *all of us*.

GK

Orange Juice

And we know that in all things God works for the good of those who love him.

Romans 8:28

The Long Haul

The Big Breakfast

When you step into the Christian faith, your life changes forever. For one thing, absolutely everything has a meaning. God, you see, is so excited to get involved in your life that he steps right in there and begins straight away to walk in you and with you. And because he has great plans for you, he gets involved in everything that comes your way.

That's the important bit to remember. He walks with you, working for you in all the life situations you might meet. How is it that we get this crazy idea that God is somehow making the kind of plans for us that take us *out* of the normal rough-and-tumble? That's not how it is. At the end of the day, God's agenda is to make sure we become like Jesus. He walks with us while we make the same journey as everybody else. The difference is, he makes the journey worth it.

Continental

God is in this for the long haul. Working for our good sometimes means that he allows us to face some very tough situations. Looking back, we can see his master plan.

Coffee

Lord Jesus, thank you that you walk with me and know how to make everything worth it.

RS

Orange Juice

I tell you that in the same way there will be more rejoicing in heaven over one sinner who repents than over ninety-nine righteous persons who do not need to repent.

Luke 15:7

Party Time

The Big Breakfast

The original edition of *Breakfast with God* was the first book I ever wrote and was therefore very precious to me. I wrote it all on my laptop computer. I sweated over the words and themes while on long car, plane and train journeys. Sometimes it flowed easily. Sometimes I struggled with fresh insights as I pulled over to the side of the road to jot down another possible idea on a scrap of paper that I always manage to lose anyway! This book is my baby. So you can imagine my bowel-shaking panic when my computer crashed while I was writing and the man in the shop told me I had lost everything.

But you can imagine my heart-shattering joy when, a day later, the shop called me back to say they had managed to save a few things from my desktop, one of which was the *Breakfast with God* manuscript.

We are God's *magnum opus*, his inspired creation and his precious baby. No wonder there is one humdinger of a party in heaven when that which was lost gets found – or, as *The Message* puts it, when one sinner's life gets rescued.

Continental

Mary had been coming to our church for a few months before she got saved. I told her about the party in heaven that would go on late into the night because a precious daughter who was lost had been found. Mary turned up at my house the following night with a bottle of bubbly. She wanted to carry on the party here on earth! And why not?

Coffee

Sometimes it is only when we recall how lost we once were that we can begin to appreciate the greatness of a God who relentlessly pursued us until we were found again. Say thank you to the God who went out on a limb to rescue you.

DB

Orange Juice

Before I formed you in the womb I knew you, before you were born I set you apart.

Jeremiah 1:5 NIV

He Knows, You Know

The Big Breakfast

It is difficult talking about being "set apart" or called for God's work, because for some people God writes stuff in the sky, and for others, they spend their whole life seemingly trying to make the right decisions in the dark, without any help from the great careers adviser in the heavens. For me the greatest moments of call could nearly all be put down to fascinating coincidences, so I probably sit somewhere in the middle between the miracle merchants and the rest of us.

I've got two kids on the way (they'll be born by the time you read this), and because their mum has been ill, loads of people have been praying for them. Funnily enough, one thing that all that prayer won't have changed is God's view of them. He knows them already, he knew them even before they were a ball of cells. When they get to know God, he will be introducing himself to people he knows really well: like a Spice Girls' fan finally meeting the band, God has loved us like crazy even before we knew who he was.

That is the starting point for Jeremiah and it's the starting point for us too. He knows us better than we know ourselves, so maybe he might have a good idea of what use he could put us to ...

Continental

"Why was I chosen?" [asked Frodo.]

"Such questions cannot be answered," said Gandalf. "You may be sure that it was not for any merit that others do not possess: not for power or wisdom at any rate. But you have been chosen, and you must therefore use such strength and heart and wits as you have."

*J.R.R. Tolkien, **The Lord of the Rings***

Coffee

Just think about how much God knows you and loves you, and thank him.

SH

Orange Juice

. . . that your ways may be known on earth, your salvation among all nations.

Psalm 67:2 NIV

Worldwide Worship

The Big Breakfast

As island-dwellers, the British are perennially conscious of their coastal weather system. On one particular day in the 1930s, the whole of the south coast was hidden in a deep and impenetrable fog. The response of a certain British newspaper was to run the headline: "Fog in Channel – Continent Cut Off". It never occurred to the writer that it is the island, not the mainland, that gets cut off on such days.

At the heart of worship, there is a world-embracing dynamic. God's desire is to be worshipped in all the earth – in every people group. Our problem is that our worship is so often fog-bound. Our prayers end where our national boundaries stand. We know that in theory God seeks worshippers from every tribe and tongue – but our own needs loom larger in our minds.

It is hard work to keep alive the global vision of God's purposes – but it is work to which we must commit ourselves. God longs for our worship to be deeper – but he also wants to make it wider!

Continental

Wherever you live on earth, less of the planet is close to you than far from you. How might this reality be reflected in worship and prayer?

Coffee

God of the global, widen my vision of your love. Lord of the local, deepen my awareness of your work.

GK

Orange Juice

Do not conform to the pattern of this world, but be transformed by the renewing of your mind.

Romans 12:2

Swim Against the Tide

The Big Breakfast

I grew up in London. When I was a kid, I would go Christmas shopping with Bernie, my "best bud" from school. We would start at Piccadilly and work our way up to Marble Arch. Nothing too adventurous in that, I hear you say. But we would always go against the flow of people. It seemed to be an unwritten shopper's rule that you had to "go with the flow". Our little adventure was to swim against the tide and suffer the tutting of weary bargain-hunters and the incessant battering of over-filled shopping bags in the process. We would always win eventually and would reward ourselves with a McDonald's shake at Piccadilly Circus.

Following Christ in the third millennium demands that we must run counter to our culture. It means not letting this world squeeze us into its mould. Where have you found yourself being tempted to conform recently?

The adventure of our faith is to make a break from the norm and stop following the crowd. We must learn to ignore some of our culture's unwritten rules and stick to the Master's plan. The result? I promise you this: the reward at the end is even sweeter than any strawberry shake!

Continental

I always thought that God's will for my life would be boring. This verse reminds me that God actually wants to bring out the best in me. His will for my life is good, not bad; it's pleasing, not dull; it's perfect, and I could never improve on it.

Coffee

The Message brings this verse bang up to date: "Don't become so well-adjusted to your culture that you fit into it without even thinking. Instead, fix your attention on God. You'll be changed from the inside out."

DB

Orange Juice

... a person who hates being corrected is stupid ... the wise listen to advice.

Proverbs 12:1, 15 NCV

The Most Excellent Advice Book

The Big Breakfast

I know a man who will never accept that he's made a mistake. It is just amazing to watch. Even if his mistake is a genuine slip-up, he wriggles and squirms, trying to make himself out to be Mr Innocent. It's become a standing joke. David (not his real name) is truly Mr "I Never Make a Mistake"! The sad thing, of course, is that nobody takes him seriously any more.

I love the way the Bible is full of such excellent advice. Look at this proverb: you're stupid if you don't let other people tell you when you're getting it wrong; you're smart when you listen to good advice. What could be simpler? Yet for some of us, it seems, such advice is so hard to follow.

Continental

Why would someone not want to take advice? Nobody gets everything right. Could it be that old devil called pride again?

Coffee

There are a few things that God hates with a passion. Pride is one of them. Think about it.

RS

Orange Juice

I am not ashamed of the gospel, because it is the power of God that brings salvation to everyone who believes.

Romans 1:16

Power!

The Big Breakfast

Why would anybody be ashamed of the gospel? Well, we all know the answer to that question. Most of us will have found ourselves in a position where it is much easier to keep quiet than to admit that we are Christians. I'm supposed to be a "professional" Christian, but there are still parties I go to where I just want to enjoy myself and not feel like I'm God's ambassador all the time. "Ashamed" might be a bit strong, but "embarrassed" – maybe that's more like it.

So why shouldn't I be ashamed? Because this gospel – this good news – is that God is powerful. "Yeah, yeah," I hear you say. "So what? I know that – he wouldn't exactly be God if he wasn't, would he?" Well, that's true, but we don't generally live as if it were true.

And what's amazing about this statement is that the power of God comes from the good news and not the other way around. God's work through Jesus in saving us is the most powerful force in the universe, so grab hold and prepare for a ride!

Continental

"I'm not ashamed of the gospel, I'm not ashamed of the one I love," sings Martin Smith. What about you?

Coffee

May God shield me,
May God fill me,
May God keep me,
May God watch me,
May God bring me
To the land of peace,
To the country of the King,
To the peace of eternity.

ancient Celtic prayer

Orange Juice

I know your deeds, that you are neither cold nor hot. I wish you were either one or the other! So, because you are luke-warm – neither hot nor cold – I am about to spit you out of my mouth.

Revelation 3:15-16

You Make Me Sick

The Big Breakfast

"Knowing them inside and out, God looked at the church in Laodicea and said, 'I am sick to death with you – you make me want to puke!'" (Bloomin' Obvious Version – Colour Pictures Edition).

I remember my parents, teachers and some football coaches saying something similar to me at various times when I was a kid. It wasn't that they didn't want the best for me. It wasn't even that my parents had stopped loving me. It was pure exasperation. Passion you can channel. Rebellion you can sort. Lukewarmness is a cancer that still has no cure.

The homeless cry out for shelter, and we are too busy painting the walls to the new church extension. The hungry cry out for food, and we are too busy attending conferences on reaching the lost. The poor cry out for money, and we are too busy overloading our credit limits. The outcast cries out for acceptance, and we are too busy debating the theology of their lifestyle.

Being busy is one thing. Being busy with kingdom stuff is another. One is the lukewarm life of empty religion. The other is nothing short of Christian fanaticism. Which one are you?

Continental

I wonder what God would say to the church in Essex or Edin-burgh or El Paso today? I wonder what God would say to you and me today? I wonder what God would say? I wonder ...?

Coffee

"If you have ears, listen to what the Spirit says" (Revelation 3:22 CEV). So, listen up or lose out!

DB

Orange Juice

May the nations be glad and sing for joy, for you rule the peoples justly and guide the nations of the earth.

Psalm 67:4 NIV

Justice Just *Is*

The Big Breakfast

There are some journeys that, no matter how short the distance, seem to take forever. The journey from the heart to the wallet is one. For many of us, the journey from worship to justice is another.

Worship is associated with God and us, with his work in our lives and with our feelings in response to his actions. The wider dimension of public justice belongs to some other arena – that of campaigning, social action and politics.

There is no such problem for the writer of this psalm. The peoples of the earth will worship God because he is just. The ways of God are good news in a nation, bringing with them gladness and justice. People will be caused to worship God, the psalmist contends, in response to the justice that he brings. Justice is as much a part of worship as singing.

Where the coming of "Christians" to a nation brings with it not justice but oppression, the God in whose name they come is not worshipped!

Continental

We speak of a God who receives our worship, who hears our prayers and songs. God listens, also, for the voice of justice in the earth.

Coffee

As a song rises to the ears of God, as my prayer like incense comes to him, let justice also rise and the fires of mercy burn.

GK

Orange Juice
Reckless words pierce like a sword, but the tongue of the wise brings healing.

Proverbs 12:18 NIV

The Show Must Go On

The Big Breakfast
Have you watched much of that confessional TV stuff? You know the kind of thing. Two sisters haven't talked for a year. One of them comes on and talks about it in front of a live audience. The other sister is listening backstage. She is not too thrilled about what's being said about her. Eventually the two sisters are sitting there together, sorting it out in front of the whole world. The show will get a higher rating if the sisters have a good go at one another. Words that pierce like a sword.

Sometimes our words can be intentionally cruel because we feel hurt, let down or betrayed. We deal with our pain by hurting another person. Sometimes we use cruel words because we feel threatened, jealous or maybe a little less important than someone else. Sometimes we're just plain careless.

As followers of Jesus, every word we speak is important. Our words should never pierce like a sword, because that destroys. Rather, we should look for ways to build people up. Wise words are good for building up.

Continental
Are there times you look back to and wish you could cut out your tongue, because of something you said? Remember, wise words bring healing.

Coffee
Lord Jesus, please prompt me before I open my mouth, so that I speak words that build people up rather than stab them in the heart.

RS

Orange Juice

And because of Christ, all of us can come to the Father by the same Spirit.

Ephesians 2:18 CEV

A Backstage Pass

The Big Breakfast

I was once involved in an event at the Royal Albert Hall in London with none other than British supersinger Cliff Richard himself. Security was very tight. Nobody could get access to the stars who were performing unless, like me, they had a little pass around their necks with the words ACCESS ALL AREAS. It meant I could look in the royal box, wander around backstage, sit in the green room, stand on the stage, and even rummage around Cliff's underwear drawer. (The latter option I declined on account of the fact that there are some things better kept a mystery in life.) I could have sold that pass for thousands to some of those Cliff fans.

The apostle Paul desperately wanted the Ephesian Christians to know that they had access to all areas – a backstage pass to the Father, authorized by Jesus Christ himself. Now they could sit with royalty, enjoy heavenly hospitality and co-star with his Son in life's unfolding drama.

Continental

We make appointments to see doctors. We schedule time to meet with work colleagues or clients. We are summoned to see teachers or judges. Yet we are invited to rush headlong into our Father's arms 24 hours a day, 7 days a week.

Coffee

"Christ now gives us courage and confidence, so that we can come to God by faith" (Ephesians 3:12 CEV). That is freedom to tell him anything – he's never shocked. And confidence to know he won't judge – his Son has already taken the blame.

DB

Orange Juice

But the chief priests ... were angry when they ... heard the children shouting praises to the Son of David ... Jesus answered. "Don't you know that the Scriptures say, 'Children and infants will sing praises'?"

Matthew 21:15-16 CEV

The Power of Words

The Big Breakfast

It is a beautiful scene: Jesus arrives at the temple, surrounded by his disciples. Of course, the children don't fit in – this is a religious building! The priests are absolutely furious because these children are making a noise in their beloved Temple, but even worse, they are uttering blasphemy!

I can see the smile of Jesus as he responds to the priests. It is undoubtedly a neglected theme of the Bible that when adults refuse to listen to God, he just moves on to the next generation (see, for example, Gideon, Samuel, David and many others).

Continental

When churches used an image of Jesus similar to the famous picture of the South American revolutionary Che Guevara, with the punchline, "JESUS: Meek. Mild. As if', there was a huge outcry. Why?

Coffee

These priests had somehow become fossilized over the years, but revival can start with the young. Talk to God about your own religious tradition and ask him to shake it up, if it needs to be.

SH

Orange Juice

May the peoples praise you, O God; may all the peoples praise you. Then the land will yield its harvest, and God, our God, will bless us.

Psalm 67:5-6 *NIV*

Man Bites Dog!

The Big Breakfast

The oldest rule in journalism is this: "Dog Bites Man" is not news; "Man Bites Dog" is front-page news. This verse is one of the Old Testament's "Man-Bites-Dog" headlines.

The expectation of God's people in Old Testament times, still very evident in our century, is that a good harvest leads to praise. When the crops come in, and our barns are full, we will give thanks to our God or gods. It is a deep human instinct to offer thanks for gifts received.

But this psalm says something different – it says that praise leads to a good harvest! When we praise God, when we rejoice in the justice of his rule, *then* the land will yield its harvest. It is as if the very soil we work with is programmed to respond to the praise of its Creator.

This biblical principle is often misapplied by the salesmen of a comfort-fit prosperity gospel. But it remains true – praise works. Put first things first – offer your life as worship – and let God take care of the harvest. Where God is rightly worshipped, fruitfulness flows.

Continental

We may feel that we should invest heavily in our working lives, so that we can praise God in plenty – but God calls us first and foremost to invest in our worshipping lives, and leave the plenty in his hands.

Coffee

God my provider, whose praise is the substance of the very air I breathe, help me today to put first things first, and worship you before and above all else.

GK

Orange Juice

The Lord is good and his love endures forever; his faithfulness continues through all generations.

Psalm 100:5 NIV

Stop Paddling Around

The Big Breakfast

I took two of my boys swimming today. But this was no ordinary swimming pool: it was called a subtropical paradise. This meant you did very little swimming and a great deal of sliding down tubes, negotiating white water rapids and squeezing into hot jacuzzi pools with oversized women in undersized costumes. The highlight for Matthew and Nathan was the regular Tarzan call and flashing lights which heralded the onset of the wave machine. We held on for dear life as the waves pounded us against the fake subtropical rocks. By the end of the session, I felt thoroughly worn out and slightly eroded at the edges.

The psalmist reminds us that God's pounding love for us isn't like some rogue wave that wanders gently up the beach every few days and then slinks back out to sea. It's forceful, it's enduring, it's incessant, it never gives up, and it erodes away the rock-hard hearts we harbour deep within.

Maybe it has been a while since you went out into the deeper waters of God's goodness. Steal some precious time now. Other stuff can wait – it must wait. Let your soul swim. Let the power and majesty of that long-lasting love crash into your consciousness again this day.

Continental

I worshipped recently in an ancient church building over 600 years old. We sang songs and read words about the enduring love of God, from centuries past, words repeated by generations of followers. We have a great heritage to our faith because we have a God who endures forever. You are part of something that will go on and on.

Coffee

When you watch a gripping TV drama, it often concludes with the caption: "To be continued …" The faithfulness of our God is like that; it is "to be continued" in your generation. Don't miss the next enthralling instalment.

DB

Orange Juice

A gentle answer turns away wrath, but a harsh word stirs up anger.

Proverbs 15:1 NIV

War of Words

The Big Breakfast

It was a war zone. That was what it was like. The missiles were vicious. They cut to a ribbon in seconds. Neither side would give in. What does that sound like? You and your sister having a row over a new shirt you bought that she wore first? Some of the politicians who are supposed to be running our country having a ratings battle in the run-up to an election?

I started to follow Jesus when I was 16. It was a very clear thing for me. I knew he wanted me to follow him and live by his guidelines. Why couldn't I do it, then, when my sister had a go at me? She seemed to know how to press that button and off I'd go, yelling at her as loudly as she yelled at me. It got me down. One day I found this verse in Proverbs. I began to put it into practice. It wasn't always easy. I really wanted to yell back. God helped me not to, however, and my sister and I became very good friends.

Continental

Kindness and gentleness aren't difficult. They just take practice.

Coffee

Lord Jesus, I want to be your follower in everything I do. Help me to remember that includes the words I speak.

RS

Orange Juice

The King will reply, "Truly I tell you, whatever you did for one of the least of these brothers and sisters of mine, you did for me."

Matthew 25:40

Serving Jesus

The Big Breakfast

Matthew 25 should carry a health warning: "Do not read this chapter if you want your life to stay the same." After reading this chapter you have two choices: carry on living your life, being a bit "spiritual", maybe even going to church, and end up on the scrapheap; or step outside your boundaries and go and serve Jesus.

That's one of the problems with so much of today's spirituality, Christian and not: fundamentally, it's a kind of God-induced therapy, with the sole aim of helping ME sort out MY problems and – if I'm lucky – helping ME become a better person (whatever that means!).

There has always been a tension in the Church about this passage, because it seems to go against the whole "God loves you and all you need is faith and you'll be saved" message, which I totally agree with. But I *also* agree with James: "You have faith, show me it. I'll show you my faith by how my life has been changed" (my version of James 2:18). There is no getting round this: if you're a Christian and your life isn't different for it, something's wrong. One of the ways Jesus gives us to check on our own changed-ness is this chapter. When we serve the poor, we serve him.

Continental

"If a man be gracious and courteous to strangers, it shows he is a citizen of the world."

Francis Bacon

Coffee

Is there someone you know who you need to serve as if they were Jesus?

SH

Orange Juice

These are the numbers of the men armed for battle ... men of Issachar, who understood the times and knew what Israel should do – 200.

1 Chronicles 12:23, 32 NIV

Connect with Your Culture

The Big Breakfast

As King David selected his "mighty men" to rule over Israel he included, among his soldiers and brave warriors, 200 futurologists who knew the trends and how the people should respond to them.

I met a man recently who is paid by nations and huge multinational companies to live ten years in the future. They want to know what is happening and how to shape their organizations accordingly. He holds virtual conferences, advises virtual companies on future patterns of life and work and is paid a virtual fortune for doing so!

Unless the Church learns to connect with our culture we will continue to answer yesterday's questions. If we are to regain the role of "prophet to the nation", we need to be like the men of Issachar "who understand the times". For you it may mean occasionally listening to pop music instead of Christian radio. It may mean buying a daily newspaper, getting involved in local political issues. Are you wrestling with the daily dilemma of connecting with our culture while not getting contaminated by it? Where have you got into a ghetto and where have you compromised your convictions? This is a bloody battle, and none of us is exempt from the front-line.

Continental

I often get asked how we can make Jesus relevant to our culture. I always say we can't. Jesus has always been relevant to our world. It's just that the Church has cleverly disguised a contemporary Christ in organized religion.

Coffee

One eminent church leader of old said, "The true Christian holds the Bible in one hand, a newspaper in the other and applies them both simultaneously." So grab hold of your newspaper and your Bible today and put them both into action.

DB

Orange Juice
God will bless us, and all the ends of the earth will fear him.

Psalm 67:7 NIV

The Fame Game

The Big Breakfast
Probably the most famous billboard advert in history was put out by the Democratic Party in the 1960 US Presidential election.

John F. Kennedy was running against Richard Nixon. The polling couldn't have been closer, and on the eve of the final, crucial vote, the Democrats knew they had to pull something out of the hat to tip the scales in their favour. The next day America awoke to billboards that held a huge photograph of Nixon and asked one simple question: "Would you buy a used car from this man?"

As well as becoming a legend in communications studies, this campaign illustrates a universal truth: in politics and PR, appearance is everything. It is a truth with which the Hebrew mind would have been at home. There is a passion – a jealousy – in the Old Testament for the reputation of God.

The whole project of worship and obedience is geared to this outcome: that God should be famous to the ends of the earth.

Continental
Just how famous God becomes – how widely and deeply his fame spreads – may depend, in the end, on what kind of billboards our lives become.

Coffee

In the closest circles of my life, *Lord, may your fame spread.* In the furthest reaches of my world, *Lord, may your fame spread.* From the outset of my day to the ends of the earth, *Lord, may your name be known.*

GK

Orange Juice
Your word is a lamp to my feet and a light for my path.

Psalm 119:105 NIV

Read It Right

The Big Breakfast
A friend rang me in a bit of a state the other day. Her best friend had just dropped a bombshell. She was leaving her husband to go and live with someone else. Her husband was a good man. He had always been kind and they were good friends, but she didn't love him any more. She did love the other person. My friend was devastated. The couple whose marriage was about to get blown into a million pieces was one of the few Christian partnerships she admired. The most upsetting thing of all was the way her friend used the Bible to justify what she was about to do. "God's okay with this," she said.

The Bible is the best way to discover what God is really saying, through his clear guidelines for us. We do need to read it properly, however, and that takes patience and practice. Then we'll discover that it is much more than a rule book. It is a wonderful revelation of God and all he wants for us, which is very good indeed.

Continental
We don't apply our lives to the Bible. We apply the Bible to our lives. Think about the difference, then go and do it.

Coffee
Lord Jesus, I confess that I sometimes find the Bible hard to understand. Please help me, and show me how to help myself.

RS

Orange Juice

When Jacob awoke from his sleep, he thought, "Surely the Lord is in this place, and I was not aware of it."

Genesis 28:16 NIV

A New Fragrance

The Big Breakfast

Debbie is the best nurse I have ever been to bed with. Well ... she's the only nurse I have ever been to bed with, and she is my wife. It makes that opening line much less attention-grabbing.

Before we were married, she trained at the hospital for sick children in London. She loved her four years of training, apart from a three-month stint in a psychiatric hospital outside London. The shifts were long, and the pain-filled patients often frightening and abusive. Her small room was more like a cell. It had bars at the only window, and that looked out on to just a brick wall opposite.

On one particular occasion, the whole experience nearly broke Debbie. She had gone beyond tears of loneliness and began thinking it was time to quit. Nothing I could say or pray seemed to help, so I brought her a bunch of yellow flowers. She came off a late shift that night and the sweet smell arrested her gloom and the bright yellow colour lit up her face. She almost heard the warm sound of the Father's voice saying, "You are my fragrance in this stale place, it's you that I choose to bring my colour into these grey tormented minds." Surely the Lord was in this place and she had not been aware of it.

Continental

As Jacob woke up he got a new perspective on his circumstances. What a great way to kick-start your mind at the beginning of another day.

Coffee

Does your world seem caged in and colourless? Maybe you need to wake up. To look again today and see the evidence of God's profound beauty in the most simple of ways.

DB

Orange Juice

Jesus ... knelt with his face to the ground and prayed, "My Father, if it is possible, don't make me suffer by making me drink from this cup. But do what you want, and not what I want."

Matthew 26:39 CEV

Alone

The Big Breakfast

If you have ever seen the musical *Jesus Christ Superstar* you'll know that this scene is the real heart of the piece, not the dodgy disco title track. For me, it perfectly encapsulates Jesus' pain that God had put him in this inescapable position, and yet his willingness to obey his Father, even when he couldn't completely see the way forward. It is the night before his arrest, and Jesus is in the Garden of Gethsemane begging God for a way out of what is about to happen.

Maybe we have this idea that Jesus approached his own torture and slow death with a kind of secret pleasure, knowing that he was going to get his own back on his enemies when – ta-da! – he rose from the dead. I don't think so. As much as the Cross, Gethsemane tells us the price Jesus was willing to pay for us. He's surrounded by his closest friends and allies, all asleep, and he has to face this night alone.

There is no equivalent. I'm sitting here at my computer trying to think of a nice modern-day analogy, but there just isn't one.

Thank you, Jesus.

Continental

Jesus had many options open to him that night: he could have begged Judas not to betray him, he could have run away, he could have died defending himself, he could have prepared a brilliant defence for Pilate. What would you have done?

Coffee

Is there an area in your life where you need to say to God, "But do what you want, and not what I want"?

SH

Orange Juice
And he kissed all his brothers and wept over them.

Genesis 45:15 NIV

You Don't Owe Me!

The Big Breakfast
The possibility of total forgiveness is demonstrated in the life of the Amazing Technicolor Joseph. Tricked and deceived by his own brothers, he was robbed of his inheritance and sold as a slave.

Years later, the tables were turned. Joseph had gained wealth and prestige, and it was the brothers who stood before *him* to ask his help. It was within his power to have them thrown into jail. At the very least he could humiliate them publicly, and let them know how deeply he was wounded.

Joseph did none of these things, however – he wept before his brothers and embraced them. This was only possible because the debt they owed him no longer existed.

It is not enough to say, "I forgive"; you have to back it up by wiping out the debt – so much so that when you are given the opportunity for revenge, you will pass it up. This is the measure of the forgiveness with which God has forgiven us – and it is the measure with which he urges us to forgive those indebted to us.

Continental
There are some for whom the debt to be forgiven has a crushing, years-spanning weight. God neither demands nor expects glib obedience. Forgiveness is a place we are journeying to – even if, for some, the journey is long.

Coffee
Help me, God of the second chance, to cancel the debts of those who owe me. Where this is a hard journey, help me to take the first small steps.

GK

Orange Juice
Your two breasts are like two fawns, like twin fawns of a gazelle that browse among the lilies.

Song of Songs 4:5 NIV

God Invented Sex

The Big Breakfast
I asked one of the lads in our church youth group what his favourite Bible verse was, and he came up with this one from Song of Songs. Being a minister, I obviously discounted it immediately. But to tell you the truth, that bothered me. If it's in the Bible, why shouldn't I use it? Then I walked past a graffiti poem on a station wall:

Sex is evil
Evil is sin
Sin is forgiven
So get stuck in!

It must have been sprayed by someone with a dodgy church history. Look at the religious language they use. But where did they ever get the idea that God was anti-sex? Didn't he create it in the first place? Jesus was a sexual being. He was tempted in every way and yet he never sinned. Sex is not evil. I remember from my biology class at school that the sex life of a newt involved the male depositing a sack of good-ies on a leaf and then leaving it for the female to insert herself. Thank God today that he created you human and not amphibian, and say sorry to God for the times you have misused this great gift. And start again.

Continental
When God created sex he knew how powerful and yet how destructive it can be. So he created a strong container to put it in. He called it marriage. A place where two people leave their parents and cleave commitment to each other in the ceremony of marriage, and then, and only then, do they get down to the "one flesh" bit (Matthew 19:5).

Coffee
Imagine writing such intimate words on a card to your beloved. Try it and you'll probably get a slap in the face. Yet it is that same outrageous intimacy that Song of Songs says our beloved God longs to share with you, his lover.

DB

Orange Juice

"The LORD has left me; the LORD has forgotten me." The LORD answers, "Can a woman forget the baby she nurses?... Even if she could forget her children, I will not forget you. See, I have written your name on my hand."

Isaiah 49:14-16 NCV

Gift-Wrapped Answers

The Big Breakfast

I read a comment recently which was made by a Christian person who was having a tough time: "I am sick of Christians offering me gift-wrapped answers when my world is falling apart."

How is your world today? Did you jump out of bed full of energy, skip to the bathroom, dash downstairs for coffee and orange juice and run out into the sunshine excited about what lay ahead of you? You did? What kind of coffee do you drink? I want some!

Or did your day start with a heavy black cloud hovering over you, your feet like lead, your heart so sore that you feel you'll never be free from the pain?

It may be that both of these pictures are way too dramatic. You're neither elated nor in despair. Our lives do have highs and lows, however, and everything in between. It is part of the deal. What doesn't feel like part of the deal is God's silence during the dark and cloudy days. It's at times like these that we need him most, so how come it feels as if he's away on vacation?

Continental

Part of our growing as Christians can only happen in the dark place where God appears to have abandoned us. In these moments, trust what you *know* of God, not what you feel.

Coffee

Your name is written on the palm of God's hand. It is impossible for him to forget you.

RS

Orange Juice

Therefore, I urge you, brothers and sisters, in view of God's mercy, to offer your bodies as living sacrifices, holy and pleasing to God – this is your proper worship as rational beings.

Romans 12:1

Body Worship

The Big Breakfast

Don't worry about today's title – I haven't suddenly gone all fitness-crazed on you. In fact, I have to say that I think today's body-fascism is one of the most powerful strongholds of the enemy in the West. No, I'm talking about worshipping God with our bodies. And that doesn't mean liturgical dance or shaking violently either.

If we had a chance to ask God what way he preferred to be worshipped, I suspect he would say, "With your lives". I can't imagine anything pleasing God more than people who love him so much that they will do anything for him. As someone with a slightly sick sense of humour once said, the problem with living sacrifices is that they have a tendency to crawl off the altar. Those that stay there are therefore even more precious to God our Father.

Worship is so often nowadays connected with singing the right songs and going to the right conferences. Let's leave all that behind and reach out after Jesus, living in a way that will have people turning their heads and knowing that he really does exist.

Continental

"Worship is the submission of all our nature to God. It is the quickening of conscience by his holiness, the nourishment of the mind with his truth, the purifying of the imagination by his beauty, the opening of the heart to his love, the surrender of the will to his purpose."

William Temple

Coffee

Read through the William Temple quote on this page a few times, until you have fully understood each clause and are ready to ask God that it be true of you.

SH

Orange Juice

After the death of Moses the servant of the Lord, the Lord said to Joshua son of Nun, Moses' aide: "Moses my servant is dead."

Joshua 1:1-2 NIV

The Past Is Past

The Big Breakfast

Stating the obvious or what! Of course Joshua knew that his boss had died. After all, the Israelites had been mourning his death for thirty days (Deuteronomy 34:8). So why did God feel it necessary to tell him what he already knew? It was to bury the past, once and for all, and to begin a brand new chapter in Joshua's life story.

I spent a year working alongside the missions agency Christians in Sport some time back. My main role was the summer sports camp. My great friend Steve Conner had pioneered this amazing event, growing it to near capacity in a very short space of time. To say I was nervous taking on this new task was an understatement. Steve had done such an unbeatable job, and I didn't want to let him down. I remember sitting in a hotel lobby in Cambridge, sharing my anxiety with a good friend. He ordered us both another cappuccino, pulled his Bible out of his briefcase and turned to this verse. I realized again that no matter how successful the past was, it was the past. I sense that, for many of us, our pasts are still hampering our futures. It is time to let go, to hold a funeral service for the days that are gone and to christen a new dawn, a new tomorrow.

Continental

"We have trained men to think of the future as a promised land which favoured heroes attain – not as something which everyone reaches at the rate of sixty minutes an hour, whatever he does, whoever he is."

C.S. Lewis, **The Screwtape Letters**

Coffee

God's promise to Joshua and to you gives fresh motivation to a weary soul: "As I was with Moses, so I will be with you. I will never leave you nor forsake you. Be strong and courageous . . ." (Joshua 1:5-6).

DB

Orange Juice

Dear friends, let us love one another, for love comes from God. Everyone who loves has been born of God and knows God.

1 John 4:7

My Love Is Your Love

The Big Breakfast

Everyone who loves touches God. Whoever gives love celebrates the presence of God in their life in the measure in which they give that love.

Love is the sign of God in the creation. If God were not present, set loose by the power of his Spirit to roam the roads of the cosmos, there would be no love. Every time a child is loved, God is worshipped. Every time, for the love of another, we overcome the love of self, God is worshipped.

It is quite possible to put love to the wrong use, just as it is possible to experience corrupt and selfish forms of love. And it is quite possible to love in the name of other gods, or of no god. But the underlying reality, as sure as chickens lay eggs, is that love comes from God.

Continental

No one can contend that the hand of God has never been at work in their life unless they have never loved or been loved.

Coffee

If not for love, we could not know the name of God. If not for love, we could not seek him. If not for love, we would not feel the need for God. If not for love, we could not meet him.

GK

Orange Juice

To the Jews who had believed him, Jesus said, "If you hold to my teaching, you are really my disciples. Then you will know the truth, and the truth will set you free."

John 8:31-32

Walk the Walk

The Big Breakfast

Morpheus, in the movie *The Matrix*, says to Neo, "There's a difference between knowing the path and walking the path." Jesus and Morpheus both have this right, don't they? Jesus is telling people to follow what he tells them. Why? Because his words will give them what they need to get it right. To get what right? The way to live, of course.

Morpheus has got a few things sussed out. You can acquire the knowledge, but you need to walk the path to make that knowledge any use. Jesus has explained that acquiring the knowledge from him is a start, but you then have to walk the path. By that he means you have to live by the good things he's told you. Do it his way, and you will be free.

I wonder what he means by "free". My guess is that Jesus is letting us know that in our lives we will come across many ways to live which seem good, but his way is the only one that guarantees us good choices.

Continental

I get very sad as I listen to some of the song lyrics around today. Popping pills to get rid of the pain is a theme that comes up too often. If only people would look to Jesus.

Coffee

Just as Morpheus does for Neo, Jesus has shown us the path. We must make the choice to walk it. That's a choice we need to make every day.

RS

Orange Juice

When you see the ark of the covenant of the Lord your God ... you are to move out from your positions and follow it. Then you will know which way to go, since you have never been this way before ... Consecrate yourselves, for tomorrow the Lord will do amazing things among you. *Joshua 3:3-5 NIV*

Stop Hiding

The Big Breakfast

A high-ranking officer enters to find a nervous private cleaning his rifle.

OFFICER: Come here, soldier. Here are your new orders. *(He pulls an official-looking piece of paper from his tunic).* When you and your division see the big G and his army on the move, come out from your safe areas and follow. Otherwise you will get left behind – or worse, get lost in the woods. This is a new order and supersedes all other orders, as we have not been this way before.

End message.

PRIVATE: Right, sir ... yes, sir. I will be on the lookout, sir.

OFFICER: *(pauses)* A word in your ear, my boy.

He glances around surreptitiously then speaks in a quiet voice.

Clean yourself up because the word in the officer's mess is that tomorrow the big G is planning to do some amazing things!

Newly appointed Joshua was about to take his people into the Promised Land. But first they were to consecrate themselves, which meant to wash – both inside and out. As you follow God into today's battles, take time to get clean. As you step into the shower, let the torrent of God's forgiveness overwhelm you. Now watch as God does "amazing things among us".

Continental

These officers insisted on vigilance because the people had never gone this way before (v. 4). Do you always seem to tread the same paths spiritually? Are you feeling stale in your devotion? Ask God to lead you along new paths so that you can find wonder again and say, "I've never been this way before".

Coffee

Maybe the "amazing things" of our faith always seem to happen to others because we are not willing to leave our current positions, get cleaned up and become authentic followers.

DB

Orange Juice

We bring nothing at birth; we take nothing with us at death. The Lord alone gives and takes. Praise the name of the Lord!

Job 1:21 CEV

In Sickness and in Health

The Big Breakfast

Recently I heard a terrible story about a woman from the Dangerous Sports Club who had broken her pelvis being thrown out of a medieval catapult built by her boyfriend. The newsreaders that were trying to convey this story to me just couldn't do it: their laughter got the better of them. It wasn't that this lady's pain wasn't real, it was just that the situation had reached comic proportions: TV cameras were there to record the abject failure (or was it success?) of this latest attempt to do something stupid.

Job's story has something of the comically tragic about it: it is so bad that you have to smile at the guy. It's probably some biological defence mechanism: we just can't help being happy that it's not us! Yet Job had something that was perhaps more precious than all that he lost: a faithful heart. That's special.

I had a friend at college who told me that he had decided not to be a Christian because God hadn't provided him with good enough friends. Pardon? Aren't you getting God and a mail-order catalogue a bit mixed up here? Still, that's how it is with many Christians. As long as everything is okay, I'll worship you, Lord. But as soon as anything goes wrong, you're out the door and I'll be trying out the old Feng Shui.

Continental

"Faithfulness in little things is a big thing."

Chrysostom

Coffee

If you can, try writing down something that might look a bit like a psalm. Remember that the psalms in the Bible included both complaint and praise together, verse by verse: don't feel ashamed of letting your bad feelings out along with your praise.

SH

Orange Juice

Whoever does not love does not know God, because God is love.

1 John 4:8

Sentimental Sediment

The Big Breakfast

Each of us has our own strange habits and obsessions. One of mine is the need to clean stainless-steel sinks.

There is something that offends me in the fact that stainless steel is so quick to get stained – and there is nothing better to stain it with than tea and coffee leftovers. These regularly build up a presence in our sink and from time to time I will go at it with bleach and scourer until it shines again. The sight of a gleaming sink satisfies me deeply!

There is a staining, though, that is not so negative – the stain of love. This is the sediment that builds up in our lives when we pursue the way of love. Just as tea poured down a sink will leave a residue, so love poured through our lives leaves its mark.

I have recently been challenged to explore the difference between being a Christian and being Christ-like. The former can be an institutional, historic commitment – the latter can only be a changed life. Christian or Christ-like – the acid test is love.

Continental

What is the test of Christian growth? How do you assess your own progress? The answer lies in a simple question: Do you love more?

Coffee

Father, even when I love at my best, I do not love enough. At my worst I barely love at all. Flood me, I pray, with the love that bears your name.

GK

Orange Juice

So Jacob was left alone, and a man [God himself, as Jacob eventually realized] wrestled with him till daybreak.

Genesis 32:24 NIV

God Picks a Fight

The Big Breakfast

I've had a few nights like that. It is often in those "alone times" that we fight in our inner selves and try to pin God to the canvas on an issue. I guess it is also in those "alone times" when God finally has our full attention and picks a character-building fight with us in order to toughen us for the journey ahead.

I once spent three hours locked alone in my parents' porch. Although I missed an important meeting with some church leaders, I ended up with an unscheduled appointment with the Almighty himself.

I wrestled with a God who let me miss such a strategic meeting. But God fought back. He wrestled with me because my daily to-do list had become more important than my daily devotion, and it had been so long since I had been in the company of the King. It wasn't long before the Spirit of God had turned my temporary prison into a temple of worship and I had become a hostage of a holy God instead of a slave to a grueling schedule. Where is God getting tough with you right now? What are the issues that bring you to blows with him? Or have you given up the fight, stepped out of the ring and taken an early shower?

Continental

Jacob calls out to God mid-struggle, his arms locked around his shoulders, his voice full of gritted-teeth determination: "I will not let you go unless you bless me." Now that's the kind of battle cry that would put a stop to our constant complaining.

Coffee

Jesus, you know how I long for your gentle comfort, yet I commit myself again to your discipline and your judgement because I know you do this through the lens of love.

DB

Orange Juice

God does not see the same way people see. People look at the outside of a person, but the LORD looks at the heart.

1 Samuel 16:7 NCV

The Year I Was 16

The Big Breakfast

I was speaking once to a class of 80 high-school girls. What a fantastic group they were. Energetic and peachy-faced, they reminded me of those crazy days of falling in love one moment and wondering where your eyesight was the next ... the war with acne, with parents or teachers, and with all those other stupid people who seemed to be out of the Dark Ages ... the discoveries that belonged only to the year I was 16.

I smiled to myself. Most of it had a familiar feel – except for one thing. They were all on a diet. Yes, all of them. I couldn't believe it. The whole "I'm too fat/too thin" routine in itself was no surprise. It goes with the territory of being 16. To find a *whole* year group deeply unhappy with how they looked, however, was just terrible. I looked around that schoolroom and wanted to weep. They were beautiful, absolutely lovely, but they felt ugly. Who had filled their heads with such a lie?

Continental

We all want to be beautiful, to have a face that's our passport to acceptance. God means it when he tells us that what we are on the inside is much more important.

Coffee

Inner perfection glows. People see it on your face. It gives a beauty that never fades, that draws people to you because you're good to be around.

RS

Orange Juice

This is how God showed his love among us: He sent his one and only Son into the world that we might live through him. This is love: not that we loved God, but that he loved us.

1 John 4:9-10

The Mirror Cracked

The Big Breakfast

For all that we are witnesses to the love and power of Christ, we are not the final measure of God's love. We know that our love is partial, dimmed, obscure and corrupted by self-interest. We know that we will never love enough.

The work of love in our lives is like the slow erosion of rocks in the flow of waves or a river. It is like the growing and maturing of a forest; like the way a city, year by year, expands its boundaries. It takes time – and usually far more time than we expect. Love is a long-term investment plan – cash it in early, and the returns will be disappointing.

Our fear, as this time so slowly passes, is that the picture others see of Christ in us will not be enough. We wonder if our lives will let God down.

But here is the good news. God has taken the initiative to pour his life into Jesus for precisely this reason: so that perfect love is made visible. Jesus is the benchmark of love.

Continental

It is to Jesus, not to the Church, that we look to see the fullness of love displayed. He is the light. We are at best broken mirrors.

Coffee

Thank you, Father, that when my love fails, the love of Christ remains. Thank you that when little of you is visible in my life, everything of you is seen in Jesus.

GK

Orange Juice
Cast all your anxiety on him because he cares for you.

1 Peter 5:7

Chuck It All at Jesus

The Big Breakfast
So what's making you anxious today? What's eating away at you deep inside? According to medical research, anxiety and worry are proven to be the root causes of a great number of physical illnesses. The effects of stress and guilt fill our hospital waiting rooms on a daily basis.

There is a great story about the author Sir Arthur Conan Doyle. As a prank, he sent a note to twelve London socialites. It simply read, "Flee at once. All is discovered!" Within twenty-four hours they had all left the country. I guess many of us live with an undiscovered past that causes guilt to rise and worry to set in.

Whatever worry it is that has stolen sleep from you recently, the secret of finding freedom and peace is in this verse. We need to do some casting, some lobbing, some chucking, some picking it up with both hands and throwing it as hard and as far as we can. And where do we aim? At him, at Jesus, at the Prince of Peace, at the one who had no sin yet became sin for us. That's where!

Continental
Don't fret or worry. Instead of worrying, pray. Let petitions and praises shape your worries into prayers ... Before you know it, a sense of God's wholeness, everything coming together for good, will come and settle you down.

Philippians 4:6-7 MSG

Coffee
What foolish follower of Christ leaves worry at heaven's door and yet continues to pick over it when the Master says, "You're under my care now and I'm dealing with this one"? So let it go!

DB

Orange Juice

Worship the LORD with gladness; come before him with joyful songs.

Psalm 100:2 NIV

If Music Be the Food of Love . . .

The Big Breakfast

Think of a piece of music that makes you *feel* something. Even if you're not into music, you surely know someone who is the opposite: music provides a constant soundtrack to their life. If you're unlucky, you might sit next to them on the bus, listening to that annoying *szztin szztin* sound coming out of their Discman.

But when you stand looking out at the ocean or at the top of a hill, or look down a microscope at the wonders of a human cell, or marvel at the complexities of the human mind, and say, "God made that", the same is true of music. He needn't have bothered, we could have managed without it, but God wanted to make something that expressed beauty and emotion in a way that is beyond explanation, just as he is.

Music was made for the worship of God, even though some people forget it. They may think that music was made to get young girls drunk on a Friday night so not-so-young men can get them into bed, but it's not true: every note, every chord was created by him. So use it! And that goes for all the arts too . . .

Continental

"Anyone who does not find [God] in his wonderful work of music is truly a clod and is not worthy to be called human!"

Martin Luther

Coffee

Find time to play some music, read a good book, go to an art gallery – or do something else you enjoy that will help you to worship God.

SH

Orange Juice

And who knows but that you have come to royal position for such a time as this?

Esther 4:14 NIV

Halt the Evil Moment

The Big Breakfast

The right place at the right time. When we follow Jesus, there are a million times in our lives when we'll be in the right place at the right time. We are his hands and his feet. We are his messengers, passing on his story to others around us. We need to realize that where we are today, the people we spend time with and the opportunities that come our way are, in a strange way, organized by him. Jesus works in us and through us to impact the world around us — even though we don't quite know how he does it!

God really cares about the world he made. He hates to see people ignore him and do things their own way. It leads to injustice, to broken people and broken communities, to violence and death. As people who follow Jesus, we are strategically placed to bring his fragrance into every situation. It is a fragrance that has power to halt an evil moment. Esther was chosen to be queen for such a moment. She halted a Jewish holocaust long before Hitler was around.

What does he have for you to do?

Continental

We want our world to be a place where people do good things to one another. We know it isn't. Today you are where you are so that God can reach in and halt evil.

Coffee

Lord Jesus, use me today to make a difference right in the place where you've placed me.

RS

Orange Juice

Dear friends, since God so loved us, we also ought to love one another.

1 John 4:11

Cosmetics with a Conscience

The Big Breakfast

Anita Roddick took a simple idea – cosmetics with a conscience – and built from it a global commercial enterprise.

One of the great qualities of The Body Shop is that principle and values are so close to the surface. The primary principle – central from day one – is the refusal to sell cosmetics tested on animals.

Roddick was able to grow a chain of stores very fast because she was able to guarantee that this principle would be present in every shop and reflected in every product. The passion of the founder is transferred, with considerable success, to every product bearing The Body Shop name.

It is this same quality – which can be described both in terms of shared values and of brand loyalty – that the apostle John is asking for. If God has so loved us, then surely we, of all people – we who come under his banner and retail his brand – should be marked by that same love.

Continental

If those who own the name of Christ do not live in the love of Christ, who will?

Coffee

As you have loved me, Lord, teach me to love. As you accept me, teach me to accept. You tolerate my failures – teach me tolerance, Lord.

GK

Orange Juice

The Lord had said to Abram, "Leave your country, your people and your father's household and go to the land I will show you."

Genesis 12:1 NIV

Fanatical Faith

The Big Breakfast

He has to be one of my all-time Bible heroes. Not so much from his list of impressive achievements but more from what he had to give up to get them. He left the whole kit and caboodle to "go to the land that I [God] will show you". He had no idea where he was going, only a deep sense of God calling him there.

Imagine you wake up one morning, grab a bowl of frosted flakes and jump in the shower. As the Jojoba Haircare Mousse froths its way down your face, you hear a strange heavenly voice rise from beyond the steam: "Leave this house. Give it to someone who really needs it. Cash in your savings plans, sell the motor and scribble a quick note to the folks. Wave farewell to work and the gang and get yourself to the airport post haste."

"You expect me to give up ... what will my friends say? ... and my folks! You can't be ... where am I going anyway?"

"Don't fret, just go and I'll give you more details en route."

Maybe it was this kind of fanatical faith that gave Abraham's picture pride of place in God's great hall of the faithful. It is stunning to see what faith like this can achieve. What have you got to walk away from to walk closer with him?

Continental

I have often heard preachers smugly expound that "Faith is spelt R-I-S-K". I always think, "No, it's not. It is spelt F-A-I-T-H, and anyway, what's so risky about stepping out into the centre of God's will for your life? It's actually got to be the safest place to be!"

Coffee

"By faith Abraham, when called to go to a place he would later receive as his inheritance, obeyed and went, even though he did not know where he was going" (Hebrews 11:8). Get yourself a good faith lift today.

DB

Orange Juice

These people honor me with their lips, but their hearts are far from me. They worship me in vain; their teachings are merely human rules.

Mark 7:6-7

Truth and Spirit

The Big Breakfast

This is the tough one. As Christians we walk a very fine line. We are called to worship God however we feel; yet we mustn't get into meaningless routine and ritual, which, let's face it, does tend to happen when we try to worship when our heart's not in it. It is obviously something that Jesus felt passionate about, because he talks quite a bit about it.

The key seems to be this balance, which is really, really hard. Not enough truth, and you float off into the clouds in a haze of spiritual ecstasy (well, we can dream, can't we?); not enough spirit, and we crumble and die, but of course we do it with doctrinal purity. The only way out of this, as far as I can see, is Jesus.

Because Jesus is the source of the Spirit, and describes himself as the truth, if we want to worship God rightly, we need to completely immerse ourselves in the person of Jesus. Read the Gospels over and over again. If that's too hard, get hold of a copy of *The Book of God* by Walter Wangerin, which contains the story of Jesus in an easier form. Do whatever you need to do in order to keep your worship alive. Jesus said it himself: "If you know me, you know God."

Continental

"The person who really knows God will worship him."

Seneca

Coffee

Focus on Jesus in some way, either remembering a story about him or just conjuring up an image of him in your mind. Worship him now!

SH

Orange Juice

Jesus said to her, "I am the resurrection and the life. Anyone who believes in me will live, even though they die."

John 11:25

Don't Mention the "D" Word

The Big Breakfast

"I feel strongly that death does not exist." Those are the words from a recent interview with Brian Blessed, the actor and explorer who undertook a climb up Everest in 1993. I was intrigued by the way he thought about death. For him it was the next phase in life, a place to move on to that would eventually bring him back to where he had started.

Do you ever think about death? It seems a long way off, so why get upset about it? Unless, that is, you have already been forced to feel its painful effects through the loss of a close friend or member of your family. Death upsets us. Relationships and friendships that matter a lot get interrupted by death, and very often we simply don't understand why.

Jesus has been there. He has made it through death. He doesn't take away the pain of being separated from someone special. He does make sense of it, though, because he gives meaning to the other side of death.

Continental

Jesus is the only person who can make sense of death, because he is the only person to have beaten it. Ask him to help you understand what that means.

Coffee

Lord Jesus, death scares me. Show me what it means to believe in you and to have life even if I die.

RS

Orange Juice

"*Abba*, Father," he said, "everything is possible for you. Take this cup from me. Yet not what I will, but what you will."

Mark 14:36

My Daddy

The Big Breakfast

I flew from Beirut to Jordan on the day that Yasser Arafat was on the lawn of the White House signing the Middle East peace treaty with Benjamin Netanyahu. Not the best plan I have ever made. Security everywhere was tight. I sat quietly panicking in the airport's "final departure" lounge.

The moment was broken by the cries of two little Jordanian girls who had temporarily lost their parents. With tears rolling down their cheeks, one cried for "*Imma*" (Mommy) while the other sobbed "*Abba*" (Daddy). At the thought of being separated from their parents, all formality went as they cried out. As Jesus wrestled with his mission in the Garden of Gethsemane, he too cried out. Not to the Almighty or to the King of Kings, but to his daddy. I don't think it was the nails that Jesus feared the most: it was being separated from the Father he loved.

Maybe today you feel like a lost and abandoned child in a crowded world. You used to sit so safely in your Father's arms, and you long for those days again. Throw away your pride and cry out loud again for *Abba* to come and rediscover his child.

Continental

Don't send a memo to God requesting a meeting at his earliest convenience vis-à-vis a few hitches in your life plan. Stop and realize how intimate he wants to be with you. Start to dwell on the truth that everything is possible for him, even among the twisted branches of your Garden of Gethsemane.

Coffee

This resurrection life you received from God is not a timid, grave-tending life. It's adventurously expectant, greeting God with a child-like "What's next, Papa?" God's spirit touches our spirit and confirms who we really are ... father and children.

Romans 8:15 MSG

DB

Orange Juice

No one has ever seen God; but if we love one another, God lives in us and his love is made complete in us.

1 John 4:12

When Love Came to Town

The Big Breakfast

Conception is one of the more enjoyable activities written into God's creation order. Through the passion and love of a couple, something new begins. Darkly, secretly at first, in a hidden place, a new life begins to grow.

In time the new form becomes visible. Later still, through birth, we welcome a new being to the human family. But even this is just a stage – the growing goes on. And when physical growth has ended, years later, and decline sets in, there are still senses in which the growing goes on to the very point of death, and beyond.

Life itself is a never-ending adventure, a journey to the deepest reaches of eternity. In the same way, love is a journey towards completeness. When we let God in, something begins in and amongst us. It is a growing thing. Love may at first take hold in secret places, but in time it will break the surface. And the growing will go on forever.

God has committed himself to this process – he will never stop loving us until his love is made complete in our being.

Continental

When we receive God, love comes to town. A new force and power becomes present in our lives and community.

Coffee

O Lord our God, when Christ comes, love comes. You make everything new. Transform the poverty of my being to reflect the riches of your love.

GK

Orange Juice
You will be my witnesses in Jerusalem, and in all Judea and Samaria, and to the ends of the earth.

Acts 1:8

May the Force Be with You

The Big Breakfast
When you know Jesus and how important it is to have him in your life, how do you tell others? This is a question with which many of us struggle. Everybody seems to have their own answer to what it means to find spiritual togetherness. Richard Gere, we're told, wears something called a "spirituality bracelet". It reminds him of the inner peace he's searching for. Then there's the command, "Don't think, feel – and may the Force be with you", given by Liam Neeson as the Jedi Qui-Gon in the movie *Star Wars: The Phantom Menace*. Spiritual matters are really important to many people. There is a big search on for the spiritual path or journey that will fill the inner gap, and every week some new experience is promoted. If only Jesus could be seen more clearly.

Well, that's our job. I recently read a great quote from a church pastor: "When the world doesn't know what to believe, we need to stand up and tell them God's story in a way they'll be sure to get it."

Continental
God's story is about loving people unconditionally. Our friends will understand the story a whole lot better if we love them unconditionally.

Coffee
Lord Jesus, give me your heart for those around me who don't know you, and help me to serve them for your sake.

RS

Orange Juice

For this reason I remind you to fan into flame the gift of God,
which is in you through the laying on of my hands.

2 Timothy 1:6

Light the Fire Again

The Big Breakfast

Last night was a cold, wintry evening as we sat with friends
around a roaring log fire. As the evening went on the fire
cooled. Where there had once been a blaze of searing heat
there now remained only a grate of charred ashes. However,
somebody noticed the problem, quickly picked up a poker and began vigorously
prodding and poking the dying embers. As if from nowhere, the fire found new
energy and began to blaze again, warming our cold toes and doing the job it was
designed to do.

Do you remember the time when your soul burned with a passion to achieve
great things for the kingdom of God? What put that fire out?

Recently I sat chatting to a 35-year-old man whose dreams from his youth had
now grown cold. "I had such big plans," he said, as he told me the story of how he
had been prayed for by his church and was planning an inner-city outreach project.
"I got married, had kids, and got this job offer with a huge salary and company BMW.
I just can't seem to find a way back. My passion is dying. I feel like I've lost my dreams."

If you are going "to fan into flame the gift of God that is in you" it may take some
vigorous prodding and poking to start the fire blazing once more. Don't let it grow
cold.

Continental

The philosopher Søren Kierkegaard once said, "Life must be
understood backwards; but ... it must be lived forwards." Look
back to those dreams of old and fan them into flame once more.

Coffee

Don't start blaming everyone else for stealing your gifts and your
passion away. Paul's reminder to Timothy was for him to do the
fanning. It is your responsibility.

DB

Orange Juice

Jesus called out with a loud voice, "Father, into your hands I commit my spirit." When he had said this, he breathed his last.

Luke 23:46

Famous Last Words

The Big Breakfast

If the words of Jesus are important to us, then his *last* words must be especially so. How did he choose to use the breath that, even as he used it, was being squeezed from his body by the unbearable heaviness of dying?

He chose to commit himself to God. These are words of lifelong habit. Jesus did nothing in the moment of death that he had not done in every moment of life. At the temple at the age of 12, in the wilderness when he was 30, with his disciples, with the crowds, alone in Gethsemane – at every landmark in the life of Christ there is abandonment to the love and will of the Father.

These are also words of hope. In Psalm 31:5, the same words are used by a writer who knows God as a rock and refuge, and looks with hope to be rescued from an enemy's trap. For Christ, no matter how great the pain or how frightening the prognosis, the central reality is that the Father can be trusted. This is a cry not of blind desperation but of intimate trust.

Continental

When you face pressure, what emerges – desperation or trust?

Coffee

"Father, I abandon myself into your hands; I give myself, to you without reserve, and with boundless confidence, for you are my Father."

Charles de Foucauld

GK

Orange Juice

Honor your father and your mother, so that you may live long in the land that the Lord your God is giving you.

Exodus 20:12 NIV

I Just Don't Love Her

The Big Breakfast

This thing about honouring your parents: it's pretty easy, isn't it? Certainly, they get on our nerves from time to time, nagging about a tidy bedroom, a clean and respectable appearance, good table manners, getting a good job, and so on. But they're not a bad pair really, as parents go. So if God wants them honoured, that's fine.

Well, for some of us it's not fine, not that easy. A good friend said to me recently about his mother: "I just don't love her, so how can I honour her? But God says I must." This wasn't just a "shrug the shoulders and get on with it" kind of comment. He was having a truly bad time about it. His mother had been emotionally abusive to him all his life, especially through his growing-up years. He had promised himself that he would never allow hate to creep in. Now, though, he neither loved nor hated. He felt nothing. I didn't know all the ins and outs of this relationship. What I did know, however, was that he regularly spent time talking with her. He gave her birthday cards. So actually he *was* honouring her. It just didn't feel like it.

Continental

The painful experiences that happen to us sometimes seem to make God's commandments look impossible. They're not. We just need to allow him to show us how to go about it.

Coffee

Lord Jesus, I'm slowly realizing that to do what you command sometimes means that my head and my heart haven't quite caught up with one another. Help me to do what you want me to, no matter how I feel.

RS

Orange Juice

We are not fighting against humans. We are fighting against forces and authorities and against rulers of darkness and powers in the spiritual world.

Ephesians 6:12 CEV

Get the Perspective Right

The Big Breakfast

Sometimes the prayer described here is called "spiritual warfare", which is fine by me – although to imagine that there are some kinds of prayer that *aren't* spiritual warfare seems a bit wrong-headed to me. Whenever we get involved with God in his business, we are involving ourselves in the struggle. And who is the struggle against? Not your boss, nor a demanding teacher, nor the person who picks on you for being a Christian. When people sin against us, we need to remember Jesus' words on the cross: "Father, forgive these people! They don't know what they're doing" (Luke 23:34).

Maybe you think this is all too much like *X-Files*. Maybe the idea of all kinds of weird creatures flying around all over the place is beyond your threshold of belief. Well, tough. Just imagine I'm talking about ideas rather than actual beings, but always remember the message: people are not our enemies and never will be. We are to turn the other cheek, to bless those who curse us. This is a radical message, one that will get you into trouble.

Continental

Why is it that the neo-Marxists are the ones with a band called Rage Against the Machine and it takes Chuck D of Public Enemy to tell us to "Fight the Powers that Be"?

Coffee

Spend some time remembering the good things that God has done for you: that in itself is an act of spiritual warfare.

SH

Orange Juice

Therefore let us move beyond the elementary teachings about Christ and be taken forward to maturity.

Hebrews 6:1

Moving On

The Big Breakfast

I love the story about the young girl who falls out of bed one night with a great thud. Mum and Dad rush upstairs to find her sitting up in a daze, rubbing her head. "What happened?" Mum asks. "I think I stayed too close to where I got in," she replies.

Maturity in Christ means not staying too close to where we got in. It means moving on in all walks of life. My youngest son has just moved from the womb to the world. My middle son is moving on from mashed-up soft stuff to proper cereals. My next lad is moving on from nursery to big school. My wife is moving on from attending a small group to leading a small group. I am moving on from just typing sermons to learning PowerPoint presentations. Our church is moving on from news-sheets to web pages. Even my mother-in-law is moving on from landlines to mobiles. We all need to move on or we will stand still.

If my kids stayed with porridge and pre-school they would never grow. If Debbie and I stayed with the tried and tested ways of working we would never develop. If the Church sticks with yesterday's communication methods it will never be heard.

Don't go back over the old lessons you learnt about Jesus. Go on to grown-up teaching.

Continental

Peter the Great, who was once the Tsar of Russia, said, "I have conquered an empire but I have not been able to conquer myself." We need to make that inner journey if we are ever to grow up in Christ.

Coffee

The CEO of General Motors once told a group of employees, "Sometimes it's not incremental changes we need, but to go out on the lunatic fringe!" What fringe do you need to step out on to today in order to kick-start your "growing up" in Christ?

DB

Orange Juice
O Lord, our Lord, how majestic is your name in all the earth!
You have set your glory above the heavens.

Psalm 8:1 NIV

The Wonder Years

The Big Breakfast
A story is told about the movie star John Wayne, who was
not known for the depth of his intellect. When filming the biblical epic *The Purple Robe,* he played the centurion at the foot
of the cross. The director was not convinced by Wayne's rendition, in cowboy drawl,
of the line, "Surely this was the Son of God."

"Say it with awe, John – say it with awe!" he cried through his megaphone.

Wayne acknowledged the instruction, and on the next take, drawl unchanged,
said, "Awe, surely this was the Son of God."

Wayne is not alone in struggling to articulate awe in the contemporary context.
In an age of machines and bureaucracy, in which prosperity, leisure and security are
ensured through technological wizardry, words like "majesty", "wonder" and "awe"
come strangely to us.

But there is an awe, a majesty, invested in the earth, and it points us to God. The
recovery of wonder is a project in which the Christian can profitably and legitimately
invest energy and passion.

Continental
If the wonder of the created order is a sign of the majesty of
God, it is ironic that those most inspired by the earth are often
not believers at all.

Coffee
Father, the glory of the earth is *your* glory. The majesty of the skies
is *your* majesty. The wonder of the stars is *your* wonder. I give you
praise.

GK

Orange Juice

Then Jesus told his disciples a parable to show them that they should always pray and not give up.

Luke 18:1

Doing Something Practical

The Big Breakfast

Jesus tells his followers to take prayer seriously. Do it all the time. No excuses, just keep praying. That's his message. Is that how things are for you? I imagine that, if you are anything like the rest of us, prayer often gets squeezed out by things that seem more important. Or perhaps prayer itself doesn't make much sense. Doing something practical would seem to make a lot *more* sense.

Perhaps we come to our senses when the important matters in our lives just can't be sorted out by doing something practical. Jesus has a very clear message. Pray all the time. Pray about everything that is happening in your life. Pray when you're happy. Pray when you're sad. Pray when you're in trouble, afraid, lonely, struggling to make sense of your life. Pray and don't give up.

The story Jesus goes on to tell shows us how prayer makes a difference when we're in trouble. Pray all the time, but especially when there's a problem that needs sorting.

Continental

Praying when we're in trouble can be a desperate struggle. Don't give up hope. Jesus says that things do change when you pray. Ask people in South Africa or Northern Ireland.

Coffee

Is anything too hard for the Lord?

Genesis 18:14 NIV

RS

Orange Juice
But to you who are listening I say: Love your enemies, do good to those who hate you, bless those who curse you, pray for those who mistreat you.

Luke 6:27-28

Beat the Grudge

The Big Breakfast
Get the bigger picture with this one, please. The verse doesn't tell us to walk away from those who hate us or treat us badly. There is no sense of mere tolerance here. We are clearly commanded to do them good, to offer them a blessing and to pray for them.

I knew a man who disliked me so much that he twisted the truth about me publicly, spread damaging rumours about my character privately and told my closest friends that they should abandon me. Everything within me wanted to hurt him. Everything within God wanted me to love him, to bless him and even to pray for him. If it hadn't been for the advice of a wise friend, I might well have gone with my emotions and missed the adventure of going against the grain.

I began by reluctantly praying God's very best for him. That's where my attitude slowly started to change. I vowed never to speak badly of him publicly, and made every effort to talk well of him in private. I even sent him a gift as a blessing.

I discovered that real freedom would never come from revenge, but only from real love. I also discovered that I could never have behaved that way but for the love of good friends and the grace of a great God.

Continental
Winston Churchill once remarked that we should listen to our friends *and* our enemies, as they are both telling us the truth from a slightly different perspective. When the rocks of criticism fly, we must learn not to build a wall with them but to use them to build a solid foundation for our character.

Coffee
Jesus starts with, "But to you are listening ..." Don't go deaf on God; instead, deal with whatever issue it is today, before your head hits the pillow.

DB

Orange Juice

From the lips of children and infants you have ordained praise because of your enemies, to silence the foe and the avenger.

Psalm 8:2 NIV

No Contest!

The Big Breakfast

What comes out of the lips of children? Faltering words, giggles, spit, puke, chewed food, half-eaten lollipops that attach themselves to car seats with an adherence worthy of superglue.

God is not revealed in the sentimental perfection that we imagine in children until we spend time with them. He is in the intricacy and intimacy of the world he has made – with all its mess and muddles. The danger of this psalm is that we picture a soft-focus image of angelic sterility – and then impose that image on our worship.

But our God is a real-world God. We love our children when their faces are dirty, when they are hidden in unspeakable mess, when the smell that rises from them would be at home in a farmyard. We bond with them because, in the midst of the mess, there is a miracle happening – new life, formed and growing; the sheer joy of innocent, unsullied love. The enemies of God are silenced by such joy. Against power and sophistication, the miracle of infancy wins every time.

Continental

This is praise: not a world delivered from ambiguity and pain, but a God who brings to us, in the midst of ambiguity, the miracle of life.

Coffee

The world was made to praise you, Father. Where I fail to do so, infants and rocks will shame me by their song.

GK

Orange Juice

Stand firm then, with the belt of truth buckled around your waist, with the breastplate of righteousness in place, and with your feet fitted with the readiness that comes from the gospel of peace.

Ephesians 6:14-15

The Armour

The Big Breakfast

Paul starts to talk about "the armour of God", and this is where you switch off, right? If you have grown up in the Church, then you probably know this bit off by heart, and your mum has a picture of a Roman soldier in a drawer somewhere, the poor guy wielding a ten-foot "Sword of the Spirit", used in your imagination for killing dinosaurs.

But how much thought have you given to "the readiness that comes from the gospel"? If you were to actually live what you believe and pray that God would give you opportunities to do the right thing today, the battle would be half over. You would just need to pray for the ability to see what the Father is doing and to follow him – what Paul calls "readiness".

Praising God is a great place to start in prayer, but how often do you pray for readiness and righteousness? Yep, me too. I'm resolving to pray differently as I write this.

Continental

One of the characters in the film *The Matrix* says, "It's the difference between knowing the way and walking the way." Prayer is about your life with God, the day ahead and all your futures. Never let your prayer life get divorced from the rest of your life.

Coffee

Pray for readiness to do right today: "God, I want to see what you're doing and work with you, just like Jesus did. When I go to bed tonight, I want to know that you've answered this prayer."

SH

Orange Juice

Do not get drunk on wine, which leads to debauchery. Instead, be filled with the Spirit.

Ephesians 5:18

Get Drunk!

The Big Breakfast

My initial years as a Christian were spent with believers whose passion for God was only surpassed by their disdain for alcohol. I remember one older gentleman explaining away the apostle Paul's advice for Timothy to "take a little wine to help his stomach trouble" as meaning he should rub it on (1 Timothy 5:23)! I was often sternly reminded about the first part of this verse, which in itself is excellent advice – "Do not get drunk". It was only in later years that I grasped the importance of the "be filled with the Spirit" bit. Is Paul suggesting that the infilling of God's Spirit is akin to having a skinful of best Beaujolais? In some ways, yes.

Wine makes people lose their inhibitions, it makes them dance like constipated octopuses and not bother about what anyone else thinks. It frees their emotions to express inner feelings. Being filled with the rich wine of God's Spirit gives freedom to worship, to embrace the passion of our love affair with Jesus. He enables us to express our affection for each other with genuine honesty and vulnerability. Pay a visit to heaven's vineyard today and swap the headache of too much booze for the heartbeat of the Father's best vintage.

Continental

Nancy Astor wrote in the *Christian Herald* back in 1960, "The only reason I don't drink is because I wish to know when I am having a good time." Do your fun times rely on a glass in your hand? Can you still laugh and play without the drug of drink? What spirit are you addicted to?

Coffee

"Wine makes you mean, beer makes you quarrelsome – a staggering drunk is not much fun" (Proverbs 20:1 MSG). How easy would it be for you to fast from alcohol for a month?

DB

Orange Juice

... the judge refused to help her. But afterwards, he thought to himself, "Even though I don't respect God or care about people, I will see that she gets her rights. Otherwise she will continue to bother me until I am worn out."

Luke 18:4-5 NCV

Never Give Up

The Big Breakfast

This poor woman: she has no money, so she can't pay a bribe; she has no man in her life to fight for her. She has only one way out. All she can do is to keep pleading, no matter how hopeless the situation seems, hoping to wear the judge down.

The judge says of himself that he's corrupt. He can't be shamed into doing what's right. He doesn't care what people think of him. And as for God, well, he has no fear of God either.

What does the story have to say to us? I think it's something like this: keep praying. Keep coming to God with your requests. Be persistent. If a corrupt judge is eventually worn down by the pleading of a widow, how much more likely it is that God – who is loving, kind, compassionate and just – will answer you and help you.

Continental

Prayer is a mystery. It isn't about "wish lists", nor is it about changing God's mind. That would be to misunderstand Jesus. It is about bringing genuine need to God and not giving up.

Coffee

Perhaps the key is to remember that we come to a loving Father not a twisted judge. His response to our prayers can always be trusted.

RS

Orange Juice

Our Father in heaven ...

Matthew 6:9

The Ultimate Overview

The Big Breakfast

Why do tennis umpires sit on elevated chairs? Why is the weather best understood through satellite imaging? Why do eagles hunt from such a great altitude? The answer, in every case, is 20-20 high-sight. You get a view of a situation from a great height that you cannot get on the ground.

Prayer, according to Jesus, is rooted not only in *who* God is – the Father who made us and loves us – but also in *where* God is. Heaven is the ultimate vantage point, offering an overview of our needs that is invisible from any other angle.

Those four words cited above – almost certainly the most-quoted words in the Bible – capture the twin reality that is the engine-room of biblical prayer. Because God is in heaven, he is distant from us, far enough away to take an eagle's-eye view of our lives and to lead us well. Because he is our Father, that distance does nothing to dent his commitment to us. Prayer is a message sent over the wire to Headquarters. At the same time it is a word whispered in the ear of a concerned parent.

Continental

"Sometimes you're further than the moon," writes Martin Smith of the band Delirious? "sometimes you're closer than my skin." Both God's distance from us and his closeness to us are necessary for the effectiveness of prayer.

Coffee

Father, I know so little of prayer. Standing with your first disciples in their ignorance and need, I echo their words: "Lord, teach us to pray."

GK

Orange Juice

Jesus asked a third time, "Simon ... do you love me?"
Peter was hurt because Jesus had asked him three times if he
loved him. So he told Jesus, "Lord, you know everything. You
know I love you."

John 21:17 CEV

Do You Love Me?

The Big Breakfast

We are quite limited when we use the word "love" in the
English language. We have to use the same word to say, "I
think I love you, Doris," as we would use to say, "I'd love a bag
of chips." The ancient Greeks were far more expressive:

Phileo love was the love of things or friends.

Agape love was unconditional love – the kind of love God has for his children.

After the resurrected Jesus has finished his breakfast with Peter, he asks him three
times, "Peter, do you love me?" The first couple of times Jesus asks, "Peter, do you
agape me – love me unconditionally?" Yet both times Peter answers, "Lord, you
know that I *phileo* you – love you as a friend." Eventually Jesus asks a final time, but
this time he says, "Peter, do you *phileo* me?" "Yes, Lord," Peter replies. "You know
that I *phileo* you."

Was Jesus dropping his standard? Letting Peter off the hook? I don't think so. I'm
convinced that he was saying to Peter, "You know the kind of love I long for from
you, but let's start from where you are." God longs for our exclusive attention today,
yet he begins with our faltering affection.

Continental

Before Jesus was crucified, Peter told him he would die for him.
What happened? He ended up denying Jesus three times. It is this
same Peter that Jesus reinstates and of whom Jesus says, "I will
build my Church on you." Gives us all hope, eh?

Coffee

Jesus doesn't run through a "why did you deny me three times?"
debate with Peter. He simply asks, "Do you love me ... I mean
really love me?" How would you respond to that same question
asked of you today?

DB

Orange Juice

However, when the Son of Man comes, will he find faith on the earth?

Luke 18:8

Jesus: The True Source

The Big Breakfast

Faith isn't about how we feel. This is hard to take in. "If it feels right, do it." You've probably heard that a lot recently. Don't misunderstand me: how we feel is very important. God made us body, mind and spirit. Jesus honours our wholeness when he tells us to love God with all of who we are – our heart (emotions), mind (intellect), soul (spirit) and strength (physical body). Sometimes, though, our mind or our understanding must lead the way. Getting to know God well will make that a great deal easier.

Being a follower of Jesus, which means having faith in him and God, isn't just about our own wants and needs. It is also about other people. Jesus asks if he'll find faith on earth. I guess he wants to know if those who say they are his followers are actually getting on with the job – the kingdom job of fighting injustice, speaking out on God's good and pure ways to live, and telling the world how important it is to honour him. Will the Son of Man find faith on earth?

Continental

Maybe faith isn't the most difficult bit. Crystals, palm readings, special bracelets – these all need "faith" in order to work. Seeing Jesus as the true source of faith – now that's a whole lot harder.

Coffee

Lord Jesus, I'm beginning to understand that by doing things that demonstrate my faith in you I'll show others where true faith is found.

RS

Orange Juice

Take the helmet of salvation and the sword of the Spirit, which is the word of God.

Ephesians 6:17

The Fight

The Big Breakfast

I live in Leeds, England, and up here in the cold, frosty north, somebody thought it would be a good idea to house all the stuff from the Tower of London that nobody gets to see. So, we have a huge grey building called "The Royal Armouries" in which people run around in medieval armour and pretend to chop each other's heads off. Obviously just the right kind of entertainment for us northern savages.

I must admit it's not really my cup of tea. What I have become aware of, though, is the significance of a knight's helmet and sword. The helmet was a sign of his place in the pecking order: the fancier the helmet, the more noble its wearer. Likewise with the sword: Excalibur, King Arthur's sword, could be wielded only by a king.

So these two things tell us something about our identity: we are children of the King and we have the best weapon available to us. What is that weapon? The word of God. Now, I know that we all immediately assume that means the Bible, but don't forget that God continues to speak to us today. Keep listening – it's your best weapon!

Continental

For the word of God is alive and active. Sharper than any double-edged sword, it penetrates even to dividing soul and spirit, joints and marrow; it judges the thoughts and attitudes of the heart.

Hebrews 4:12

Coffee

Prayer is as much about listening as it is about talking. Either spend a few minutes in quiet or read a psalm, and allow God's word to soak into you.

SH

Orange Juice

Blessed are you who are poor, for yours is the kingdom of God.

Luke 6:20

How Poor Do You Have to Be?

The Big Breakfast

What kind of a deal is that? The kingdom of God is yours if you are poor? I mean, how poor do you have to be in order to qualify for this "once-in-a-lifetime-never-to-be-repeated" offer? Is Jesus talking about the poverty of a student with no grant, a huge debt and only the smell of last night's curry for breakfast? Or is it the poverty of the bag lady who pushes her life in a shopping trolley from doorway to doorway? Or maybe he means the heartbreaking poverty of the starving African child or the homeless Kosovan refugee?

I struggled with this verse for so long until I sat over a fairly-traded decaffeinated coffee with a friend of mine who has travelled to some of the world's nations with Tearfund, a Christian development and relief organization. "So how poor do you have to be, Dave?" His answer was swift, and one he had made a thousand times before in as many such meetings. He simply amplified the verse for me: "Blessed are you who have seen everything the world has to give and realize that the most it has to give is poverty." He repeated it, then talked some more.

I nodded in the appropriate pauses, but I listened to none of it. Something had happened deep in my soul – I had understood. Do you, too?

Continental

The phone rang as I wrote this piece today. It was a man who has walked out on his faith, his job, his home and his friends for a woman he loves but can never have. Now he wants to taste God's kingdom again. I read him this verse from *The Message*: "You're blessed when you've lost it all. God's kingdom is there for the finding."

Coffee

When you wake up to the fact that there is something better in life than money or sex, fame or power, then – and only then – is the kingdom of God truly yours!

DB

Orange Juice

You made him a little lower than the heavenly beings and crowned him with glory and honor.

Psalm 8:5 NIV

Maybe Angels

The Big Breakfast

Some childhood games surface in almost every culture. Hide-and-seek and tag are two of them. Another is a game played on the seashore, at the very boundary of ocean and beach.

The game consists of running forward as the waves recede, until you are almost in the ocean itself, then retreating up the beach as fast as possible when a new wave comes in. The objective can be simply expressed: to get as far into the ocean as you can without getting wet.

This is the unique possibility that God has carved out for women and men in the creation: to get as close to heaven as it is possible to get without actually leaving the earth. The phrase "a little lower than the heavenly beings" implies that once you get "higher" than women and men, you leave the earthly sphere altogether. Whatever God has poured into his creation, he has given to women and men a special place at its head. There is no higher calling in the universe than the call to be human before God.

Continental

We are earth-bound – made for earth and deeply tied to its rhythms – yet in our hearts we sense the possibility of heaven.

Coffee

A child of the earth, I long for the freedoms of heaven. A child of heaven, I long to see the kingdom come to earth.

GK

Orange Juice

But we have this treasure in jars of clay to show that this all-surpassing power is from God and not from us.

2 Corinthians 4:7

The Start-Up Group

The Big Breakfast

If Jesus had sent the profiles of his twelve disciples to a management consultant and asked for an opinion on his choice of recruits, what do you think the response would have been? "You're off your trolley, Jesus! This lot are a complete disaster. Peter doesn't know how to control his temper, nor does he have any natural wit. Matthew comes with a very poor reputation. I wouldn't have him in your start-up group. Much too risky ... You do have one good one. He's good with money, he's astute, he understands that strategy is important. Yes, I'd keep Judas Iscariot and get rid of the rest!"

Jesus, of course, would have ignored such advice. It was those eleven original disciples (minus Judas) who started the Christian Church. Since then, millions and millions of people have joined. It is estimated that throughout the world every day, 63,000 people become Christians and 1,600 churches are planted.

Continental

We are like jars of clay that break easily. Jesus doesn't have his eye on strength and ability when he's looking for disciples. Rather, he's looking for a willing jar to carry his message.

Coffee

Lord Jesus, it's amazing to think that those unlikely disciples were your start-up group. I'm no different, yet you choose to use me too. Thank you.

RS

Orange Juice

Yet to all who did receive him, to those who believed in his name, he gave the right to become children of God.

John 1:12

Are You Receiving Me?

The Big Breakfast

The doors are locked and bolted, the windows barred. A repossession order in hand, the landlord stands at the threshold. The papers prove that he is the rightful owner – the law is on his side and his ultimate victory is assured.

But there is a standoff. His determination to gain entry is matched, ounce for ounce, by the determination of those within to resist.

So he changes tack. Rather than force entry, he announces to all those who will recognize his right of ownership and make themselves known, that a place will be kept for them in the house once repossession is complete. They have one last chance to join the winning side.

But to do so will mean breaking ranks with the rebels. It will mean acknowledging the illegitimacy of the occupation and identifying with the lone figure at the door. It is a hard choice to make – especially from within the occupied home. But the promise is there – a full pardon, and the right to live now the life that is promised for the cosmos.

Continental

Making the choice, identifying with Christ, means breaking ranks with those with whom we have shared the occupation. It is a new allegiance that will often run counter to allegiances we have held in the past.

Coffee

Jesus, who stands at the door of our lives, we welcome you. Jesus, who knocks, and will not come in without invitation, we receive you. Jesus, who promises a new kind of life here and now, we worship you.

GK

Orange Juice

Come, let us go up to Bethel, where I will build an altar to God, who answered me in the day of my distress and who has been with me wherever I have gone.

Genesis 35:3 NIV

Practical Holiness

The Big Breakfast

What is Jacob to do? His sons have slaughtered an entire village (Genesis 34), and, for all Jacob knows, there could be an army on its way right now to wipe out his entire family, God's promises or not. Jacob listens to God, who tells him that his real home is Bethel, the place where Jacob first met God in a powerful way. Maybe Jacob was running away, but maybe he was also realizing that his real home, however dry and dusty that might be, would always be the place where he met God.

In my church we have tried to make a big deal of being "in the world but not of it". Lots of people have got jobs as a way of meeting people and not just for the money. For some people this has been brilliant, and we have seen other people getting to know God through them. For others, it has not been an easy ride at all. They discover that there are lots of people seemingly having a good time out there. In order to survive, they need to find their own "Bethel" – a place where they can meet God and call it "home".

Continental

God is where we belong. If any other thing is central to our lives, we will always be homeless.

Coffee

Is your "Bethel" a real or imaginary place? Resolve to spend more time there.

SH

Orange Juice

Instead, they were longing for a better country.

Hebrews 11:16

A Better Place to Live

The Big Breakfast

Russian comedian Yakov Smirnoff writes, "Coming from the Soviet Union I was not prepared ... On my first shopping trip I saw powdered milk – you just add water and you get milk. Then I saw powdered orange juice – you just add water and you get orange juice. Then I saw baby powder and I thought to myself, wow – what a wonderful country!"

These few words from Hebrews ignite again a soul-wrenching longing for a better nation than the one we have now.

A country where locksmiths go out of business because stealing doesn't exist.
A country where divorce courts remain empty because couples remain faithful.
A country where maximum security becomes minimum occupancy because killing stops.
And a country where my team always wins the league.

Michael Jackson's "Man in the Mirror" was right: "If you want to make the world a better place, take a look at yourself and make a change." It is the only way to see the dream become reality.

Continental

A little lad was throwing washed-up starfish back into the Mediterranean Sea. An intrigued tourist asked how he intended to make a difference to so many. The boy simply picked up another, tossed it back into the cool water and said, "I made a difference to that one, didn't I?" Start small, but make sure you start!

Coffee

You might not be able to change everybody's world everywhere, but you can change somebody's world somewhere. Whose world do you want to make a change in today? Go do it!

DB

Orange Juice

The devil who rules this world has blinded the minds of those who do not believe. They cannot see the light of the Good News.

2 Corinthians 4:4 NCV

Expose This Lie

The Big Breakfast

We live in a world of lies. Satan, the Devil, the evil opposer of God and his kingdom, is alive and well. He blinds people. He's been at it for a long time. In the very beginning it was Satan who told Adam and Eve that they'd be okay if they ignored what God told them and did their own thing.

Are you aware of some of his big lies today? The latest cool, trendy thing that promises to ''make life a blast''. The idea that wearing great gear will solve your image problem. The pressure never to be without a boy/girl partner, because that will sort the need to belong. The idea that good sex will solve the search for love.

Who's he kidding? Who are we kidding? Great gear is wonderful, but it won't change how we feel inside. A loving relationship is a great gift and sex in the right context is enormously special, but belonging runs much deeper than that. We live in this sea of lies every day. Satan must laugh out loud at times. Our job, those of us who follow Jesus, is to expose his lies.

Continental

Expose the lies of Satan by speaking God's truth in every situation. Satan is enjoying a free rule because of our silence.

Coffee

Lord Jesus, I'm not always sure how to speak your truth in the situations in which I find myself. Please show me how.

RS

Orange Juice
You made him ruler over the works of your hands; you put
everything under his feet.

Psalm 8:6 NIV

A Steward's Enquiry

The Big Breakfast
The unique place of women and men in the creation is not
only a statement of human identity. It is also a job description.
We have work to do.

Throughout the biblical witness, there is an emphasis on this notion of caring on
God's behalf for the world. The term most often used for this role is "stewardship",
which carries with it the idea of accountability. We have a task, and we will be taken
to task.

With trembling hands, God holds out to us the totality of the world he has made
and loves. Like Paddington Bear, we find a label on it saying, "Please Look After This
Planet".

The property handed to us is not some vacant lot, some square of barren
ground – it is the tumbling, sparkling, precious product of the artist's hand. Imagine
an author asking you to look after a lifetime's worth of unpublished manuscripts –
texts into which he had poured his life. God trusts us with his treasures because he
loves and honours us, because we're family.

Continental
We know that we are called to trust God. We speak less
frequently of the flip-side of the same coin. God, deeply and
genuinely, trusts us.

Coffee
Thank you, Father, for the trust you have placed in me. Help me,
day by day, to make good that trust.

GK

Orange Juice

Prepare for war! Rouse the warriors! Let all the fighting men draw near and attack.

Joel 3:9 NIV

Take the King's Shilling

The Big Breakfast

We must get away from the idea that church is a Sunday-school picnic complete with fondant fancies and warm lemonade. We must recapture the image of a small mud-splattered army who meet together each week for the commanding office, to heal our battle scars, lead our war cry and roll out the strategy for the coming offensive.

We must lose the image of the Church as a convalescent home for retired or just tired soldiers. We only retreat in order to prepare again for advance. God doesn't have a divine, MASH-like helicopter that rescues us from life's battles and drops us back in the warmth of the officers' mess. If he did have such a helicopter he would drop the winch and on the end of it would be Jesus himself, who promises to walk through the battlefield with us.

Until late in the nineteenth century, the British army recruited men by giving them the King's Shilling. That coin would have been a small fortune to those men, and taking it meant they were officially conscripted – no backing out. Many fought in bloody wars. Many lost their lives.

Hear the cry again this day – "Prepare for war!" Gladly accept the King's Shilling as a sign of your commitment to the cause.

Continental

We live in enemy-occupied territory. Our forces are outnumbered and out-resourced. Yet when the Spirit of God fell on 120 followers in that Upper Room, all heaven broke out and all hell ran scared as together they turned the known world upside down. The devil may seem a mighty foe, but our God is the almighty champion.

Coffee

Missionary C.T. Studd once said, "I don't want to live within the sound of chapel bell, I want to run a rescue shop within a yard of hell." Where are your priorities?

DB

Orange Juice

We have renounced secret and shameful ways; we do not use
deception, nor do we distort the word of God.

2 Corinthians 4:2

God Goes Online

The Big Breakfast

Well, there's www.beliefnet.com, www.gospelcom.net,
www.spiritchannel.com and www.ibelieve.com. God has
gone online. Websites are now available for the ever-
growing numbers of net-surfers looking for answers to reli-
gious questions. An estimated 600,000 sites exist (and this figure doesn't include
home pages for churches and religious organizations or groups). A recent survey
suggested that a quarter of all net-surfers have visited sites for religious purposes.
Apparently this makes it as popular a subject as sex!

This is great news. The hunger for spiritual answers gives us, as followers of Jesus,
a wonderful opportunity to tell people about him. For a change we'll be answering
the questions they're asking. There's an interesting warning in this verse from 2 Corinthians, however. As we share God's story with people, we must do it openly. We
must be up-front and honest in speaking the truth God has given us without changing
any of it. That's not always easy, because some of God's truth can be offensive to
people. We need to tell it as it is, nonetheless.

Continental

The gospel, God's story, is his story not ours. We must tell it
as it is and allow God to deal with the consequences.

Coffee

Lord Jesus, sometimes it is tempting to tell people what they want
to hear rather than the truths you show us in your word. Help me
to avoid that temptation.

RS

Orange Juice

... I was seeing the brightness of the Lord's glory! So I bowed with my face to the ground, and just then I heard a voice speaking to me. The Lord said, "Ezekiel, son of man, I want you to stand up and listen."

Ezekiel 1:28-2:1 CEV

Don't Get Down, Get Up!

The Big Breakfast

The first prayer meeting I remember going to as a new Christian was at the home of a friend from school. There were about ten of us and, obviously, I didn't really know what to do. Still, I learned soon enough that one of the most important things about prayer is position. Even if I never actually said a word, I could show everyone else that I was praying by leaning forward in my chair and looking at the floor.

Perhaps this shows that I only partly understood how big God is. If I had really met him, I would no doubt have ended up on the floor, just as Ezekiel did. He saw God in a scary way and did what most of us would do: since you can't run away from a God who is everywhere, at least you can bury your face in the ground and hope for the best ...

And then God says, "Get up! I want you to stand before me; you've got nothing to hide!" God's like that: along with the justice comes mercy; along with the immenseness of the Creator of the universe comes the voice of a friend.

Continental

"Leonard Thynn leaned across and whispered in my ear, 'He knows a different God to the one I do. His God's nice.'"

The Sacred Diary of Adrian Plass

Coffee

Why not try praying in a different position than the one you normally use? Even if you are sitting on a bus right now, you could always stand up, or just cup your hands as a sign of openness to God. It can make a difference!

SH

Orange Juice

Then Peter stood up with the Eleven, raised his voice and addressed the crowd: "Fellow Jews and all of you who live in Jerusalem, *let me explain this to you.*"

Acts 2:14 (emphasis added)

Let Me Explain

The Big Breakfast

As a preacher, I spend most of my time *proclaiming* the story of God: in schools, at church, on the streets and in people's homes. But not Peter. He spent his time *explaining*. God had spoken quite well for himself by all the miraculous things he had done previously. Peter merely said, "Let me explain them to you". To be honest, I'm getting fed up with all this proclamation. I want to do some explanation.

You're well again despite the prognosis – let me explain ...

You've found a job when they said you never would – let me explain ...

You've found a partner when they said you were still on the shelf – let me explain ...

You feel a peace you can't understand, you've lost that bitterness deep within, you can forgive now after all these years and you don't know why? Let me explain ...

Let the work of God in your life speak for itself today. Then hear yourself repeating Peter's words – "let me explain".

Continental

It is not often that our words about God demand any explanation from our friends. It is more likely to be things such as spending some time with the social outcast, being honest on this month's expenses claim or choosing to see the best rather than fuel the rumour. Does your life provoke that kind of explanation?

Coffee

There should be things in our daily lives that can be explained only by God. Reflect on those things in your life.

DB

Orange Juice
Hallowed be your name.

Matthew 6:9

Cleaning Up God's Image

The Big Breakfast
Computer-based graphics and imaging programmes offer a range of "clean-up" tools, from image sharpening to de-speckling. My favourite is a command called "Remove Noise". This analyses the bit-map of an image and looks for random pixels that don't contribute anything useful and are getting in the way. It is the digital equivalent of blowing across a chalk drawing to remove the dust without disturbing the picture.

This process is something like what is at work in the phrase "Hallowed be your name". To ask that the name of God should be honoured is the same, in Hebrew culture, as asking that his character should be known and seen. We are praying here that the clutter and distractions of our lives – the dust and debris that stops us seeing God for who he is – might be swept away, until the Father can clearly be seen and known.

Whatever else this important phrase means, it is a "Remove Noise" command for our life of prayer.

Continental
A number of people have experienced trouble on the Internet when hackers have been able to hijack their name and use it to access suspect websites and even to make purchases. In what senses have we hijacked the name of God?

Coffee
Father, as we learn to pray and grow in faith, may our prayers – and our actions – be a true reflection of your character and name.

GK

Orange Juice

If you love me, you will obey my commands. I will ask the Father, and he will give you another Helper to be with you forever – the Spirit of truth.

John 14:15 NCV

From Friend to Brother

The Big Breakfast

Do you remember how tough it was to get your maths homework done? If calculus and trigonometry weren't your thing, it was total torture with no way out. Maths was one of those subjects everybody had to pass. It was always great when a friend who understood it better gave you some help.

The Holy Spirit is a bit like that friend. Firstly, he *is* a friend, a really good friend. He's there to help, especially as we try to understand all the things Jesus taught. The Holy Spirit will help us make sense of it, and will remind us about it as time goes on.

His job is bigger than that, though. He reveals Jesus himself to us, and to those who don't believe. As he does that, he shows very clearly what sin is, and also shows that sin (living for ourselves not God) has consequences. I guess that's the link shown in this verse. Jesus says that if we love him, we will obey him. The Holy Spirit will teach us about Jesus and help us to love him.

Continental

Brian Jones, the round-the-world balloonist, said of his co-pilot Bertrand, "We took off as pilots, we flew as friends and we came home as brothers."

Coffee

The Holy Spirit will stick with us the whole way, first as our friend and then as our brother.

RS

Orange Juice

Those who try to keep their life will lose it, and those who lose their life will preserve it.

Luke 17:33

Protect Life or Pursue It?

The Big Breakfast

One commentator said that no other saying of Jesus is given such emphasis in the gospels as this one. This is a big thing to grasp. Jesus tells his followers that there are two ways to look at life: keep it or let it go; protect it or pursue it.

As you walk life's road you will inevitably come to Decision Junction. The rickety signpost points left towards "Cosy Town – via Pipe and Slippers Lane". The road is busy and well lit this way, with flashing neon signs advertising take-it-easy restaurants and don't-get-too-involved family fun parks. The sign also points right towards "Adrenaline City – via Adventure Boulevard". The road here is a steep climb, and not many choose to take it. However, the rumour is that it's a long haul to the top but, boy, is the view worth it!

So which road will you take today? The safe route that says if I don't take part they won't criticize me? Or the adventurous route where the adrenaline rush of active involvement pulsates constantly through your veins?

You see, whichever route you choose you'll arrive in heaven. But choose the wrong route and you'll have no stories to tell when you get to your destination.

Continental

Imagine if Jesus had chosen to protect his life rather than vigorously pursuing it. Safeguarding his reputation would have kept him away from prostitutes, the poor and the pious. Safeguarding his life would have kept him away from criminals, critics and, ultimately, the cross.

Coffee

"If you grasp and cling to life on your terms, you'll lose it, but if you let that life go, you'll get life on God's terms" (*The Message*). Decide what you need to let go of today.

DB

Orange Juice

So you are no longer slaves, but God's children; and since you are his children, he has made you also heirs.

Galatians 4:7

Heirs and Graces

The Big Breakfast

There is a sense in which our adoption into God's family looks to the past. It sees the poverty and slavery from which we have been delivered, and rejoices in the God of liberation. In another sense, it is a present experience – enjoying the companionship and security of God, the perfect parent.

But there is a third dimension to our adoption, in that it has a future tense. All that was lost in the Fall, all the Creator's ambitions for his human friends, all the cosmic significance of the role to which Eve and Adam were called – all this is restored to us once more, as we are called not children only, but also heirs.

To enter into the parenthood of God is to enter into a destiny beyond our imagining. It is this future dimension of the Cross that gives it irresistible power – the power of hope for the hopeless, the power of inheritance for the dispossessed.

Continental

There are promises of God that are fulfilled the moment we come into adoption – the promise of forgiveness is one. But there are other promises – the fullness of healing and restoration – that may remain in the future for us.

Coffee

God of my adoption, Father, Son and Spirit, thank you that you have dealt with my past history, you have transformed my present experience, and you have given me a future full of promise.

GK

Orange Juice

"But about that day or hour no one knows, not even the angels in heaven, nor the Son, but only the Father. As it was in the days of Noah, so it will be at the coming of the Son of Man … They knew nothing about what would happen until the flood came and took them all away. That is how it will be at the coming of the Son of Man." **Matthew 24:36-37, 39**

Hold on a Minute!

The Big Breakfast

Here is a statement from Jesus which must always be in our minds when we start getting into thinking about when God winds up the world as we know it. Jesus once said that when he returned (an important part of God's plans for the end of the universe), it would be as unexpected as when a thief breaks into your home in the middle of the night.

Lots of Christians from around the world spend huge amounts of time, money and energy trying to work out when Jesus is coming back, despite the fact that Jesus himself said we'll never know. It may be that we'll die before Jesus returns, or it may be that today's the day …

Continental

"Limited by mortality, yet destined for liberation, in hope the universe waits: God's purpose shall be revealed."

The Iona Community

Coffee

If you knew that the world was going to end in a week and that you would then meet Jesus face to face, what would you do during that week?

SH

Orange Juice

Now this is eternal life: that they know you, the only true God, and Jesus Christ, whom you have sent.

John 17:3

The Big-Time Search

The Big Breakfast

A survey of Internet users recently revealed that a quarter of all surfers have used the net for religious purposes. Sites offer religious instruction on how to raise your child, or how to read the Bible, and there's even one offering users an online confessional box. Of enormous interest is the question, "Is there eternal life?" People want to know, "What happens when we die, and can we be sure God won't let us down on that one?"

Eternal life is about knowing God now – today, while we're still alive. It is not about "pie in the sky when I die". How is it that we've missed that? Everyone's looking for real life. This explosion of interest on the Internet is only one piece of evidence for that. The search for spiritual meaning is on, big time.

Jesus tells us that knowing him and knowing God now, as well as after we die, is what life is all about. Why are we keeping this amazing truth to ourselves? It was never meant to be the best-kept secret in the world.

Continental

Have you noticed how many new religions there are around today? Jesus makes it clear that he is the way, the truth and the life (John 14:6).

Coffee

Jesus knows that our friends won't always understand why we want to know and follow him. That's why he promised to pray for us (John 17:9).

RS

Orange Juice

He came to that which was his own, but his own did not receive him.

John 1:11

Home Switched Home

The Big Breakfast

You've had a long and tiring journey. You are jet-lagged, but glad to be home. You park in your own drive, walk to your own front door and put your own key in the lock.

But the lock doesn't turn. You try other keys, but nothing fits. When you see movement in the house, you knock on the door. A total stranger comes and informs you that the house is no longer your home. It has been occupied by the Revolutionary Army of Something-or-Other and has been declared a Stateless Zone. The locks have been changed and you will not be given access. Until you can get a court order and police back-up, you are homeless.

This is your home – your property. Not only do you own the title deeds – you even built the place with your own hands. Inside are your belongings, your memories. But you are outside – left out in the cold.

Jesus came to a planet over which he has rights of ownership and occupation – he came to his home. It is we, the tenants, who have refused to give him access.

Continental

Imagine the President of the United States being refused entry to the White House. Imagine Bill Gates being thrown out of Microsoft HQ as a trespasser. Now picture God, unrecognized within his own creation.

Coffee

Take your place, Lord Jesus, in my heart and home. May you find warmth and welcome, and sustenance and rest.

GK

Orange Juice

These bodies will die, but the bodies that are raised will live forever. These ugly and weak bodies will become beautiful and strong.

1 Corinthians 15:42-43 CEV

He Loves Your Body!

The Big Breakfast

What does God think about you? Does he like you? Does he like your body? Hmmm. What do you think? Well, despite what most people seem to think about life in God's new world, we will have bodies. Okay, so our bodies won't be exactly the same, but we will still be em-bodied. This is really important: we are not just spirits living in bodies short-term. God sees us as whole people and is not just concerned with the invisible bits of us.

I have a friend who hates her body. I know she's not the only one: there are millions of people in the West who suffer greatly with problems to do with their self-image. The Devil tells them that their bodies are ugly because they don't look like Kate Moss/Lara Croft/Britney Spears/insert your own ridiculous role model here. God's love of our bodies provides us with a challenge: we must fight the voices that say bodies are only beautiful if they look a certain way.

Yet there is good news for the person who feels that their body lets them down: we get a new one! What will it be like? Well, perhaps the best model for that would be Jesus, who was able to do amazing things with his resurrection body, but was still identifiable as the guy everyone knew.

Continental

"What we call the beginning is often the end
And to make an end is to make a beginning.
The end is where we start from."

T.S. Eliot

Coffee

Tell God which parts of "you" you would like to take with you into your new life, and which parts you would like to leave behind.

SH

Orange Juice
Whatever you do, do it all for the glory of God.

1 Corinthians 10:31

Total Dedication

The Big Breakfast
I love this verse. Total dedication to the cause. A cry to go above and beyond the call of duty. Billy Graham once received a letter from a communist who was breaking up with his girlfriend. It oozes with infectious dedication:

We communists do not have the time or the money for many movies, or concerts, or T-bone steaks, or decent homes, or new cars. We have been described as fanatics. We are fanatics. We have a cause to fight for and a definite purpose in life … There is one thing which I am in dead earnest about, and that is the communist cause. It is my life, my business, my religion, my hobby, my sweetheart, my wife, my mistress and my bread and meat. I work at it in the daytime and dream of it at night … I cannot carry on a friendship, a love affair or even a conversation without relating it to this force which both drives and guides my life … I've already been in jail because of my ideals, and if necessary, I'm ready to go before a firing squad.

This kind of fighting talk stirs the heart again to dedication, especially if we were to live our lives for Christ as this communist did for his cause! Don't lose the sense of passion that has exploded in your soul today.

Continental
"Let us not rust out. Let us not glide through the world then slip quietly out without having blown the trumpet loud and long for our blessed redeemer. At the very least let us see to it that the Devil holds a thanksgiving party in Hell when he gets the news of our departure from the field of battle."

Missionary C.T. Studd

Coffee
God, hear my prayer. I want you to know that whatever I do this day, I do it for your glory. Because I know that whatever you do this day, you do it for my best.

DB

Orange Juice

Stop judging by mere appearances, but instead judge correctly.

John 7:24

X-Ratings

The Big Breakfast

The potato and avocado salad was the star dish. Everyone was raving about it. Why? TV chef Jamie Oliver, who made cooking cool, was the reason. It was just one of many sexy cook-ups from his popular TV series. How is it that good old potato salad with a bit of avocado thrown in gets to be sexy? And that's not all that gets the X-rating these days – shoes, furniture, cars, breakfast television ... even kitchen weighing scales can be dubbed "sexy"!

If the image is right, it'll be a runaway success. The cosmetic companies are onto this as well. Courtney Thorne Smith (alias Georgia from *Ally McBeal*) is Almay's new cover girl, Cindy Crawford is selling Foster Grant sunglasses and Shania Twain is reportedly $5,000,000 better off thanks to Revlon ColorStay.

How is it that we still get caught up with "image"? God isn't impressed. He's much more interested in what's going on inside, in the state of our hearts and minds.

Continental

Sex symbol Brigitte Bardot said, "I am what I am. I have wrinkles. Even if I had a face-lift, what about the marks etched by life on the heart and soul? You can't get those lifted."

Coffee

Lord Jesus, the pressure to follow the in-crowd is all around me. Help me to step aside, to listen for your perspective and follow your lead.

RS

Orange Juice

Now Moses was tending the flock of Jethro his father-in-law, the priest of Midian.

Exodus 3:1 NIV

Falling Into Failure

The Big Breakfast

If you're going to fail, fail in style. Moses had tried to act on behalf of his birth-tribe, defending a slave against one of his own adopted people, the Egyptians. But it all went pear-shaped, and he found himself in exile, living in the rocky, infertile hills of Midian, scratching an income tending sheep – a job beneath contempt for an Egyptian.

Brought up in the palaces of Pharaoh, in the abundant fertility of the Nile River valley, Moses was trained to reign. As a non-Egyptian, he would never be the Pharaoh himself – but the film *Prince of Egypt* is right in showing that he was destined to be the ruler's close confidant.

From celebrity to slavery, from royalty to rejection, Moses had fallen as far as it is possible to fall and still be conscious. But God had never given up on this impetuous ruler. Late in life, just as the slow decline was beginning, the Redeemer stepped in.

Past mistakes need not rob us of God's future. It ain't over 'til the fat bush burns.

Continental

What disqualifies you from making something of your life for God? Too young? Too inexperienced? Tried too many times already? Take a look at Moses and think again.

Coffee

Father of failures, God of the good-for-nothing, hope of the has-been – let your redeeming fire touch my life this day.

GK

Orange Juice

In the year that King Uzziah died, I saw the Lord seated on a throne, high and exalted ... Above him were seraphs, each with six wings ... calling to one another: "Holy, holy, holy is the Lord Almighty; the whole earth is full of his glory."

Isaiah 6:1-3 NIV

God Steps In

The Big Breakfast

I don't know if you have had an experience of God like Isaiah's, but I haven't, and I would probably need a change of underwear if I ever did. I once felt God forcing me down onto the carpet, and I think I saw some fire out of the corner of my eye, and that was enough for me! Isaiah got to see God on his throne and was obviously terrified.

Not everyone gets a call like this one, but boy, it would help in those what-*am*-I-doing-believing-this-stuff? moments. It's okay to feel useless in the presence of God. In fact, I suspect any other attitude is probably a bit of a mistake. The awesomeness of God tends to get played down a bit nowadays, in our new Jesus-is-my-best-friend world. Isaiah met the Creator and Sustainer of the universe!

Continental

"You cannot know God as your friend until you have known him as your enemy."

Martin Luther

Coffee

Remember a time when you became aware of the bigness of God. Try to recapture how you felt at that time. If you've never had that kind of feeling, try reading Isaiah chapter 6 and entering into the story as much as you can. How would you feel?

SH

Orange Juice
The harvest is past, the summer has ended, and we are not saved.

Jeremiah 8:20 NIV

The Saddest of Verses

The Big Breakfast
I think this is the saddest verse in the entire Bible. "Harvest past" – it is like turning up for a party and everybody's gone. The party happened and you missed it.

"Summer gone" – it is like going off on a sunshine holiday with your sun protection factor 25 in one hand and your paperback thriller in the other, only to discover the hotel closed, the sky clouding over and the locals cleaning up.

"Salvation missed" – it is like watching a sky full of shooting stars, standing slightly scared by the ocean's edge on a blustery day, or watching a baby being born, and thinking, "Maybe there is a God in heaven … ah, but what the heck."

The harvest is past, the summer is gone, and we are not saved – it is all too late. Why didn't I do something about it before?

I read this to a friend who's not a Christian. "That's me!" he said, in a surprised tone of voice, "I've often looked at the world around and the intricacies of the human body and wondered if God really did exist. But I always banished the thought from my mind as stupid."

Continental
Arthur Koestler, who wrote the classic *The Ghost in the Machine*, once bleakly commented, "God seems to have left the receiver off the hook, and time is running out." The truth is that God came in person to planet earth two thousand years ago with a rescue plan. If time is running out, it's our problem.

Coffee
"That time has come. This is the day for you to be saved" (2 Corinthians 6:2 CEV). Put it off no more.

DB

Orange Juice

The Lord will guide you always; he will satisfy your needs in a sun-scorched land and will strengthen your frame. You will be like a well-watered garden, like a spring whose waters never fail.

Isaiah 58:11 NIV

Ground Force

The Big Breakfast

A recent trend in broadcasting is programmes offering home and garden transformations – the UK's *Changing Rooms* and *Ground Force* and the US's *Trading Spaces* are just a few examples of the genre.

We love these shows because we believe that our homes and gardens can and should reflect our prosperity and status. By implication, we establish a graduating scale of abundance. The successful will have designer interiors. The *really* successful will have designer interiors *and* landscaped gardens. And the really super-successful will have designer interiors and landscaped gardens with a water feature!

But all of this is not as new as we may think. In Isaiah's day the same was true – there was no image of abundance and fruitfulness more perfect than that of a well-watered garden. The longing, then as now, was for Eden restored. The image is used here as a graphic promise: the selfless compassion of this chapter will not lead to want and misery, but to an abundance of life beyond imagining. Live this way, and God will give your life a *Ground Force* make-over!

Continental

If you picture your life as a garden, what kind of garden is it? What would you ask the *Ground Force* team to change?

Coffee

"Creator, Father of all, you give me life, you give me love, you give me yourself. Help me to give my life, my love, myself to you."

David Adam

GK

Orange Juice
Be still, and know that I am God.

Psalm 46:10 NIV

Be Still: Settle Yourself

The Big Breakfast
Nothing manages to be unhurried these days. We buy a cappuccino to go. There isn't time to drink it in the café. We wish we had 30 hours in every day, 8 days in every week and 20 months in every year. There's never enough time.

God says, "Be still and know me." Stop all this crazy running around. None of it matters as much as you think. Have the courage to stop dead, now, and have a good long look at yourself.

There's a great story in the New Testament about this kind of busyness. Mary and Martha have invited Jesus to dinner. Martha runs around the place getting everything prepared, while Mary simply sits and listens to Jesus. You can just imagine Martha's tone when she's had enough of being the kitchen slave. "Lord, don't you care that my sister has left me to do the work by myself? Tell her to help me!" (see Luke 10:40).

"Be still," God says. The most important thing is to take time with God. The rest will fall into place.

Continental
We were created for a relationship with God and with one another. How come our lives have got so out of control that there's time for neither?

Coffee
Lord Jesus, I know I'm far too busy, that I squeeze you and other people into second place. Forgive me, and help me to change.

RS

Orange Juice

"Woe to me!" I cried. "I am ruined! For I am a man of unclean lips ... Then one of the seraphs flew to me with a live coal in his hand ... With it he touched my mouth and said, "See, this has touched your lips; your guilt is taken away and your sin atoned for."

Isaiah 6:5-7 NIV

I'm Not Worthy!

The Big Breakfast

Isaiah represents a major leap forward in the Bible's understanding of how God deals with sin. While the early Israelites had a complex set of laws and rituals, here Isaiah's penitence is enough for him to receive forgiveness from God. Indeed, all that we've read so far has more in common with Jesus' story about the Pharisee and the tax collector (Luke 18:10-14) than with the usual idea of the nasty Old Testament God with a big beard and even bigger lightning bolts. Here we have this mad conflict: one minute we think that we've had it because God is so great and just, and then the next minute he's offering salvation. Phew! Thank you, God!

Sometimes we forget this amazing miracle about God: "Who is a God like you, who pardons sin ...? You do not stay angry forever but delight to show mercy" (Micah 7:18 NIV).

Continental

Jesus said, "For all those who exalt themselves will be humbled, and those who humble themselves will be exalted" (Luke 18:14).

Coffee

Imagine an angel coming to you with a burning coal and offering to touch anything that is "unclean" in the sight of God. Will you let the angel take away your sin, even though the purification might be painful? Even if you're not ready to have everything burnt up, talk to God about it.

SH

Orange Juice
Your kingdom come, your will be done.

Matthew 6:10

Have It Your Own Way . . .

The Big Breakfast
We are all kingdom-carriers. Each of us has a sphere of activity and influence over which we are able to exercise authority. Much of this is inward and unseen, but it spills over into our visible lives. At times our "kingdom" only matters to us, but there are also times when others are drawn into our sphere.

To ask that God's kingdom come is not to pray for some fundamentalist state in which the whole of life looks like church. Rather, it is to pray that more and more of the visible world will be drawn into the sphere of God's influence and rule – that rebellion will end and obedience to God will break out like springtime.

We want God's will to be done because God has all the best ideas about how things should be. Everything in the creation is designed, at its heart, to respond to the expressed love of its Creator. Things function best when they function in God, where the response of love is heartfelt and unhindered. It is for this condition that we pray.

Continental
As I pray "Your will be done", I must be willing to change where I am the hindrance, and I must be willing to co-operate in the fulfilling of God's purposes.

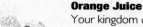

Coffee
Father, I want what you want for my life and for the world. And where I find it hard to want what you want, I want to want what you want!

GK

Orange Juice

If a man shuts his ears to the cry of the poor, he too will cry out and not be answered.

Proverbs 21:13 NIV

The Not-So-Secret Diary

The Big Breakfast

The Not-So-Secret Diary of a Frustrated Christian (aged 35 and a bit)

Sunday

Decided to walk home from church. Why is it you never hear church people say, "Oi! It's my turn to sit on the front row this morning"? Preached about prayer. Why is it you never hear people say, "I was so enthralled with your talk that I never noticed you went twenty minutes over time"?

Monday

Wanted to start the week in prayer. Ended up trawling through endless third-world charity letters. Chucked the lot.

Tuesday

Day off. Decided to also have a day off from praying and go and spend some money on myself.

Wednesday

Got bothered by the *Big Issue** salesman, along with a bloke on a blanket with his dog. Took sanctuary in a teashop. Thought I could pray there. Read the paper instead.

*A magazine sold on the streets by the homeless.

Continental

If we don't listen to the poor in our world, God in heaven says he won't listen to you and me when we pray. Is that why your prayer life seems so rusty? Is that why answers seem so few and far between?

Coffee

Author and activist Jim Wallis said, "Many Christians gladly get converted from their sin but never get converted to the poor." Begin that process today. At the very least, buy a copy of *The Big Issue* or check out its website (www.bigissue.com) or *Sojourners Online* (www.sojo.net).

DB

Orange Juice

You are God's children whom he loves, so try to be like him.
Live a life of love just as Christ loved us and gave himself for
us as a sweet-smelling offering and sacrifice to God.

Ephesians 5:1 NCV

Imitators

The Big Breakfast

Paul makes a strong statement here. "Be like God". The NIV
translation says "be imitators of God". Does this means that
we should be mimics, like Rory Bremner or Will Ferrell? No,
because that's a copycat, sometimes mocking form of imita-
tion. We are called not to copy God, but to allow him to transform us from the
inside out, so that we become like him almost without knowing it. "Let Christ be
formed in you" is another way of expressing this. Then we'll be living the life of love
that God has planned for us.

The mission of Jesus was to bring about a new way of living, one that's driven by
love. What does that mean? I guess it means that we come to understand the shift
from religion to relationship. No longer is faith just a rule-book existence or merely
a philosophy for living. It is a transformed life that comes out of a dynamic relationship
with Jesus.

Continental

John Lennon sang, "All you need is love ..." He was right. All
you need is the love of God transforming everything you are
and everything you do.

Coffee

Lord Jesus, come round my way today. Please work your transforming love in my life, so that I can be like you and love like you.

RS

Orange Juice

Then the Lord said to [Moses], "What is that in your hand?"

Exodus 4:2 NIV

Bring and Buy!

The Big Breakfast

When Moses meets God at the burning bush he is beginning to warm to the possibility of freedom. All the passion he felt when he first rediscovered his Hebrew roots, when he saw the slavery of his people and longed to act, is coming back to him. Decades of forgetting are being peeled away.

But he is not yet sold on God's call. He wonders what weapons he will have if his first approach is rebuffed. With sharp insight, he foresees the stubbornness of the Hebrews – and asks God what the backup plan might be. God's answer is the timeless, universal, unchanging question that he puts to each of us: "What do you have in your hand?"

We seek God for *his* gifts – he seeks ways to use *ours*. We ask him, "What can you give us?" He asks us, "What do you bring?" We see faith as a supermarket for buying new gifts – God sees it as a bring-and-buy sale where no one arrives empty-handed. Before God overwhelms you with some new gift, he will always ask you, "What do you have in your hand?"

Continental

Consider the areas of your life in which you are longing for God to act. Ask yourself. "What do I have in my hand?"

Coffee

Lord God, all that I have in my hands – my talents and my lack of talent, my background and my brokenness, my humanity and my helplessness – I bring to you.

GK

Orange Juice

See, my servant will act wisely; he will be raised and lifted up and highly exalted.

Isaiah 52:13 NIV

The Man

The Big Breakfast

When Isaiah wrote about God's servant, he was thinking primarily about the terrible state that God's people were in and how their faithfulness would eventually be vindicated. Little did he know that his immediate prophetic insight into the affairs of Israel would take on such significance when Jesus appeared on the scene! There's a lot of that kind of prophecy in the Bible: there is an immediate meaning and a kind of subtext, a God-given bigger picture.

It is good to be reminded of this truth: while God is looking right at us, he's still aware of what's going on around the universe, and vice versa. In an age where we're expected to work, look after our family, have a beautiful body, go on holiday *and* be holy, we should remember that God is the original multi-tasker.

Continental

In this upwardly-mobile world, are you prepared to follow God's wise servant and maybe even be downwardly mobile?

Coffee

Is there someone you know who is often seen as an outsider or a reject? Pray for that person; maybe you could try to spend some time with them.

SH

Orange Juice

It was now about noon, and darkness came over the whole land until three in the afternoon, for the sun stopped shining.

Luke 23:44-45

Who Gets the Blame?

The Big Breakfast

I remember the eerie feeling of watching the midday sky turn cold and dark during a recent total eclipse. But what happened in the three hours of darkness when the carpenter from Nazareth ended his days on a torturous wooden cross?

God was apportioning the blame. He blamed his own Son, his own spotless lamb, who had never committed a crime in his life; never done anything wrong.

He blamed him for the twisted crime of the paedophile.

He blamed him for the dark heart of the terrorist.

He blamed him for the murderous mind of the serial killer.

He pointed the finger of blame at his own Son for every wrong thought that has ever tempted you into sinful action.

In those dreadful hours of darkness when the sun stopped shining, the God of heaven lifted the burden of guilt from your shoulders and loaded them on to the Son he loved. Then he sent him to hell in your place. Worship God today. Even if it means getting in late, stop and hold an audience with a God whose love for you goes beyond your wildest imaginings. And say thank you ... thank you ... thank you.

Continental

I meet many people who blame God for the pain in their lives. They blame him for the death of a loved one, for the handicapped child or the raw deal of a partner's fury. The truth is, they are two thousand years too late. God has already blamed Jesus for all the sin that causes all the pain in all our lives.

Coffee

Eventually Jesus cried out, "Father, I put myself in your hands!" (Luke 23:46 CEV). "Dad! I'm coming home!" He went home to prepare a place for you (John 14:2). Let the hope of that homecoming crack a smile today.

DB

Orange Juice

In him and through faith in him we may approach God with freedom and confidence.

Ephesians 3:12

Approaching God

The Big Breakfast

It is all down to Jesus. Do you see that? In him, through faith in him, we can approach God. That's awesome. We've lost some of the wonder that ought to grip us when we read a verse like this. First-century Jews were in such awe of God, in such fear of him, that they wouldn't use his name. The very idea that they could approach him in freedom and confidence was something they could not have imagined.

Life in the Spirit, the new order Jesus has brought about for us, is about discovering how incredible the love of God is. It is a love we can discover through faith in Jesus, and only Jesus. What sets Christianity apart from all other religions? It's the *relationship* we can have with the living God. That's what it's all about. It isn't a philosophy, or a way of thinking. It's a friendship with the greatest person ever.

Continental

What would it mean to you if Prince William, the heir to the British throne, wanted to be your friend? You might be awestruck by such an idea. Friendship with God is much bigger than that.

Coffee

Lord, I haven't understood the real meaning of this verse at all. Forgive me. Please give me a sense of it today and an understanding of what it cost you.

RS

Orange Juice
What is man that you are mindful of him, the son of man that you care for him?

Psalm 8:4 NIV

Living in Skin

The Big Breakfast
In 1887 the artist Paul Gaugin painted what he thought would be his last work. Planning to end his own life, he intended the painting as a kind of visual suicide note.

Its title was etched onto the canvas itself, and captured the turbulence not only of Gaugin's life, but of the turn-of-the-century world in which he lived. It was called *Where do we come from? What are we? Where are we going?*

In bringing the three questions together, Gaugin was echoing the voice of the Psalms. In our own day, we often speak of the first and last of the three, but the middle question gets less attention. What are we?

The contradictions of the creation – its holding together of animal savagery and spiritual peace – are wrapped up in the very fabric of our human nature. It is our humanity that points us to God, but it is our humanity that makes it hard to reach him. The lowest depths and the greatest heights in the universe are alike found in the human heart.

Continental
There are many mysteries in the universe, but two of the greatest are these: What is it that makes us human, and why is it that God loves us so?

Coffee
What is humanity? *Father, teach us to know you.* That you are mindful of us? *Father, teach us to love you.*

GK

Orange Juice

I would gladly be placed under God's curse and be separated from Christ for the good of my own people.

Romans 9:3 CEV

Belonging

The Big Breakfast

To say that our racial and ethnic identities should not be too important within the church of God is not to say that they disappear. I am still a European, an Englishman, a Yorkshireman, a Leeds United supporter, etc. These loyalties still have meaning for me.

Paul was a Christian who had grown up as a devout Jew. Becoming a Christian didn't suddenly turn off his ethnic identity. Instead, his love for his people increased as his own tribal loyalty was amplified by God's love for the Jews. Paul even goes so far as to say he would be willing to sacrifice his own salvation if only the Jews would come to know Jesus.

That's Paul's job: to care for those in his home, his family, his tribe. If he didn't care for them, pray for them, share the gospel with them, then who would? The person who said "Charity begins at home" wasn't saying that we should look after our own family at the expense of others; rather that we should not ignore those close to hand in our desire to love those on the fringes.

Continental

Becoming a Christian made Paul love his people even more than he had done before. Many Christians love the Church so much that they neglect their family and neighbourhood. Christians need to have their feet planted firmly in the soil of their communities, because the Church can grow nowhere else.

Coffee

What "tribes" do you belong to? How can you share Jesus' love with those tribes?

SH

Orange Juice

I'm completely worn out; my time has been wasted.

Isaiah 49:4 CEV

Clear Vision

The Big Breakfast

Why does so much of what we do in life feel like hard work but with very little purpose? I think it's because we so often lose our focus. The end goal has gone fuzzy on the horizon. I went to Disneyland a few years back. If you ask the ticket-collectors, road-sweepers or entertainers what their role is, the answer is always the same: "To make people happy who come to Disneyland". They have a clear goal, and it works.

In 1789 William Wilberforce came before the British parliament to plea for an end to slavery. Twenty years later, just days after his death, his life's vision became reality.

In 1907 Henry Ford told the world that he was going to make cars affordable for the average man. The world sniggered, but a decade later millions of Model T Fords rolled off the production line at just $290 each.

The sheer power of a clear vision. It ignites passion in the soul and makes dreams come true. A lack of vision will always lead to frustration. Do you know why you do what you do? Is it clearly stated? For one famous hospital in London it is "Child first and always"; for our church it is "Helping people to make life work". What is it for your life, your church, or your workplace?

Continental

Bill Hybels, pastor of one of the largest churches in the United States, says, "Vision is a picture of the future that creates a passion in you." Have you got the kind of dream where nothing will stop you fulfilling it – not money, not reputation, not anything!

Coffee

Author Charles Swindoll said, "Vision is essential for survival . . . it encompasses vast vistas outside the realm of the predictable, the safe and the expected. No wonder we perish without it!"

DB

Orange Juice

I pray that Christ will live in your hearts by faith and that your lives will be strong in love and be built on love.

Ephesians 3:17 NCV

The Life That's Different

The Big Breakfast

If the outworking of God's love in us is absent, then we haven't spent enough time with him. To train or push ourselves to be good, caring, genuine people is to miss the point. We're all created in his image, so everyone will show something of him. Gentleness, kindness, compassion – these are the kind of attributes we admire and hope to find in people. They are there in every human being because every human being shows something of God, our Creator.

The fruit of the Spirit is different. It is the life and love of God, formed in us and shared through us. This is hard to grasp. What is our part? What do we have to do so that this will come about? Well, nothing. Nothing, that is, except spend time with him, and determine to allow nothing to get in the way of our relationship with him. Jesus didn't go through the horrors of the cross to produce a new variety of rule-book Christian. He faced Golgotha because he wanted people who would show the world what he's like.

Continental

Let's stop "doing" the Christian life. Step aside and allow God to *be* the Christian life through you. Then you will love as he loves.

Coffee

The focus of Christianity is God, not ourselves.

RS

Orange Juice

As he was leaving the temple, one of his disciples said to him, "Look, Teacher! What massive stones! What magnificent buildings!"

Mark 13:1

The Tallest Idea in Town

The Big Breakfast

The Sydney Opera House, the Sears Tower in Chicago, Paris's Pompidou Centre ... every major city of the world has its stand-out architecture. Big buildings house big ideas – we project our values in bricks and mortar. These projections of ambition and hope become the language of the city – the daily headlines of the urban skyline.

To the disciples, the temple was simply the most imposing and the most solid building in their lives. Set at the heart of Jerusalem, its huge walls rose above the neighbouring houses to overshadow daily life for all concerned. The message was loud and clear: the traditions of this temple were immovable at the heart of this community. The biggest ideas in town were ideas associated with the temple. For the disciples, as for all Jews of their day, this was the uncontested conclusion, and every time they saw the temple they were reminded.

The message of our day is the same but different. What are the temples of our day? They are threefold: shopping malls and banks, arts and entertainment institutions and, tallest of all, telecom towers.

Continental

To read the message of the urban skyline is to hear the heart of the city.

Coffee

"May the glory of your kingdom which the saints enjoy surround our steps as we journey this day."

Adapted from **Celebrating Common Prayer, London, Mowbray, 1994**

GK

Orange Juice

And on the seventh day hold a sacred assembly and do no regular work.

Leviticus 23:8 NIV

Stop It!

The Big Breakfast

Some of us have the problem that work (whether it's paid work, schoolwork, or even volunteer projects) just gets in the way of our life; for others work is their life. Such people have a tendency to look down on the nine-to-fivers as weak-willed slackers. They understand the meaning of *real* work – except, of course, they know nothing about life. That's the terrible problem of the professional classes in the West: men and women who spend their whole lives working in order to build a family that's falling apart through neglect. God knew what he was doing when he instituted the Sabbath.

It is so annoying. Imagine it's harvest-time and the corn is ripe. You go out and begin harvesting, but then the sun goes down and it's Friday night. You *have* to stop for 24 hours, or else you'd be breaking the law. It's maddening! A few weeks ago I went on holiday and took my computer with me to try and finish this book. Only I didn't: by a string of coincidences it never got into the car; so I had two weeks of holiday in which I couldn't do any work. It was wonderful!

We need to learn what "Sabbath" means for us today. God's priorities on that day began with him, but included family and community as well. How can we get that time back? We need it if we are ever going to change our country.

Continental

"It is your work in life that is the ultimate seduction."

Pablo Picasso

Coffee

What does your Sabbath look like? Do you need to make more space for yourself, friends, family, God? Why not ask God what your priorities should be?

SH

Orange Juice

So here I am today, eighty-five years old! I am still as strong today as the day Moses sent me out; I'm just as vigorous to go out to battle now as I was then. Now give me this hill country that the LORD promised me that day.

Joshua 14:10-12 NIV

Hold on to the Dream

The Big Breakfast

What kind of an old person will you be? If you read these verses, you'll discover that this old man, Caleb, had a dream from God that he kept for forty-five years. Not even old age was going to rob him of it. So he took a risk: with his pension book in one hand and his false teeth in the other, he went for the hill country that God had promised him all those years back.

You will never get anything of value unless you hold on to a dream and then take a risk to see it happen. I reckon every bloke remembers his first kiss with a girl. I may have looked cool on the outside when I puckered up to Debbie, ready to minister to her through the laying on of lips, but inside was sheer panic. What if I missed! And I clearly remember the night I asked her to marry me. My emotions had never known such chaos. I was as nervous as a frog in a biology class. What if she said no? I took a risk and got something of great value – my dream girl. I'm only glad that God didn't do a Caleb on me and make me wait 45 years! You never get anything of value unless you take a risk.

It is interesting to note that Caleb wanted the hill country. Dreams can often be an uphill struggle, but it's there that we meet with God.

Continental

Helen Keller once interviewed a young girl who was both blind and deaf. She asked what could be worse than having those two disabilities. The girl replied, "Having your sight but having no vision."

Coffee

Henry Ford said, "The poor man is not the man without a cent but a man without a dream." If you haven't got a dream, find someone who has and let it rub off on you. If you have – go for it!

DB

Orange Juice

With God's power working in us, God can do much, much more than anything we can ask or imagine.

Ephesians 3:20 NCV

Take God By His Word

The Big Breakfast

The power that's at work in us is the same power that raised Jesus from the dead. Ephesians 1:20 tells us this. Now that's incredible. What kind of power is it that can raise a person from the dead? This is the awesome power which is only found in the living God.

As you think about this today, do you get just a tiny feeling that something might be missing? Where is this kind of power in *your* life?

Could it be that we're not prepared to take God at his word? The "much, much more" of this verse is God saying, "I can and I will fill you with my Spirit. I have the power to do that – but I want your love." Think about it. The first and greatest commandment is to love God with all your heart and soul and mind and strength. Have the faith to believe how crucial that is.

Continental

"I don't know how to love him," you might protest. No you don't – but as in other relationships, such knowledge will grow as you spend time with Jesus.

Coffee

Love is a decision. Decide today to love God with all your heart, soul, mind and strength.

RS

Orange Juice

They were not God's children by nature ... God himself was
the one who made them his children.

John 1:13 CEV

Womb with a View

The Big Breakfast

Where you are born, how you are born, to *whom* you are
born – these factors affect our lives very deeply.

To be born on the wrong side of the tracks; to be born
into wealth and title; to be born and unwanted – we each
carry both the burdens and the blessings of our birth. We are not predetermined
by our birth like automatons, but we are profoundly shaped by its circumstances.

Right at the start of his Gospel of new birth, John wants us to know that the
rebirthing he is talking about is a different quality of birth. There is the possibility of
a new start, a new injection of DNA, a whole new inheritance to come into. In our
first birth, the choices, characters and circumstances of our parents shape us. In the
new birth, we become heirs of God. For John, the encounter with Christ is not just
a fork in the road of life; it is an entirely new road to walk.

Continental

John is saying "Whatever else you do or don't understand
about Christ, understand *this:* the choice to follow Christ is a
choice to begin a new kind of life."

Coffee

Thank you, Father, for the DNA of Jesus. Thank you for the new
birth that leads to a new kind of life. Thank you for giving me the
right to become your child.

GK

Orange Juice

Our enemies were trying to frighten us and to keep us from our work. But I asked God to give me strength.

Nehemiah 6:9 CEV

Cape Fear

The Big Breakfast

I wish, somewhere in the Bible, it said, "And once you become a Christian everything will be SUPER TWINKY" (to quote a T-shirt my friend has) – but, of course, it doesn't. Instead, we get enemies who try to frighten us. This time the bad guys are trying to stop the rebuilding of the walls of Jerusalem, and it's a great illustration of how the enemy has a go at us: (1) He wants us to be afraid, so that (2) we will get discouraged and (3) God's work won't get done. It's a pretty simple tactic. Sports people always talk about the psychology leading up to big matches and fights. The best thing you can do is to get the opposition afraid of you.

So what's Nehemiah's response? "Lord, finish the work off for us so we don't have to be in danger"? Nope. "Lord, make the bad guys go away so that we'll be safe"? *Nada. Non. Nein danke.* Nehemiah prays that God will give him the strength to keep going, whatever. Scumbag!

If you read through the whole of Nehemiah you'll see that he often talks to God, as if to say, "I'm doing this for you, so you'd better back me up." And it's true: he takes the tough decisions in a way that our modern politicians could only dream about.

Continental

You will need to persevere so that when you have done the will of God, you will receive what he has promised.

Hebrews 10:36

Coffee

If you are in a situation where you are afraid, or seemingly not achieving what you set out to achieve, just repeat Nehemiah's prayer: "Now strengthen my hands" (Nehemiah 6:9 NIV).

SH

Orange Juice

Unless I see the nail marks in his hands and put my finger where the nails were, and put my hand into his side, I will not believe.

John 20:25

Doubt Is Not Wrong

The Big Breakfast

I drove back buzzing from an incredible worship service last week. It was probably the best talk on discipleship I had ever heard. It was probably the best talk on discipleship I had ever given! Yet as I drove home through the darkness, I started to wonder if there really was a God in heaven. Are we just making all this up? Is it all no more than clever fantasy?

How could my heart jump so quickly from devotion to doubt? I turned to Thomas for solace. He wasn't there when the resurrected Jesus first appeared to the disciples. He had given up hope and run away. I find it incredible that so many of us doubters run away from the place where we will find help rather than run towards it. Thomas should have been in the Upper Room the first time. After all, he wasn't the only one who was afraid: the other disciples had locked themselves in there for fear of the Jews (John 20:19).

But Jesus came back a second time just for him, and said, "Peace be with you". One of the last recorded conversations of Jesus was with a man racked with doubt. So take heart today. Doubt isn't wrong, it isn't a sin. In fact, faith is developed as we walk through the furnace of doubt!

Continental

"Then Jesus told him, 'Because you have seen me, you have believed; blessed are those who have not seen and yet have believed'" (John 20:29). That's us! We've not seen him, yet we believe, so that makes us the blessed ones.

Coffee

Tennyson was once quoted as saying, "There is more faith in honest doubt, believe me, than in half the creeds!" Simply reciting the facts doesn't show faith: it just shows memory. Yes, you can doubt your faith at times, but you can also pray, "I do have faith! Please help me to have even more."

DB

Orange Juice

Be kind and compassionate to one another, forgiving each other, just as in Christ God forgave you.

Ephesians 4:32

The Countercultural Life

The Big Breakfast

Life in the Spirit is a countercultural lifestyle. Oh yes, you'll find compassion and kindness in most people, especially when there's a major disaster. The human heart responds magnificently. It is the mark of the Creator.

The life we live through Jesus' power is altogether different. We don't turn it on and off as we choose. It flows from the life of God within us. We take no credit. Kindness, compassion, love for others, a patient spirit, a humble, forgiving heart free of envy and self-interest: these are the marks of the life lived in the power of the Spirit.

I was made to feel very ashamed the other day. A Christian colleague came to speak to me about a matter I considered very trivial. I was very busy at the time. I snapped her head off. Then I felt terrible. Her response to me was to offer to pray with me. I felt very small indeed. She was kind. She was living in the Spirit.

Continental

We are called to kindness and a forgiving heart. Anger is the oxygen that fuels the fire of unforgiveness. Submission to God's Spirit puts the fire out.

Coffee

Lord Jesus, help me. Pray for me, that I might become a God-filled person, not a me-filled one.

RS

Orange Juice
Give us today our daily bread.

Matthew 6:11

Enough Is Enough!

The Big Breakfast
There is an ancient Hebrew proverb that offers a valuable expansion of this brief petition. It would have been familiar to Jesus, and was almost certainly in his mind when he taught this prayer.

It reads: "Give me neither poverty nor riches, but give me only my daily bread. Otherwise, I may have too much and disown you and say, 'Who is the Lord?' Or I may become poor and steal, and so dishonor the name of my God" (Proverbs 30:8-9 NIV).

The author fears two forms of poverty: the grinding, physical poverty that drives women and men into crime and desperation, but equally the spiritual poverty of forgetfulness that comes with wealth. Both are snares that can tear the unwise believer away from God. The petition, "Please God, don't let me be poor" is counterbalanced by the petition, "Please God, don't let me be rich."

In contemporary culture, the first is a prayer we pray daily – with our lifestyles if not our lips. The second is a less familiar cry.

Continental
One of the tasks we accept when we take on the praying of this prayer is the task of finding out just what "enough" should mean for us. It takes time and effort, but it liberates us to pray with total faith to receive our daily bread.

Coffee
Teach us, Father, to understand the meaning of "enough". Forgive us when, through greed, we ask too much of you, and when, through fear, we ask too little.

GK

Orange Juice

I replied, "I'm not a good speaker, Lord, and I'm too young."

Jeremiah 1:6 CEV

The Wayne's World Effect

The Big Breakfast

It is one of my favourite movie moments. Wayne and Garth and friends are piled into a tiny car listening to Queen's "Bohemian Rhapsody". As the heavy bit at the end of the song kicks in, the entire ensemble headbangs in time to the music. Sublime. Wayne and Garth introduced a variety of stupid phrases into the English language in the 1990s, the two most common of which were "Not!" and "We're not worthy!"

This latter was used whenever our two anti-heroes got remotely near anyone even mildly famous. Sad, sad, sad – but then, I guess that was the idea. I suppose saying it in front of God is a bit more excusable, but Jeremiah's whining is not a good start. After God has said, (a) "I know you" and (b) "I want to use you," Jerry decides to act dumb, literally.

Why can't he speak? Because he's young. Some things never change. I've been in churches where a twenty-five-year-old dealing millions on the stock market is handing out notice sheets. Like Jeremiah, we think, "Oh no, I couldn't be a leader; I'm under forty. Why don't I sit at the back and start a burping competition?"

Continental

We know that God is always at work for the good of everyone who loves him. They are the ones God has chosen for his purpose.

Romans 8:28 CEV

Coffee

Are there things that you are afraid of doing because of how others perceive you? It may not be age, but some other prejudice or insecurity. Talk to God about your own fears or any barriers that others may be putting in your way.

SH

Orange Juice

Do not judge, or you too will be judged. For in the same way you judge others, you will be judged, and with the measure you use, it will be measured to you.

Matthew 7:1-2

Judge and Be Judged

The Big Breakfast

When I was in my early twenties I left a career in retail marketing to become an evangelist with a British missions team called Saltmine. I was very green when I started. Not long after I joined, I went to speak at a large church in London. I had got there early to set out some of my advertising material, and then took my place on the platform, watching the suited Sunday congregation slip into the service during the first song.

In the crowd I noticed a small crumpled lady dressed in a dirty raincoat held together with string. Carrying two well-worn carrier bags, she barged her way through the well-dressed worshippers and found a seat right on the front row. It was almost as if she was a regular and someone had saved her a seat there. I leant across to the minister and made some derogatory comment about "waifs and strays" and security problems in this part of London. "I'd be careful how you judge," he replied. "Edna has led more street people to Jesus than I can begin to tell you about. She doesn't have a glossy brochure to advertise her ministry and she never goes to conferences, but she's the best evangelist I know."

Jesus was right: God will be as hard on you as you are on others. It hit me square in the face!

Continental

I may have wanted the ground to swallow me up but I learnt a valuable lesson that day: don't judge or you will be judged! Put this one into practice and you will be spared the embarrassment of opening your mouth as I did and putting your foot right in it!

Coffee

The composer Sibelius said, "A statue has never been set up in honour of a critic." Train your tongue to reduce the negative and accentuate the positive.

DB

Orange Juice

For to us a child is born, to us a son is given ... And he will be called Wonderful Counselor, Mighty God, Everlasting Father, Prince of Peace.

Isaiah 9:6 NIV

Hear Ye ... Hear Ye ...

The Big Breakfast

Christmas brings out the kid in us. There's just something about it: parties and presents; great food and super TV; oh, and those carols about the baby Jesus in the manger. I always look forward to Christmas. But where does the baby Jesus story fit in with the rest of it?

Well, in some ways it doesn't. Mind you, God loves a party and he gives great presents. But those aren't the important bits. Isaiah tells us what it's really about: God, the Almighty, coming to earth as a baby. Imagine!

"Hold on," you say. "Isaiah wrote his book long before Jesus arrived in that stable!" Well, yes he did. So what we have here is God making an announcement. The incredible bit is that God gives this news at a time when people were so afraid of him, so in awe of him, that they were scared even to use his name. So to be told that God would become like them and would be born to a human mum and dad was mind-blowing!

Continental

What is the most amazing thing that has ever happened to you? Now multiply that by a thousand million – and you still aren't close to the Incarnation!

Coffee

Don't allow the Christian story to become so familiar that it seems ordinary. Instead stop, look, listen and then worship with all your heart.

RS

Orange Juice
What may be known about God is plain to them, because God has made it plain to them.

Romans 1:19

I'm Over Here!

The Big Breakfast
If you're looking for cold logic, don't watch children playing hide-and-seek. If they're young enough, they will happily stand in the middle of a room, in full view of everyone, and "hide" by covering their eyes. Logic dictates that to be hidden you must be out of sight, but infant logic knows only one rule – if I can't see you, you can't see me!

Or take the child who has hidden so well that no one comes close to finding her. After a time, the silence of her hiding-place and the excitement of success will get too much. There will be a shuffle and then a cough – and if all else fails she'll start singing. The point of hiding, to a child, is not to avoid being found, but to make being found fun!

Not surprisingly, God is more childlike than we are. When he plays hide-and-seek in the creation, he makes it as easy as possible for us to find him.

Continental
The world resounds with clues to the whereabouts of God. If you're listening hard enough, you will hear him singing.

Coffee
Creator God, thank you that you do not hide from us. You make your presence felt in a million ways each day. Help me, today, to find you in unexpected places.

GK

Orange Juice

He said to them, "Go into all the world and preach the gospel to all creation."

Mark 16:15

The Big Picture

The Big Breakfast

We know what the good news means to us as people, but what about the rest of the creation? We know that God cares about all kinds of people, but what about the rest of the universe?

We don't often remember that God wants to bring the whole of creation round to his way of thinking, because it is all "fallen" and in need of God's good news. This command of Jesus is scary on a number of counts: firstly, Jesus asks us to take responsibility for the whole world, and secondly, the whole world really is *the whole world*. Christians have often been at best apathetic about environmental issues, but Jesus wants us to be good news to our rivers and rainforests as well as our poor and oppressed.

Continental

"Preach the gospel to all the world, and use words if necessary."

St Francis of Assisi

Coffee

I arise today
Through the strength of heaven:
Light of sun,
Radiance of moon,
Splendour of fire,
Speed of lightning,
Swiftness of wind,
Depth of sea,
Stability of earth,
Firmness of rock.

ancient Irish prayer

Orange Juice
Those who claim to be in the light but hate a fellow believer are still in the darkness.

1 John 2:9

Stop Cursing the Darkness

The Big Breakfast
I heard a story recently about a man called George Burton. George had been going to church for years, listening to the faithful complaining about the thugs on the street corners "who frighten the old people". He decided to offer help rather than a critical cold shoulder. He convinced the church of the need, raised the cash and eventually opened the Mayflower Centre in Canning Town, London. For the commissioning service he entitled his talk "Better to light a candle than curse the darkness".

The first day the centre opened, some of the local heavies came in to check the place out. They stayed long enough to shout some abuse at the workers and then broke the windows on the way out. This same scenario was played out night after night. The church people did their best to support him, but spent most of their energy asking George why he carried on with such a lost cause. Yet the Mayflower Centre persevered and became a success. George Burton went on to write a book entitled *People Matter More Than Things*.

Are you too busy cursing the darkness to light a candle; to offer a flickering hope to a lost generation?

Continental
In the 1870s there was a young man who frequently preached to the poor around London. His methods were superbly Christ-like, yet the church leaders would have nothing to do with him. Eventually, after turning his hand to painting for a while, he committed suicide. His name – Vincent Van Gogh.

Coffee
"Anyone who claims to be intimate with God ought to live the same kind of life Jesus lived" (1 John 2:6 MSG). Allow your hearts to burst with intimacy as your hands begin to get grubby with the business of the kingdom.

DB

Orange Juice

He has helped his servant Israel, remembering to be merciful to Abraham and his descendants forever, just as he promised our ancestors.

Luke 1:54-55

A Song for the Whole World

The Big Breakfast

You're at a party. Imagine you've just been told the solution to one of those irritating puzzles, the kind of thing that usually keeps you baffled for hours. Now you've been given the answer, and of course it's so obvious, so simple. You laugh to yourself as others who aren't in the know come up with a billion complicated solutions to solve the riddle.

This verse in Luke 1 is a bit of a riddle too. Until, that is, you get the inside story. This is part of Mary's song, the one she sang to Elizabeth. Who's Elizabeth? She's the mother of John. Mary and Elizabeth were celebrating the fact that Mary was pregnant. How strange. In those days an unmarried, pregnant girl was a disgrace, not a blessing.

They were celebrating, though, because they understood the riddle. It was easy to solve if you had faith! They had faith. They knew their Bible. Isaiah 7:14 told them that the Messiah would be born to a virgin. Mary was that virgin.

Continental

Our lives, and the things that happen to us, can seem like a riddle that makes no sense. Until we look towards God, that is. He's committed to solving our riddles, putting things straight. Give him the opportunity to do just that.

Coffee

What faith challenges do you face at the moment? Learn from Mary. She was able to step out, to go to God because she knew him well through the Scriptures.

RS

Orange Juice

Is it not to share your food with the hungry and to provide the poor wanderer with shelter – when you see the naked, to clothe him?

Isaiah 58:7 NIV

Opportunity Knocks

The Big Breakfast

There is a hugely important clause in the challenge that Isaiah presents – it is the phrase, "when you see". So often, our objection to taking action for the poor comes from our sense of being overwhelmed. There are so many needs, so many causes, so many people we *could* reach out to. We don't know where to start – so we don't start at all.

Isaiah heads the objection off at the pass – you start, he says, with what you see. Before you even begin to go looking for needs, deal with the needs that are right in front of you. Who do you see, day by day – even moment by moment? Whose life could be changed by your intervention?

Like all great projects, the liberation of the planet's poor starts small. The small acts, whether offered to neighbour or stranger, will often spark off a chain reaction of obedience. Before you know it, you really will be making a difference. Don't worry, for now, about the finishing tape. Worry about getting off the starting-blocks.

Continental

A church leader who had often seen miraculous provision when those in need came to his door was once asked why he thought such "God appointments" happened to him so often. "God has to know he can trust you," he replied, "before he will give the poor your address."

Coffee

God of the poor, God of liberation, give me the eyes to see those you are bringing to me, and the courage to act on what I see.

GK

Orange Juice

Jesus entered the temple courts and drove out all who were buying and selling there ... "It is written," he said to them, "'My house will be called a house of prayer,' but you are making it a 'den of robbers.'"

Matthew 21:12-13

Speak Out!

The Big Breakfast

This is one of those famous scenes that linger in the subconscious of our nation, although ask someone what it was about, and people often go quiet. No, the temple wasn't an early shopping mall. In fact, the priests had come up with a groovy way of making money. Okay, you have to come here to sacrifice an animal, but we won't let you bring your own: you must buy one of ours! Then, in order to buy one, you'll have to use our special temple money! And, of course, we get to set the exchange rate!

Even Microsoft hasn't got that kind of monopoly. Jesus wasn't bothered by all the people hanging around in the temple courts (maybe a bit like the church car park or a huge foyer); he was bothered that they were being exploited by the ones who were supposed to be bringing them close to God. No wonder Jesus said what he said; he was mad!

Imagine spending three years trying to bring God close to the common people, and when you get to the place where people come to meet him, they have to lose the shirts from their backs to do so ... Well, wouldn't you be upset?

Continental

"Justice is truth in action."

former British Prime Minister Benjamin Disraeli

Coffee

If there is an injustice that you are angry about, bring it to God. If money and possessions are more important to you than prayer, take time to talk to God about it.

SH

Orange Juice
Don't let anyone look down on you because you are young,
but set an example for the believers in speech, in conduct, in
love, in faith and in purity.

1 Timothy 4:12

Age Doesn't Matter

The Big Breakfast
Why do we presume that youth and inexperience should
exclude us from being used by God? The disciples were young
people, most of them in their teens and twenties when Jesus
called them. He loved the buzz of working with young people.

In most churches you have to be older than Jesus to place the flowers in the
sanctuary! If I may, I would like to offer you an apology. If you are a younger person
who has got the impression that you can only serve God properly if you are over
45, married and have a different voice for when you pray – then I'm sorry. It's not
like that.

I can remember being told constantly that I was part of tomorrow's Church and
that one day I would be able to speak or lead or sing or pray. Unless, of course, I
wanted to help in the Sunday school, in which case I could begin immediately. Listen:
you are part of today's Church, and don't let anyone tell you otherwise. The skill is
this: don't let the "farties" like me look down on you because you are young, but lead
the way in speech, in life, in love, in faith and in purity.

Continental
God said to the young Jeremiah, "Don't say you're too young
... I promise to be with you and keep you safe, so don't be
afraid." Be cheeky for the kingdom today and don't be afraid!

Coffee
"Nursing infants gurgle choruses about you; toddlers shout the
songs that drown out enemy talk and silence atheist babble!"
(Psalm 8:2 MSG). Hold your head up high, walk tall and walk
humbly. Understand again today that your age must never stop
you living out your heavenly dreams.

DB

Orange Juice

While they were there, the time came for the baby to be born, and she gave birth to her firstborn, a son.

Luke 2:6-7

Seeing Stars*

The Big Breakfast

Bill Clinton came to Belfast while he was President of the United States. You just would not have believed it. Motorways were closed. No other vehicle could travel the route at the same time as the President. Trees were cut down so that he would never be out of sight. Men talking up their shirtsleeves were everywhere. Camera crews and TV networks from all over the world caught every moment of the visit and beamed it around the world. What a commotion. Nobody, absolutely nobody, missed it.

The Lord of the Universe, the King of Kings, was born in a smelly, urine-filled stable, to a teenage girl who was helped by a rough, and probably frightened, carpenter.

Take a second or two to picture this moment in history. God, who reduced himself to the size of a human foetus, allowed the manner of his coming to be unmajestic and extraordinarily humble. The world slept, but heaven was in uproar, with angels overcome by the work of the Mighty God.

Continental

The circumstances that surrounded the birth of Jesus were mind-blowing – a dangerous journey from Nazareth to Bethlehem, a filthy stable floor, an untrained midwife! Would you allow your baby to be born in such conditions?

Coffee

Think about the incredible humility of the Sovereign God, his determination to be like us. I want you to understand what it took for God to reach you. Yes, you. Has it sunk in? It's awesome. Don't waste such a gift.

RS

*Adapted from the original work by Steve Stockman, which first appeared in *Living Well*, a compilation of daily Bible readings produced by Frank P. Sellar, Adelaide Road, Dublin.

Orange Juice

While they were eating, Jesus took bread, and when he had given thanks, he broke it and gave it to his disciples, saying, "Take and eat; this is my body".

Matthew 26:26

The Words of Grace

The Big Breakfast

The power of this moment still gets me, as does the stupidity of the disciples. Jesus has been living with the knowledge that this is the time for his death for many days (probably months), and he knows that there is a traitor in their midst. Holding up the Passover bread, he reminds the disciples of when the children of Israel were in so much of a hurry to escape Egypt that they had to make unleavened bread. They are thinking of that day, many centuries before, when God saved his people, and then Jesus says it: "This is my body."

Whoa. I don't think they got it even then. They knew Jesus was special, so how could he die? That just didn't fit in with the plan. Here he was, saying what? That what he was about to do was as important as what Moses did? That he was going to save an entire people for God? They were only having dinner!

Continental

The Lord's Supper is one of the few things that Jesus asked us to do regularly. Why do you think it's so important?

Coffee

Think for a bit about each of these different meanings: *Eucharist:* thanksgiving to God for Jesus' death for our salvation. *Communion:* relationship with God and with each other. *The Lord's Supper:* remembering Jesus' life, death and resurrection. *The Mass:* feeding us and sending us out to serve God in the world. What aspect is most meaningful to you?

SH

Orange Juice

Now faith is being sure of what we hope for and certain of what we do not see.

Hebrews 11:1

What Is Faith?

The Big Breakfast

I was always under the impression that having faith was about gritting your teeth, screwing up your eyes and hoping for the best. To have enough faith to see somebody healed meant shouting your prayers louder than a football manager standing on the touch line with his side losing 4-0.

Faith is not about how loud you shout. It is not even about how much of it you have. It is about where you put it. Imagine you are standing by a lake frozen over with a paper-thin layer of cracked ice. You may have so much faith that you would willingly drive a tank over it, but you'd still sink. Why? Although you've got loads of faith, the thing you are putting your faith in is weak. Conversely, you can stand by a lake frozen over with such thick ice that they are holding a tank race across it! Yet you cross it gingerly with a rope around your waist and your life insurance policy in your hand. Naturally the ice holds your weight – but why? It isn't to do with the amount of faith you have, but the thing in which you put it.

So if your faith is more akin to Homer Simpson's than Billy Graham's, remember that it is not about how much you've got but where you place it that counts.

Continental

C.S. Lewis said, "Faith is the art of holding on to things your reason has accepted, in spite of your changing moods." No matter how you feel today, God still loves the socks off you! That's being sure, that's being certain.

Coffee

"Truly I tell you, if you have faith as small as a mustard seed, you can say to this mountain, 'Move from here to there' and it will move."

Matthew 17:20

DB

Orange Juice
Bring joy to your servant, for to you, O Lord, I lift up my soul.

Psalm 86:4 NIV

Joy Beyond Circumstances

The Big Breakfast
What a strange thing for David to say! At this point in his life he's barely hanging in there. He's looking to God for help, trusting God to get him out of this particular hard spot. But joy? Who even thinks about joy when things are really tough? It would be enough simply to get through this awful time. That would be just great. Time enough *then* to think about the better things in life.

Perhaps David had already discovered something that God wants us all to know. Our lives will have good times and bad times. Our circumstances will sometimes bring us a lot of fun, a lot of joy, and even great happiness. If you fall in love, for example, and your love is returned, it is just brilliant – there's no feeling on earth quite like it. You think your heart will burst with sheer joy. This, though, is circumstantial joy.

David lifts his soul to God. That means the whole of his life. He knows that a relationship with God is what he needs. He knows it works above everything else.

Continental
The kind of joy that David is asking God for is much deeper than the happiness that comes through pleasant circumstances.

Coffee
We're very slow to make the discovery David had made. Life will throw hard stuff at us. That's a fact. Don't blame God, though – instead, trust him for the deep joy that these circumstances will bring to you.

RS

Orange Juice

For although they knew God, they neither glorified him as God nor gave thanks to him, but their thinking became futile and their foolish hearts were darkened.

Romans 1:21

Prime Suspect

The Big Breakfast

Paul is convinced about the presence of God in the world – so convinced that he finds it hard to believe that anyone could miss it. In the mystery of creation, God is the Prime Suspect – everything points to him.

But even those who have seen the evidence can be drawn to the wrong verdict. Like the jury in a miscarriage of justice, there are those who see all that God has made, who look directly at his very fingerprints, and yet conclude that he is not there.

For Paul, this can never be the conclusion that flows naturally from the evidence – it is a choice we make. In his view, we do not begin in darkness, looking for the light of God. We begin with the light that God has given. Those who walk in darkness do so, he argues, because they have made a choice to turn off that light. For reasons of their own, they hit the dark-switch. Belief, not unbelief, is the default setting of the creation.

Continental

Just as belief and faith bring light, so unbelief brings its own kind of darkness.

Coffee

God of light and life, shine your light upon me. Scatter the darkness before my path this day. May I ever choose to walk in your light.

GK

Orange Juice

Therefore go and make disciples of all the nations, baptizing them in the name of the Father and of the Son and of the Holy Spirit, and teaching them to obey everything I have commanded you.

Matthew 28:19-20

The Main Command

The Big Breakfast

I have a friend who talks about this passage all the time, and he always begins by asking the same question: "In the Greek, one of the verbs in the main sentence (*go, make, baptize, teach*) is the main command Jesus gave, while the others are more like, 'and while you're doing that one, you should do these three as well ...' Which one is it?" Everybody says "go", when in fact the main verb in the sentence is "make".

This tells us something important about Jesus, because to me the word "disciple" says that being a Christian is a lifetime thing, so much more than "becoming a Christian". That's just the beginning of a lifelong adventure!

Continental

Are you merely a convert or are you a disciple?

Coffee

Is there someone you know well who you can pray for today, that they become a disciple of Jesus? They might be a Christian or not. As you pray, remember that making disciples is our job, given to us by Jesus.

SH

Orange Juice

The eye is the lamp of the body. If your eyes are healthy, your whole body will be full of light. But if your eyes are unhealthy, your whole body will be full of darkness.

Matthew 6:22-23

Watch What You Watch

The Big Breakfast

If you stand in the entrance hall of BBC Broadcasting House in London's Portland Place, you'll read this inscription:

To Almighty God this shrine of the arts, music and literature is dedicated by the first Governors in the year of our Lord 1931, John Reith being Director General. It is their prayer that good seed sown will produce a good harvest, that everything offensive to decency and hostile to peace will be expelled, and that the nation will incline its ear to those things which are lovely, pure and of good report and thus pursue the path of wisdom and virtue.

If some of the BBC's heads of programming reread this inscription then the programmes they commission might change drastically. What we watch and what we listen to affects the way we live our lives.

If our eyes and, I presume, our ears are the gateways to our souls, then we need to place a team of security guards around them. Take stock of the late-night TV you watch, the Internet sites you visit and the certificates on the movies you rent. They could turn off the light inside you!

Continental

Solomon's challenge is "Above all else, guard your heart, for it is the wellspring of life" (Proverbs 4:23 NIV). Maybe that's because if we don't monitor what comes into them they will become dark, full of "evil thoughts, sexual immorality, theft, murder, adultery, greed, malice, deceit, lewdness, envy, slander, arrogance and folly" (Mark 7:21-22).

Coffee

Make the psalmist's prayer your prayer today: "Turn my eyes away from worthless things; preserve my life according to your word" (Psalm 119:37 NIV). Amen!

DB

Orange Juice

Then Jesus said, "Which one ... was a neighbour ...?" The expert on the law answered, "The one who showed him mercy." Jesus said to him, "Then go and do what he did."

Luke 10:36-37 NCV

She Said Yes

The Big Breakfast

When she was asked by one of her classmates if she believed in God, Cassie Bernall said "Yes". So he shot her. We all know the story of Columbine High School in Littleton, Colorado. Thirteen young people were murdered there when two of their classmates rampaged through the school on 20 April 1999. It has been said that the two boys were cheering and laughing, saying things like, "We've been waiting to do this our whole lives!" Why? Why did Eric and Dylan do this terrible thing?

We're still shocked by the Columbine killings. It was just an ordinary neighbourhood. Why there? Why Littleton? All kinds of explanations have been given. One that struck me particularly was that Eric and Dylan had been left out of things by their peer group. They had been laughed at for being different. They felt rejected and unloved. Why did they do it? No one will ever really know. Could it be that a perceived lack of mercy and love from their classmates drove them to these appalling actions?

Continental

Mercy: the action of loving and caring because of what is in your heart, not because the other person deserves it.

Coffee

Lord Jesus, it seems to me that mercy is what your heart towards us is all about. Thank you, and please give me the same heart towards other people.

RS

Orange Juice
Is this not the kind of fasting I have chosen: ... not to turn away
from your own flesh and blood?

Isaiah 58:6-7 NIV

He Ain't Heavy ...

The Big Breakfast
In my youth, a favoured form of transportation was hitch-
hiking. Even when I was, for a time, the Personnel Manager of
a very respectable Bristol department store, I often made the
journey to and from my home in Bath by the use of my thumb.
It was cheaper than the train, and sometimes faster.

On the days when it didn't go so well, I would stand by the side of a rush-hour
street watching hundreds – even thousands – of cars go by, not one of their drivers
paying any attention to me. On occasions I would ask myself how differently I would
fare if one of the drivers recognized me. What if a member of my family was driving
by? The answer, of course, is that they would stop for me – because I would no
longer be a stranger in a suit incongruously commuting by hitch-hiking. I would be
family – and that makes all the difference.

Those who suffer, Isaiah cries, are your own flesh and blood – it is your human
family that is in need. How can you turn away?

Continental
How different would your life be if you saw those in need –
from famine victims on your TV screen to homeless people
on the street – as *family*?

Coffee
Father, I confess that, like others, I have divided humanity into
"relatives" and "strangers". Help me to extend the privileges of
family to *all* those you bring across my path.

GK

Orange Juice

Jesus said to the woman, "Your faith has saved you; go in peace."

Luke 7:50

Saved

The Big Breakfast

One word that Christians use to describe themselves is "saved". But what on earth does it mean to be saved?

Jesus had an amazing ability to annoy people who thought they had God all sorted out. He was always bursting people's bubbles, particularly when they put themselves between ordinary people and God. For example, take the occasion when Jesus was at a party held for him and a load of important people by Simon, a local religious leader. In came this woman – obviously no one had even bothered to find out her name – who started pouring perfume on his feet and kissing them. Something about her attitude to Jesus led him to tell her that her sins were forgiven, that she was "saved".

Sometimes we hang onto the wrong thing to try to get us "saved". Often it's things like going to church, believing the right things and so on, but Jesus saw faith in this woman's worship. Her humble adoration of Jesus was more important than the fancy feast the rich host offered.

Continental

What was it about that woman that made Jesus say, "wherever this gospel is preached throughout the world, what she has done will also be told, in memory of her" (Matthew 26:13)?

Coffee

"You believe that there is one God. Good! Even the demons believe that – and shudder" (James 2:19). Faith in Jesus is trust in, and worship of, God's only Son. Take time out for an attitude check.

SH

Orange Juice

If any of you lacks wisdom, you should ask God, who gives generously to all without finding fault, and it will be given to you.

James 1:5

You've Got Mail

The Big Breakfast

Subj: Re: Prayer

Date: AD 50 13:23:07 standard time

From: James@Jerusalem.freechurchserve.co.nt (James, brother of Jesus)

To: Twelvetribes@jol.com

Greetings ... Blah, blah, blah. Thanks for the recent emails. Sorry for the delay in replying but Peter spilt communion wine all over my keyboard again. Listen, I know this Christian life stuff is often a struggle. I mean, I'm family and it still baffles me at times. Being a believer doesn't exempt you from the trials and temptations of life.

If you really have no idea how to handle the next family crisis, or your donkey has failed its emissions test again, then talk to the Governor. He's never let me down, always dead keen to help. You won't have to twist his arm into helping out, he'll muck in and sort it out and won't make you feel a right idiot for asking in the first place. So ask the big man boldly, and believe it from me – it's as good as done! You can get him direct at jehovah@billgatesofheaven.org.

Continental

John Donne, the sixteenth-century bishop and poet, summed up my prayer life when he said, "I throw myself down in my chamber, and I call in, and invite God and his angels thither, and when they are there, I neglect God and his angels for the noise of a fly or the rattling of a coach."

Coffee

Ask and it will be given to you; seek and you will find; knock and the door will be opened to you.

Matthew 7:7

DB

Orange Juice

For you created my inmost being; you knit me together in my mother's womb.

Psalm 139:13 NIV

It's a Miracle Every Time

The Big Breakfast

My sister had a beautiful baby girl recently. She was three weeks early. I've never seen or held a little girl so small, so tiny, so perfect. Minute little fingernails, perfectly formed; beautiful eyelashes; gurgles; funny little contortions of her face that for now are a smile. Just four pounds, eight ounces of weight – and yet packed inside are the heart, lungs, kidneys, liver, blood vessels, muscles and ligaments that keep her alive. And a tiny brain, that vital organ that tells her to cry when she's hungry, to suck at her mother's breast, to sleep and wake, to react to light and heat and cold. When I saw her she was only six hours old.

It's a miracle. Every time it happens it's a miracle. A tiny egg that the naked eye can't see is fertilized. It grows gently and slowly, and inside it bones and flesh are joined together. A wonderful little person is formed who one day will breathe and think, laugh and cry, dance and sing. It's an absolute miracle.

Continental

The gift of life is a gift from God every time. No matter how you feel about yourself today, you're an amazing creation that was specially planned.

Coffee

A life that involves this degree of intricate creativity and engineering should never be flushed down a hospital waste chute like some piece of useless garbage.

RS

Orange Juice

Do away with the yoke of oppression, with the pointing finger and malicious talk.

Isaiah 58:9 NIV

War of the Words

The Big Breakfast

Isaiah understands the very real power that words have – the power to oppress. If you are going to do away with oppression, he says, you will need to watch what you say. Talk has power; oppression includes what we do with our words.

There is wisdom of the deepest kind here. How often we see racism begin with language. How often those who speak ill of their enemies later act ill towards them. Those who lived in Croatia and Serbia in the early 1990s, in the months leading up to the horrors of war, have testified that what eventually happened on the battlefield happened first in the media – and in everyday conversation.

It is easier to kill and maim those you have already spoken of as worthless. Violent words are seeds for violent acts. To be rid of oppression, you must strike at the very root – the tongue.

Continental

Most of us are not guilty of physical violence towards those around us – but how many of us are guilty of verbal grievous bodily harm?

Coffee

For the violence that uses neither guns nor fists, but arms the tongue with fire, *Father, forgive us.* For the oppression that knows no locks or bars, but imprisons its victims with words, *Father, forgive us.*

GK

Orange Juice

The whole company that had returned from exile built booths and lived in them. From the days of Joshua son of Nun until that day, the Israelites had not celebrated it like this. And their joy was very great.

Nehemiah 8:17 NIV

God's Party!

The Big Breakfast

The funny thing about the Old Testament is that everybody thinks it was a really terrible time and nobody ever had any fun. But boy, did these guys know how to party.

You've probably heard of the "tithe" because Christians often use the term to mean that they should give 10 per cent of their income to God's service. In Nehemiah's day, it was a bit more complicated than that. In addition to the tithe (which I'll come back to in a moment), there were two other kinds of offerings: one for the poor and one for anyone who worked for the city (including priests, choirs and soldiers). So, if other offerings covered community service and supporting the priesthood, what was the tithe for?

Parties. The tithe (which was a tenth) was used for temple worship, particularly the special feast days. All this stuff was given over to God on days like the Day of Atonement and, if this isn't too irreverent, it must have been chaos. Nehemiah had two full-time choirs that sang in the temple: the noise must have been incredible! There was always time to celebrate God.

Continental

"The Worship of God is not a rule of safety – it is an adventure of the spirit, a flight after the unattainable."

A.N. Whitehead

Coffee

If you normally have a quiet time with God, why not try having a loud time, and vice versa?

SH

Orange Juice

What I want from you is plain and clear: I want your constant love, not your animal sacrifices. I would rather have my people know me than have them burn offerings to me.

Hosea 6:5-6 GNB

24/7

The Big Breakfast

A man came home from work as usual, and met his wife standing in the doorway. "You don't love me any more," she barked. "And what's more, I am going to prove it to you. I am wearing something that I haven't worn for ages – since the end of the Second World War, in fact." The man made his best guess. The skirt? The shoes? The cardigan? They were all wrong. "What is it?" he asked in desperation. "It's the gas mask!" she hissed.

How could he miss something as obvious as a gas mask on his wife's face? How can we miss something as obvious as God's best for us? The prophet Hosea reminds us that the blazingly obvious way for us to love God is with consistency rather than mediocrity. God much prefers a daily relationship with us to the sacrifice of getting up earlier than most people on a Sunday to sit in a pew for an hour.

Recently I met an American basketball team from Chicago. They were telling me about the commitment needed to play basketball at the highest level, and talked about being a 24/7 kind of a person. Dedicating 24 hours a day, 7 days a week to your sport. It's that same consistency that heaven's coach demands of us if we are to play well on his team.

Continental

Stop burning those offerings to God in place of burning with a passion to walk his way. He would much rather have an honest conversation with you about your fears and your failures than a "good deed" here and there. It's about real relationship, not false religion.

Coffee

The Living Bible puts this verse even more plainly and clearly. God says, "I don't want your sacrifices – I want your love; I don't want your offerings – I want you to know me." What is stopping you from knowing him today? Push it aside!

DB

Orange Juice
Search me, O God, and know my heart ... See if there is any offensive way in me, and lead me in the way everlasting.

Psalm 139:23-24 NIV

Choices

The Big Breakfast
I think David is feeling a wee bit ashamed here. In the first part of this psalm he is very excited about the good job God did when he created us humans. In fact, you almost feel David will go into orbit because he's so excited and overcome by the wonderful way God made us. He's come down to earth now, though. "Take a look at my heart, God," he says. "It's not so wonderful in there any more."

I guess David realized something very important. When God first made things, including us, it was all perfect. Everything worked together well. But God took some risks at that time. He wanted people who would make choices, who would respond to his love and the love of other people. We make choices, good ones and bad ones. The amazing thing about God, of course, is that he wants to help sort out the consequences of our bad choices. Like David in this psalm, we need to come to God and ask him for some help.

Continental
When we become Christians we begin a journey with God that allows him to restore us to the way we were meant to be in the first place.

Coffee
When you think about yourself, do you reckon you need God's help to make the best of your potential, or will your own efforts do?

RS

Orange Juice

And forgive us our debts, as we also have forgiven our debtors.

Matthew 6:12

The Big Let-Down

The Big Breakfast

When God forgives us, there is a qualitative as well as a quantitative breadth to his mercy. He forgives us many sins, but he also forgives us many *kinds* of sin.

The sins we find easiest to spot are offences committed against God – direct, identifiable acts of rebellion. To the Hebrew mind, there is much more to sin than this. There is a deeper sense in which sin is a *failure to meet an obligation*. Our debt to God accumulates whenever we fail to meet our obligations to him. In simple terms, we sin whenever we let God down.

This becomes a dynamic definition when we apply it to those in debt to us. We are called to forgive not only those who in some specific way have sinned against us, but all those who have let us down – and even those whom we *feel* have let us down. Whenever we forgive, we are striking a blow against the spirit of the age and for the Spirit of our God.

Continental

The list of those whom we need to forgive grows longer as soon as we extend it to those whose only crime is that they let us down. More names on the list – more opportunities to forgive.

Coffee

Help me, Father, to forgive all those who sin against me, even if they just let me down. And help me to go on forgiving, daily, for as long as it takes.

GK

Orange Juice

It is my judgment, therefore, that we should not make it difficult for the Gentiles who are turning to God.

Acts 15:19

The Miracle

The Big Breakfast

The Christian church is still young and mostly Jewish, and there's been so much rumpus about the Gentiles that the leaders in Jerusalem have called a special meeting to decide what to do (see, some things never change – there will always be meetings). The Jewish Christians have heard about everything God has been doing among the Gentiles and are stunned into silence.

Then the miracle happens, James, Jesus' brother and the appointed leader of the Jewish Christians, speaks for them: "I don't think we should make it difficult for the Gentiles who are turning to God."

It sounds so easy. Yet what it actually meant was one of the most amazing sacrifices in Bible history. These Jewish Christians were willing to say to the Gentiles, "We think you're great. We have all this tradition which we love, but we realize it doesn't mean a thing to you, so don't worry about it too much. Just love Jesus with all your hearts, and that makes you our brothers and sisters."

Continental

God's ideal is that becoming a Christian and following Jesus should be the most natural thing that's ever happened to us. When it isn't that easy, let's be honest and start looking at ourselves and the things we're unwilling to let go.

Coffee

Remember a time when someone you knew helped you to grow in God. Think about what it was about them that made getting closer to God seem easy. Thank God for that person and think about how you can encourage another person in the same way.

SH

Orange Juice

In the morning, O LORD, you hear my voice; in the morning I lay my requests before you and wait in expectation.

Psalm 5:3 NIV

Facing the Dawn

The Big Breakfast

There is something quite holy about mornings. I know that some of us would replace the word "holy" with "hellish" here, but I'm convinced that there is something very precious about how we start our days. I think we miss out if we start them in a frantic rush or if we are still wiping sleep from our eyes at lunchtime.

I went for a run this morning. I did lots of thinking, seemingly without trying, and then completed the exercise with a hot, reviving shower. What a great way to start a day. How do you set yourself up for the day ahead? The author Ken Gire in his book *The Reflective Life* recounts how the Native American begins each morning.

In the life of an Indian ... his daily devotions were more necessary to him than daily food. He wakes at daybreak, puts on his moccasins, and steps down to the water's edge. Here he throws handfuls of clear, cold water into his face ... He then stands strong before the advancing dawn, facing the sun as it dances upon the horizon, and offers his unspoken orison.

How important are your daily devotions? How are you facing the advancing dawn today?

Continental

Notice the way the psalmist starts his day. He talks to God, lays his requests before him and then ... waits. No action, no giving God a hand by trying to sort it through himself. He just waits ... expectantly. Now that's real adventure.

Coffee

C.S. Lewis once said, "I am a barbarously early riser ... I love the empty, silent, dewy, cobwebby hours." Miss these moments and you will miss out.

DB

Orange Juice

Now Mary stood outside the tomb crying ... Jesus said to her, "Mary."

John 20:11, 16

I Didn't Get to Say Goodbye

The Big Breakfast

A few years ago, I had a phone call very early one morning. My brother's voice was broken and thick with tears. The next few seconds were agony. His news was clearly going to be bad. "Oh God, will I be able to cope? Will I handle it? What if I can't deal with it?"

My dad had died suddenly of a heart attack.

"Please God, tell me why. Why him? He was so young. Too young. I didn't get to say goodbye. I can't cope. I can't take this. I don't know how to handle this. I don't know how to lose him, how to exist without him. Oh God, don't you know he was such good fun? He was the big guy in our family. We all needed him. We still need him. Why? Why? Why?"

Then God spoke my name. In the middle of that moment of insanity, he spoke my name. My dad was safe. He was with Jesus. My heart was absolutely broken, shattered to pieces, but my soul was at peace.

Continental

The journey we must take can be desperately difficult at times. Jesus doesn't take us out of the really painful moments. He makes sense of them.

Coffee

Lord Jesus, I wish there was some knack to grief, but I know there isn't. Thank you that in the middle of such pain you have something personal to say to us.

RS

Orange Juice

Your people will rebuild the ancient ruins and will raise up the age-old foundations; you will be called Repairer of Broken Walls, Restorer of Streets with Dwellings.

Isaiah 58:12 NIV

Bob the Builder

The Big Breakfast

Isaiah was not called to address the unchurched so much as the over-churched. The ruins – the leftovers – of God's past glories surrounded the people of Israel. They had enough of the lingering memory of God from the past to inoculate them against his action in the present – but not enough to shake them into worship.

Isaiah's words are doubly meaningful in the context of contemporary Western culture, in which we are surrounded, often literally, by ruined churches. Is there hope, in the post-Christian West, for renewal? Is it possible to rebuild on the very ground on which the Church once stood, and has failed?

For Isaiah, the answer is yes. Our God is the God of the second chance, the God of new beginnings. In every age, with every new generation, he holds out the twin offer of reformation and renewal. But the key is obedience – a return not to the form of religion, but to the reality within it. Rebuilders start their work by getting back to foundations. Can he fix it? Yes he can!

Continental

There are times when rebuilding begins with demolition: what is left of the old must be torn down, so that the new can be built on its foundations.

Coffee

"We cannot be born anew until the old has died within us."

Paul Tillich, The Shaking of the Foundations

GK

Orange Juice

Everyone will hate you because of me, but those who stand firm to the end will be saved.

Matthew 10:22

Safe Despite the Danger

The Big Breakfast

Jesus was a master at saying stuff that people knew was true but didn't want to hear. But he isn't the type to say, "I told you so" when we try to avoid the truth and mess up. This little verse is in the middle of a big speech about what life is going to be like for the fledgling church: everyone was going to be persecuted and even kicked out of their own homes.

What's interesting, though, is that the word we translate "saved" could just as easily be translated "safe". The disciples might have asked, "So we're going to be put in prison, tortured, beaten, executed and despised, and you still want to describe us as being safe?" There is so much of Jesus' teaching that has a "now but not yet" quality to it, and this seems to include his teaching about salvation. He seems to be saying, "Even though you have a tough life, if you stick at it for me, one day you will know wholeness in every area of your life."

Trusting God is not an option for a Christian: hope for the future is central. First Corinthians 13 may say that love is the most important thing, but we shouldn't forget that faith and hope are up there as well! Hope is the power to believe that God can change the future, the ability to know that you are safe in his hands.

Continental

If nobody hates you because you're a Christian, are you doing anything wrong?

Coffee

Trusting God for the future can be hard sometimes. Talk to God about something in the future that's troubling you, and take time to see if he wants to reply.

SH

Orange Juice

Light is sweet, and it pleases the eyes to see the sun. However many years a man may live, let him enjoy them all.

Ecclesiastes 11:7-8 NIV

Today's the Day

The Big Breakfast

Are you old enough to remember the Stingray puppets? The sixties American voiceover always promised us that "anything could happen in the next half-hour". Problem is, it never really did; it was always so predictable. You just knew that no matter how desperate the situation, the little wooden puppets would save the world. This predictability eventually made the show boring for me.

My heart breaks as I meet the predictable people in life who never seem to "enjoy all their days" but endure them with a cancerous bitterness. I recently met a bus driver who had once hated his job with a passion and showed it by moaning daily to the endless streams of people who took a ride with him. Then he found Jesus, and life had a new perspective. He never gave up his job – he wasn't able to. Instead, he turned his bus into a temple. He took pleasure in greeting everyone with a smile, even on the rainiest of days. He went the extra mile to help the elderly or the mums with kids. He even won the bus company's driver of the year competition.

The way to enjoy each day is to find God in everything. Your task today is to turn your classroom or workplace into a temple, so that when you sit down for your evening meal you can say, "I have really enjoyed today."

Continental

As we "enjoy all our days" it's worth remembering Os Guinness's advice: "Christ-centred heroism does not need to be noticed or publicized. The greatest deeds are done before the audience of one, and that is enough."

Coffee

Choose to walk away from predictability and to enjoy each day, starting with this one!

DB

Orange Juice

And will not God bring about justice for his chosen ones, who cry out to him day and night?

Luke 18:7

Prayer Is an Adventure

The Big Breakfast

When Jesus talked about God's "chosen ones", the disciples would immediately have thought of the family of Israel. We can read all about them in the Old Testament. Jesus was saying that God would give them what was right and good when they prayed.

This is quite amazing. Stop and think for a moment who we're talking about. You know them: they're on every page of the Old Testament, trying God's patience to the limit, never seeming to get it right, even when it was obvious what they should do. They had sign after sign of God's goodness, and still they ran off at the first sight of trouble! It gives us hope, doesn't it? God never gave up on them.

The Old Testament is an incredible story of God's involvement in the real world of real people. He suffered with them and cared for them, teaching them how to live. He stuck with them, even if at times he had to allow them to go through hard times. He knew that was the only way they would ever come to their senses.

Continental

God was angry many times with his people, threatening to give up on them. He couldn't, though. Just as he can't give up on us, especially if we pray.

Coffee

Prayer is an adventure. Through prayer, we recognize that God is good, that he cares, but also that his way is the right one.

RS

Orange Juice

Then you will find your joy in the Lord, and I will cause you to ride on the heights of the land and to feast on the inheritance of your father Jacob.

Isaiah 58:14 NIV

You'll Get What's Coming to You!

The Big Breakfast

The abundance that the prophet Isaiah foresees for those who obey God is no less than the blessings promised to Jacob. From the very beginnings of time, God has been looking to bless his creatures.

There are promises to Eve and Adam; to Abraham and Sarah; to Noah and Moses and Jacob; to Ruth and David and Solomon and Deborah. The story of God's dealings with women and men is pregnant with his blessings. With every character, with every incident, the weight of the promise intensifies, like water building up behind a dam.

Discover the way of obedience, Isaiah is saying, and you will breach the dam. The blessing of God is not a meal but a feast. It is not a trickle but a flood. His intention is not to tickle you with small mercies, but to knock you off your feet. The longing of the creation for the blessings of God is matched by the longing of the Creator to bless. The key – the bridge between the two – is the obedience of the people of God.

Continental

The whole creation is waiting, Paul says – longing in desperate expectation – for the people of God to come into their inheritance.

Coffee

God of Eve and Adam, who walked with you in Eden – *Let your promise be fulfilled in our age.* God of Abraham and Sarah, whose longings were turned to laughter – *Let your promise be fulfilled in our age.*

GK

Orange Juice

Then Jacob put his children and his wives on camels, and he drove all his livestock ahead of him, along with all the goods he had accumulated in Paddan Aram, to go to his father Isaac in the land of Canaan.

Genesis 31:17-18 NIV

Facing Up to the Past

The Big Breakfast

How long does it take someone to admit their wrongs and atone for them? For Jacob, it took many, many years for him to go home and face up to his father Isaac and his brother Esau after he deceived Isaac and robbed Esau of his inheritance.

It is not unusual for reconciliation to take a long time. Families stay broken for life after one single argument because nobody wants to admit that they were at fault. It's hard. You're afraid of being vulnerable because the other person might take advantage of you. Well, that's true. Tough luck. We have Jesus for a role model.

In the year 2000 the Pope apologized for many of the sins of the Catholic Church over the years. It takes a lot of courage to do something like that. Part of you thinks, "Surely it's best to just forget about it and hope everyone else does." But we all know which voice that is. The person who has been wronged carries their pain round with them, and the easiest way for them to let go is for you to say sorry.

In David Lynch's film *The Straight Story,* one old man travels across the Eastern USA on a motorized lawnmower to be reconciled to his brother. It's a true story, just like our story here, and it's both ordinary and extraordinary at the same time. That's life.

Continental

Whoever says, "I will sin and repent, and again sin and repent," will be denied the power of repenting.

Jomah 8:9, from the **Mishnah,** *a collection of Jewish religious writings*

Coffee

Talk to God about any business you might have in this department, and receive his freeing forgiveness.

SH

Orange Juice

Can't you stick it out with me a single hour? Stay alert; be in prayer so you don't wander into temptation without even knowing you're in danger.

Matthew 26:41 MSG

It's Good to Talk

The Big Breakfast

My life feels like one big conversation sometimes. I have days where I go from meeting to meeting, with telephone calls in between. Even in the car, I find myself using the time to make calls on the mobile phone. So I never seem to find the time to stop and reflect unless I deliberately plan it in. Yesterday was one of the those mind-bending, meeting-after-meeting days. I had an hour's car journey early morning and, as usual, I listened to the radio for the latest news and then went to make some urgent calls. It was at that moment that a "shepherd's warning" red sky burst through the windscreen and ignited something deep in my soul.

It seemed an age since I'd had more than a grabbed conversation with God. It's tough at the best of times when you work for a boss you can't see. It's even harder when you never get round to talking stuff through with him. I switched the phone and the radio off and began to talk ... and talk ... and talk. I don't know who had missed the other more – me or God.

Switch off what distracts you today and switch back on to God, even if it's been months or years since you last spoke.

Continental

Temptation is far easier to overcome and danger far easier to avoid when prayer is important to our daily routine. Join me in the struggle of not letting our service for God take precedent over our worship of God.

Coffee

Jesus went on to say to his dozy disciples, "There is a part of you that is eager, ready for anything in God. But there is another part of you that's as lazy as an old dog sleeping by the fire." Which part will you work on today?

DB

Orange Juice

When the Son of Man comes, will he find faith on the earth?

Luke 18:8

Looking for Faith

The Big Breakfast

What is faith? That's a hard question. We've all heard those silly stories about chairs holding us up and "faith" being the fact that we believe in the chair! I don't know about you, but that kind of explanation never helped me to understand faith.

I read a helpful comment recently: "God is the focus of our faith, the purifier of our faith and the provider of faith's longings" (Charles Ringma, *Resist the Powers*, Albatross Books).

(1) God is the focus of our faith. Get to know God. Know about him. Know him as a great friend and as someone who wants to know you in return. Faith will become natural, as God becomes your Father.

(2) God will purify our faith. We need help to develop a faith that's based on reality not fairy tales. God isn't a genie in a lamp, or a heavenly Santa Claus. We often behave as if he is! God will purify our faith. Be prepared. That's usually painful.

Continental

When Jesus returns, will he find faith on earth? Don't be fooled into believing that faith in God is outdated. Like the Old Testament people, we will discover that such a notion is pure deception. Jesus is for today!

Coffee

Lord Jesus, I want my faith to grow. I don't want to disappoint you. Please give me faith when I'm tempted to doubt.

RS

Orange Juice

Immediately the rooster crowed the second time. Then Peter remembered the word Jesus had spoken to him: "Before the rooster crows twice you will disown me three times." And he broke down and wept.

Mark 14:72

The Birth of a Leader

The Big Breakfast

With the arrest of Jesus, the fast-paced narrative of Mark's Gospel hits breakneck velocity. If this were a movie, the music would be hard and driving, and the camera would cut from scene to scene with dizzying intensity.

In the middle of this tumbling drama Peter's denial emerges as a turning-point in the whole epic. Jesus has had just three years to prepare a group of disciples to carry on his kingdom work. He has already chosen Peter as their leader. But Peter is still not ready. There is too much pride in him; too much self-reliance; too much impetuous activism.

Jesus has gone – he will not speak to Peter again this side of resurrection. But here at last, in a cold, dark courtyard in the frozen moments before dawn, Peter reaches an end of himself. The time-bomb of Jesus' words predicting denial explodes, and Peter's pride is broken. He weeps uncontrollably – and in that moment, as in no other, Pentecost and the birth of the Church become possible.

Continental

It was not Peter's weakness that got in the way, but his strength. It may be the gifts we have, not the gifts we lack, that block the purposes of God in our lives.

Coffee

Thirty years later Peter wrote: "Humble yourselves, therefore, under God's mighty hand, that he may lift you up in due time" (1 Peter 5:6).

GK

Orange Juice

The Lord God said, "It is not good for the man to be alone."

Genesis 2:18 NIV

What's the Point of Church?

The Big Breakfast

There is an ancient story from the East that goes like this: the first man gets lonely, and asks God for a friend, so God creates woman. Man thinks this is great, and for a while man and woman get along just fine. Then things start to niggle, and eventually man and woman have such a fall-out that man goes back to God and says, "Please can you take woman away. I don't like her after all". So God takes woman away and leaves man to his devices. Then, guess what? Yep, that's right – after a while man returns to God and asks if he can have woman back . . .

Male/female relationships aren't the only areas where we can't make up our minds about each other. In the church we're all caught up in this strange love-hate thing with each other too. It doesn't take a brain surgeon to tell me that being a Christian on my own is hard. If you are someone who's trying to follow Jesus but is not exactly keen to go to church, you are part of an illustrious crowd which includes many well-known Christians and lots of not-so-well-known ones, like me (sometimes). It's just that the truth is that I'm even worse off on my own. We're just meant to be together, and the Church of Jesus should be the place where we discover what community is really meant to be about.

Continental

"Don't stay away from church because there are so many hypocrites. There's always room for one more."

A.R. Adams

Coffee

Lots of people complain about what the Church is or isn't doing. Remembering that as a Christian you are as much a part of the Church as any other Christian – what are you doing?

SH

Orange Juice

You have turned my wailing into dancing; you removed my sackcloth and clothed me with joy.

Psalm 30:11 NIV

Dance Into the Light

The Big Breakfast

God's double whammy! Sorrow into line dancing and sackcloth into Calvin Kleins!

He doesn't just remove your shame, he takes you down to his heavenly Retail Outlet Store and he kits you out with a brand new set of party gear. He doesn't just dry your tears, he puts the kind of smile back on your face that reaches right down to your feet and makes them dance. That's what's so precious about God. No half measures, no naked shame, no "Well-I'll-let-you-off-this-time..."

He always adds his divine Vanish Stain Remover to our garments grimed with guilt and shame. He promises to wash away all the dirt of our tears of pain and failure, and he always delivers on that promise, wash after wash after wash.

Praise is often described in the Bible as a sacrifice (Romans 12:1-2). It is tough to say thank you when your heart is breaking. But allowing the authentic sound of worship to rise up from deep within your soul brings a freedom that doesn't ignore the pain but sings in spite of it – freedom to smile again, to dance and to leave the past behind, freedom to hold your head up high and walk once more, sure of one thing: that in God's eyes the verdict still remains "not guilty"!

Continental

An old 1936 Irving Berlin song was made popular again by a recent TV advert for life insurance. I like its almost holy arrogance. "There may be trouble ahead, but while there's moonlight and love and romance, let's face the music and dance."

Coffee

The Message gives this verse a great street feel. "You did it: you changed wild lament into whirling dance; you ripped off my black mourning band and decked me with wildflowers." Dance with God this day.

DB

Orange Juice
This is the genealogy of Jesus the Messiah, the son of David, the son of Abraham.

Matthew 1:1

The Big Breakfast

So it's all to do with DNA, is it? Supermodel Cindy Crawford was asked in an interview what the secret of her success was, and she replied, "Genetic luck". What about that? It was all made for her before she was born. She has a point.

I bet you've never read this genealogy thing in Matthew chapter 1. It's just a long list of names after all, and while there are a few people you would recognize, you've certainly never heard of the rest. In fact, you probably can't even pronounce their names. What was Matthew thinking about, putting that long, boring list at the start of his book?

Well, for one thing, Matthew's long list lets us have a look at the "genetic luck" that Jesus was going to have. These people were all his ancestors – people from one generation to the next who made mistakes, told lies, slept with other people's wives, even killed one another.

Continental
The royal line of the King of Kings makes for some interesting reading, don't you think? Why did God allow this?

Coffee
God wanted to get as close as possible to us, yet stay uniquely God. Impossible? Think about it. It's the most awesome event ever to take place.

RS

Orange Juice

There was a man who had two sons. The younger one said to his father, "Father, give me my share of the estate." So he divided his property between them. Not long after that, the younger son ... set off for a distant country.

Luke 15:11-13

Drop Dead, Dad!

The Big Breakfast

The shock of this story is the audacity of the younger son. By asking to cash in his inheritance early, he is wishing his father dead. In saying, "I want it all, and I want it now", he is saying to the father who has loved and raised him, "Our relationship means nothing to me – you're worth more to me dead than alive."

When I was a sharp-tongued teenager ready to express my own pain by inflicting verbal pain on others, I had a youth leader who would give me a withering look and say, "You know how to hurt".

The son in the story knew how to hurt his father – to reject him at the deepest possible level. And sure enough, once the bank draft had been cashed, he put physical space where the emotional chasm had grown, and was gone.

If this is a picture of God's dealings with us, then it offers a compelling insight into the way God *feels* towards us. It's not the money – the quantitative measure of our sins – that matters most, but the broken relationship.

Continental

The most hurtful thing that can come between you and God is distance.

Coffee

God my Father, swallow up the distance that has come between us. Draw near, I pray, in the passing moments of this day.

GK

Orange Juice

While Peter was still thinking about the vision, the Spirit said to him, "Simon, three men are looking for you. So get up and go downstairs. Do not hesitate to go with them, for I have sent them."

Acts 10:19-20

Just Do It

The Big Breakfast

Peter had a vision and it made little sense to him until much later. Sometimes hearing from God can be like that. We may read something in the Bible and only much later do we really understand it. Or we may experience something in life and it is only looking back on it, now, that we begin to see what it was all about. That's normal. It's okay. We don't always understand everything straight away, especially when it comes to God.

Just think: one day, many hundreds of years from now, we may understand every mystery of the universe, and we will rightly feel proud of ourselves. But all we will have done is to understand something that God has made! It is like thinking we've understood humans because we've understood the wheel. Understanding God will take us a little longer – the technical term being "eternity".

So don't worry if God sometimes leaves you a bit befuddled – that's just what happens when the finite and the infinite meet. Just "get up" and "don't hesitate".

Continental

Gandhi – a great admirer of Jesus – once said that if he found just one person living out the Christian life as described by Jesus, he would become a Christian. Ouch!

Coffee

Was there a time in your life in which you can see that God was at work, even though it was hard to go through it? If so, thank God today. If not, spend a minute or two thinking about your life, and see if God shows you anything about it.

SH

Orange Juice

Even though I walk through the valley of the shadow of death, I will fear no evil, for you are with me; your rod and your staff, they comfort me.

Psalm 23:4

A Breath of Hope

The Big Breakfast

Last night a good friend died. She was my age and left a husband and three young children behind. Maybe you too can relate to the kind of grief that losing someone you love brings. Maybe, like me, your mind is full of unanswered questions and your heart numb with pain. I want you to know that the first tears to fall in your hurt were the ones that ran down your heavenly Father's cheeks.

I read the *Narnia Chronicles* long before I became a Christian. I never saw the parallel to the Christian life back then, but I do now. As I scrabble around for just an ounce of hope, Lewis's words seem very appropriate for me this morning:

> Aslan said softly, "Now the term is over: the holidays have begun. The dream has ended: this is the morning ... And for us this is the end of all the stories ... but for them it was only the beginning of the real story. All their life in this world ... had only been the cover and the title page: now at last they were beginning Chapter One of the Real Story: in which every chapter is better than the one before."

There is hope. Great hope. There always is with a God who has beaten the power of death.

Continental

My soul looked to Psalm 23 for comfort and I noticed something I hadn't seen before. It wasn't the valley of death we go through, but the valley of the *shadow* of death. You only get a shadow when there is a blazing light to create it. Right there in our darkest moments, God's dazzling light is our guide. He is with us and he will comfort us.

Coffee

Rejoice in the defiant hope of this divine declaration: "Death swallowed by triumphant Life! Who got the last word, oh, Death? Oh, Death, who's afraid of you now?" (1 Corinthians 15:55 MSG).

DB

Orange Juice

Then Jesus said to her, "Your sins are forgiven."

Luke 7:48

Keep It Simple

The Big Breakfast

What must Jesus' words have felt like for this woman? What he said was simple, direct and to the point. It wasn't a case of telling her to sign up for a class and we'll see if you can graduate. No, it was simple: "Your sins are forgiven."

When Jesus comes to us today it is still dead simple. Tell him where you've messed up, bring it to him, say you're sorry and give him the right to call the shots. You'll hear the same message: "Your sins are forgiven."

I used to work with tough kids from the inner city. Life for them had been lived by the law of the jungle – he who got the first punch in survived. The rules were made up from moment to moment. One golden rule was that you never admitted you'd got it wrong. That was to be weak, to be out of control and easy prey. Coming to Jesus and saying sorry for getting things wrong was a huge leap for these young people. It didn't need to be. Saying sorry to Jesus is not a sign of weakness but of great strength.

Continental

"I believe God wants me to quit concentrating on myself and on my own agenda and instead focus on him. He wants me to keep it simple."

Jim Aitkins, Youth Pastor from Washington

Coffee

Lord Jesus, thank you for your wonderful invitation to love you and follow you. I accept.

RS

Orange Juice
John testified concerning him. He cried out, saying, "This is he of whom I said, 'He who comes after me has surpassed me because he was before me.'"

John 1:15

A Home in History

The Big Breakfast
There are two sides to the miracle of the Incarnation. The first is the divinity of the equation – it was God himself who came. The second is its sheer physicality – it was to our ordinary world that he came.

John the Baptist gets a mention not only for his role in God's plan of salvation, but also because reference to him locates Jesus very precisely in space and time. The Word did not become flesh in some idealized, existential or disembodied sense: the Word became flesh in a specific place and time. Jesus did not "become human", he became *a* human. John the Baptist is a known figure; his name pinpoints Jesus very specifically in history.

John the Gospel-writer wants to be sure to give to Jesus a place in the flow of time – there was a time before he came, there is a time when he comes and there will be a time beyond his coming. This is history, not just theology.

Continental
For the Christian, theology (thinking about God) is rooted in history (knowing what God has done).

Coffee
Into the real world, the flesh-and-blood world, *he came*. Into real family, living in real society, *he came*. Into real, time-and-date-delineated history, *the eternal Son of God came*.

GK

Orange Juice

They said to me, "Those who survived the exile and are back in the province are in great trouble and disgrace. ..." For some days I mourned and fasted and prayed before the God of heaven ... I was cupbearer to the king.

Nehemiah 1:3-4, 11 NIV

The Broken-Down City

The Big Breakfast

Once upon a time, Ezra and Nehemiah were one book. The reason why they were separated is lost in the mists of time, but one reason might be that Nehemiah is mainly written in the first person by Nehemiah himself. Nehemiah was "cupbearer to the king", which might not sound much to us, but it made him a relatively big cheese in the world of Jewish slaves.

For reasons undisclosed, Nehemiah has not joined his countrymen in the rebuilding of Jerusalem, and only hears about the city's terrible state when one of his brothers visits him and explains that the walls are in ruins. Nehemiah doesn't know what to do, but his boss, King Artaxerxes, sees that Nehemiah is sad. Being sad in the king's presence was generally a beheading offence, but instead Artaxerxes asks Nehemiah what's up, and before long our narrator has been made governor of Judah.

There are lots of stories like this in the Bible: some nobody suddenly becomes important. What's the secret? Well, I think it might have something to do with the fact that Nehemiah obeyed God but also acknowledged the authority of the king. He didn't run away from his responsibilities, and because he respected the worldly power over him, he was rewarded by the king and was used by God.

Continental

Do your work willingly, as though you were serving the Lord himself, and not just your earthly master.

Colossians 3:23 CEV

Coffee

Nehemiah was "cupbearer to the king." What roles do you have in your life? How can you honour both God and the people who have authority over you in those roles?

SH

Orange Juice

All the days of the oppressed are wretched, but the cheerful heart has a continual feast.

Proverbs 15:15 NIV

Made for Another World

The Big Breakfast

I have often wondered what heaven will be like, probably because one day I am going to spend quite a long time there. I remember one preacher explaining eternity as a huge granite mountain. Each year a little bird would pay a visit, perch on its lofty peak and peck once before it flew off, not to return for another twelve months. When that granite mountain is eventually worn down to dust – that will be like "day one" of eternity. Mind-bending, isn't it? One thing I do know is that heaven is not just a future hope but a present reality. Eternal life begins now, not when we die. The "continual feast" has already begun.

While working with a missions team in a church near Larnaca in Cyprus, we were taken out for a traditional Greek meal. Talk about continual feast – we had course after course. I gave up counting after 36! We even stopped a few times to conga with the waiters around the restaurant and out into the high street. It was a most memorable event and it certainly cheered my heart.

Enjoy the feast today. The succulent tastes of a hope that will never disappoint, a friend who will never leave and a peace that is felt but can never be explained.

Continental

I once shared a feast with a poor family in a foreign country. Their generosity was outstanding, yet their food and table manners were questionable. Everybody but me tucked in eagerly. My host whispered in my ear, "Duncan, if pride stops you eating you will go hungry." Dive into God's banquet today. Don't be shy or you'll starve.

Coffee

In *Mere Christianity* C.S. Lewis writes, "If I find in myself a desire which no experience in this world can satisfy, the most probable explanation is that I was made for another world." Take a moment to set your soul towards heaven.

DB

Orange Juice

The next day, the Samaritan brought out two silver coins, gave them to the innkeeper, and said, "Take care of this man. If you spend more money on him, I will pay it back to you when I come again."

Luke 10:35 NCV

Bill Me Later

The Big Breakfast

You probably recognize this bit of the story of the "Good Samaritan". Have you ever asked yourself why the Samaritan would do this? He'd never met this man before. He didn't know who he was, or where he was from. He might even have been an enemy. In fact, he probably was from a community that hated Samaritans. It was one thing to get him out of the danger zone, but something else altogether to pay for his care. Who does that sort of thing?

God does. God does that sort of thing. A friend of mine was a minister in the United States for a few years. He told me about meeting a lady in a park one day. She wasn't from the same church tradition as him, but she did want to talk to a priest, she said. Her church had thrown her out because they didn't understand her lifestyle. She hated them, and God. She reckoned they had both let her down. As she talked to my friend, however, she felt understood. She felt release and healing. She turned to my friend and said, "When I couldn't find God, he found me. Thank you."

Continental

God's investment in us is a love gift. He comes and finds us to give us this gift, at no cost to us, but at enormous cost to him.

Coffee

Our salvation is free, but to follow Jesus will cost us everything we have.

RS

Orange Juice

No one has ever seen God, but the one and only Son, who is himself God and is in closest relationship with the Father, has made him known.

John 1:18

Guess Who!

The Big Breakfast

There are several things that God is not ashamed to admit – and one of them is that he is invisible from the vantage-point of planet earth. Nowhere in the dealings of the Creator with his creatures does he lay claim to easy visibility. The creature-Creator relationship is dogged by a restricted field of vision.

But John wants us to know that in Jesus this invisible God has chosen to make himself known. And he does so quietly, with little by way of cosmic fanfare. There is no universal announcement, no loud and unmissable disembodied voice. Just the barely audible whisper of a baby born in obscurity. Not only does God squeeze the fullness of his being into the tiniest of forms, but he does so without waking the neighbours.

It is as though, at the very moment when we are searching the horizon, waiting for God's big entrance, he sneaks up behind us, holds his hands to our eyes and says "Guess Who!"

Continental

God so rarely comes to us in the ways we are looking for. We watch the front door, but he calls at the back door; we expect him in laughter, but he arrives in tears; we seek him in a crowd, but he meets us alone.

Coffee

God of surprises, Father of fun, help me today to find you in the unexpected places where you hide.

GK

Orange Juice

Don't be deceived, my dear brothers and sisters. Every good and perfect gift is from above, coming down from the Father of the heavenly lights, who does not change like shifting shadows.

James 1:16-17

Changing Times

The Big Breakfast

Of one thing we can all be certain – constant change is here to stay. It only seems a breath away that the web was just something Mrs Spider lived in. We used to swap phone numbers at parties, then it was mobiles and email addresses. Vinyl records are now only seen at jumble sales. Compact discs are giving way to mini disks, while VHS video is about to exit stage left in preference to DVD. When I was at school, teachers were stamping out such discipline problems as talking in class or running in the corridors. Nowadays it's more likely to be problems of truancy or drug and alcohol abuse.

I am increasingly convinced that in this sea awash with constant change, people are desperately searching out the dry ground of certainty that previous generations seemed to enjoy. That makes our faith increasingly relevant today as we proclaim a God "who does not change like shifting shadows".

Continental

"Jesus Christ is the same yesterday and today and forever" (Hebrews 13:8). In other words, he loves you no more or less than he did the day he hung on the cross for you.

Coffee

Change is not all bad. My wife, a nurse herself, smiled as I read her *The Duty of a Nurse in 1887*. "Nurses in good standing with the director will be given an evening off each week for courting purposes or two evenings a week if you go regularly to church. Any nurse who gets her hair done at a beauty shop or frequents dance halls will give the director good reason to suspect her worth and integrity." It's good that some things change, don't you think?

DB

Orange Juice

Jerusalem, Jerusalem, you who kill the prophets and stone those sent to you, how often I have longed to gather your children together, as a hen gathers her chicks under her wings, and you were not willing.

Matthew 23:37

The Heart of God

The Big Breakfast

Picture Jesus, coming over the hill from Bethany, and this overwhelming passion ... well ... overwhelming him. This is beyond football, beyond Leonardo DiCaprio, this is God's powerful love. He speaks to the city with such longing and tenderness that I can only imagine all these roughneck disciples suddenly finding their sandals to be of great interest. Healing, we can cope with, even raising the dead, but crying – no way!

Jesus knew what was about to happen, but he wasn't crying for himself; he was crying for all that was to come. There were people alive in Jerusalem who would live to see the city ransacked and the Temple destroyed less than 40 years later. I see this moment as being just as poignant as that in the Garden of Gethsemane. Jesus is saying to the city, "If only you would turn back to God, none of us would have to go through what's going to happen."

Continental

God longs to be as close to you as a mother is to her children. Cool, huh?

Coffee

Ask God to give you a little of his heart for where you live.

SH

Orange Juice

He answered: " 'Love the Lord your God with all your heart and with all your soul and with all your strength and with all your mind'; and, 'Love your neighbor as yourself.' "

"You have answered correctly," Jesus replied. "Do this and you will live."

But ...

Luke 10:27-29

Yes, But . . .

The Big Breakfast

What are the words teenagers use most? I reckon "Yes, but ..." must be in there near the top of the list. A strange thing happens once we get past the age of eight or nine. Adults just don't seem to understand how unfair or plain stupid their expectations are. "Yes, but ..." was used a lot in my house as we grew up.

Jesus has a "Yes, but ..." being thrown at him here. "Love God with all your heart. Let me help you. Come on, it's what you were made for. And when you love me, you will grow to love your neighbour too." This is what Jesus has been trying to tell the young man. He just can't get it, though. Instead he says to Jesus, "Yes, but who is my neighbour?" Jesus must have been heartbroken. The young man hadn't heard what Jesus was saying to him. "But who is my neighbour?" was just another trick question, and both Jesus and the young man knew it.

Continental

It isn't a good idea to set out to trick someone intentionally. It often makes a fool of them, which isn't the Jesus way of living with other people.

Coffee

Lord Jesus, forgive me for the times when I say "Yes, but ..." to you. Whenever I think I know best, there's always more I can learn from you.

RS

Orange Juice

And lead us not into temptation.

Matthew 6:13

Hassled of Harrogate

The Big Breakfast

Harrogate in North Yorkshire is a nice town, by all accounts. I have only been there once, on an occasion when I chose to walk the short distance from the Conference Centre to the station.

It should have taken 10 to 15 minutes, but when 30 had passed, I knew that I was lost. I had a map, of sorts, but this was grade-A lostness – the lostness where you can't even see which way up you should be holding the map. When I eventually asked a local and found my way, I discovered that for much of my 40 minutes I had been walking in entirely the wrong direction.

When we are lost, we need help. When we are *really* lost, we need more help than a simple map can give – we need a flesh-and-blood guide who can show us how to read the map, orient us to True North, and set us on our way. The "lead us not" of the Lord's Prayer includes a "lead us": we will avoid temptations, trials and trouble when we are led by a trustworthy guide.

Continental

God does more than send us a map. He is a guide who walks with us every step of the way. What does it take to hear, and follow, his guidance?

Coffee

Father, I confess that without you I am lost. All the guide-books in the world won't help me when I don't know where to start. Walk with me. Be my guide – and teach me to trust your leading.

GK

Orange Juice

The master of the banquet tasted the water that had been turned into wine ... and said, "Everyone brings out the choice wine first and then the cheaper wine after the guests have had too much to drink; but you have saved the best till now."

John 2:9-10

Party Pooper

The Big Breakfast

This was Jesus' first miracle. If you take the time to read the whole story you'll understand that Jesus doesn't gatecrash this party: he's on the invited list, his name's on the door (John 2:2).

I find that fascinating. You see, many people think that Jesus was a party pooper, but no one invites party poopers to parties. And he proved it by turning the rancid water from the six stone foot-washing jars into a cheeky little number from God's own personal vineyard. And it wasn't just a bottle or two, not even a case ... oh no ... Jesus demonstrates again the extravagant nature of heaven by supplying this flagging party with around thirty gallons of the good stuff.

The horrified servants look on as Ben the bus boy is given the first glass drawn from the water jars and ordered to take it to the master at the top table. Surely he'll spit it out, and throw them out. The room hushes, the word has gone round. Jesus smiles as the master sips ... and sips, his only comment: "You have saved the best until last."

As I write and you read, I wonder whether heaven's switchboard is making a divine connection between my words and your soul today. He's saved the best till now!

Continental

I have often conducted the weddings of people who thought they would never find a soulmate or have prayed for people who have waited patiently for the right job. I can recall laughing with people who have looked back on where they would have been without a God who knew what was best for them and had saved it till now.

Coffee

John goes on to record the impact of this first and most extravagantly controversial of miracles. "[Jesus] thus revealed his glory, and his disciples put their faith in him" (John 2:11). How about you?

DB

Orange Juice

God said to Moses, "I am who I am. This is what you are to say to the Israelites: 'I AM has sent me to you.'"

Exodus 3:14 NIV

What's in a Name?

The Big Breakfast

God's self-declaration as "I AM" contains, by implication, its own opposite – the "I AM NOT" of the Creator. If God were to choose a name for himself, he would immediately be seen – by Israelite, Egyptian and Midianite alike – as one god among many.

Every hillside, every tribe, every region and nation – in some cases every household – had its own pet god in Moses' day. Some were more powerful than others; some were localized; some came close to overall supremacy – but none ruled unchallenged. To be a god was to join a hall of fame as full as any Hollywood roll call or sports museum of today.

By saying "I AM" (from which the Hebrew name *Yahweh*, "HE IS," was derived) God was setting himself above and beyond the crowd. I AM NOT limited by locality; I AM NOT the god of one tribe alone; I AM NOT tied to time or place. In these two words, "I AM", Moses has been introduced to the Creator of the cosmos – the in-all, above-all, once-for-all God.

Continental

No wonder the Jewish leaders were so shocked, generations later, when Jesus used the words "I AM" of himself.

Coffee

Father, forgive us for making you small and local – open our eyes to your cosmos-spanning glory!

GK

Orange Juice

You hem me in – behind and before; you have laid your hand upon me.

Psalm 139:5 NIV

God Is for You

The Big Breakfast

When God makes a decision to be involved with you it isn't half-hearted. He is totally for you. Totally. Listen to what he says in Jeremiah 32:41 (NIV): "I will rejoice in doing them good." Now those are the words of a God who is for you.

David, who wrote this psalm, understood that God was all around him, looking out for him. In fact, he couldn't get away from God and that was the most excellent thing in his life. He knew that God was totally for him. Being surrounded by God meant he felt very safe.

Continental

"If God is for us, who can be against us?" (Romans 8:31). How does that grab you? The Creator of the universe is looking out for you!

Coffee

Lord, I so often allow the problem points in my life to stop me seeing how close you are, how much you care and how much you want to help. Forgive me.

RS

Orange Juice

Jesus called in a loud voice, "Lazarus, come out!" The dead man came out, his hands and feet wrapped with strips of linen, and a cloth around his face. Jesus said to them, "Take off the grave clothes and let him go."

John 11:43-44

Funeral Chaos

The Big Breakfast

Can you imagine turning up to a funeral with Jesus, four days late, only for him to say that the corpse may be a touch yellow but he's not dead, he's just having a little doze? And that Jesus will give him the loudest wake-up call he's ever likely to hear (John 11:11)?

Jesus tells the people to remove the stone from the tomb. The dead man's sister gently suggests that he might smell a bit. Jesus replies that they might like to trust him as he is the resurrection and the life and therefore is best qualified to deal with this one, thank you very much.

Jesus calls Lazarus out by name. The only sound that's heard as the mummified figure of Lazarus appears in the doorway to the tomb is the thud of the disciples' jaws as they hit the dusty Middle Eastern ground. Jesus has to tell the boys to unwrap him and let him go!

What are the grave-clothes that have tied you up for so long? Your gender doesn't fit, so you have to keep quiet and make the tea. You've been told that you are too old for this game now, or maybe it's that you're too young and can't be trusted with that kind of responsibility.

Continental

Hear the Master's loud voice calling out to you today, "Take off those grave-clothes. Don't be bound any more. Be free ... be completely free."

Coffee

The shortest verse in the Bible is part of the Lazarus story. Just two simple words – "Jesus wept". Only nine letters, but you could fill a library with their meaning. How does the Saviour react when he sees the grave-clothes strangling his life out of you? Jesus weeps.

DB

Orange Juice

Someone in the crowd said to him, "Teacher, tell my brother to divide the inheritance with me."

Luke 12:13

Your No. 1 Job

The Big Breakfast

There's a storm brewing, a big family bust-up. Two brothers can't agree over their legacy, and they want Jesus to sort it out. Well, one of them wants Jesus to sort it out. It makes you wonder what happened before this guy got so desperate that he had to shout out at Jesus in public. Had he tried to work things out with his brother and just not managed it? Had he felt let down by his brother's attitude? Or had he just assumed that his brother would try to cheat him out of what was his by right?

Whatever the deal, one thing is clear: he wants his share. He's fighting for his rights. It must have been a big shock to him, to find that Jesus wasn't interested. "Who said I should judge or decide between you?" Jesus wasn't interested in rights of this kind. Jesus had given up all the amazing rights and privileges that were his, and had come to earth to serve people. He was hardly going to take sides in such a situation.

Continental

How do you think of Jesus? Is he Mr Fix-it for you, or a big Santa Claus who always gives us what we want? Take a closer look.

Coffee

To follow Jesus means becoming like Jesus. That means living like Jesus, which means that serving God and other people is your No. 1 job.

RS

Orange Juice
Deliver us from the evil one.

Matthew 6:13

Global Delivery System

The Big Breakfast
This final line of Jesus' prayer answers an unspoken question: When do we stop praying? What is the target toward which we are moving, as we co-operate with God in the coming of his kingdom?

If the "us" of the Lord's Prayer is not just "me and mine" but the whole world – if we pray these words as the cry of humanity to its Creator – then the question is answered. We will go on praying, and God will go on listening, until that day when the whole cosmos – every woman, man, child and created thing – is delivered from the Evil One. When the deliverance is complete across the planet, we can stop praying, and God, with us, will rest.

But until that day there is no rest. No matter how satiated my own needs might be, while there is need on planet earth, I am called to pray. We ask no less of God than that he will deliver us – all of us – from the very presence of evil.

Continental
The Lord's Prayer is not merely wishful thinking: God has promised us deliverance. There is a day coming when he will wipe away every tear. It is in the certainty of this hope that we pray.

Coffee
A resolution: Understanding that prayer must reach beyond the small concerns of my own needs, and knowing that the cry of humanity reaches to the throne of God. I resolve to pray – and to go on praying – until the day of full deliverance comes.

GK

Orange Juice
Jesus wept.

John 11:35

Tears from Heaven

The Big Breakfast
And the tears are still rolling to this day ...
He weeps over my ability to preach truth with my mouth and practise heresy with my life.
He weeps over the bride he adores who is so often heart-broken and heartless.
He weeps over communities that choose death not life, houses not homes, clean air not clean minds.
He weeps over a society that has gained possessions but lost values.
He weeps over people who understand the far reaches of outer space but have neglected their own inner space, who have beaten disease but not prejudice.
He weeps over generations who have written more but have learned less, who have developed disposable nappies along with their throw-away morality.
He weeps over a race that has faster modems but less communication, that builds worlds of leisure but has lost the art of having fun, that has more experts but more problems.
Let your heart be broken today with the things that break the heart of God. Let the tears fall.

Continental
T.S. Eliot once wrote:

The desert is not only remote in southern tropics
The desert is not only around the corner
The desert is squeezed in the tube train next to you
The desert is in the heart of your brother.

Coffee
When Jesus came closer and could see Jerusalem, he cried and said, "It is too bad that today your people don't know what will bring them peace! Now it is hidden from them. Jerusalem, the time will come when your enemies ... close in on you from every side ... because you did not see that God had come to save you."

Luke 19:41-44 CEV

DB

Orange Juice

"But God said to him, 'You fool! This very night your life will be demanded from you ...' This is how it will be with those who store up things for themselves but are not rich toward God."

Luke 12:20-21

You Can Take It with You!

The Big Breakfast

Life is a gift. Any surplus wealth we get is a gift also, because God does give surplus as a gift. Both are on loan, however. The person who thinks that security and a good life are found in material wealth is a fool. Life is good when we invest in it by being "rich toward God".

How do we become rich toward him? He has all he needs. Why would he want anything from us? And isn't this a contradiction of what we hear from Jesus elsewhere? You can't earn eternal life – it is God's freely given, undeserved gift.

There is no contradiction. There never is, even if it seems that way. We just need to understand it properly. What God wants back from us is the willing gift of our lives to him. Why? So that he can control us and remove all our freedom? No. So that he can give us the life for which we were created. On our own, we usually mess it up.

Continental

Giving our lives back to God isn't just about us. It's about pleasing God because he's worth it.

Coffee

There is only one type of wealth you can take with you when you die, and that's the investment you've made in your relationship with God.

RS

Orange Juice

When he came to his senses, he said, "How many of my father's hired servants have food to spare, and here I am starving to death! I will set out and go back to my father."

Luke 15:17-18

Amnesiacs Anonymous

The Big Breakfast

Hunger brought the Prodigal Son to his senses, but it took something more to bring him home. In the midst of his disgust and degradation, there was something he remembered – a lost fragment from his childhood – which both challenged him to go home, and gave him the courage to do so.

He had wished his father dead. He had run from him as far as he could go. He had sought peace and prosperity where they couldn't be found. Finally, he was reduced to working as a hired labourer for a man who paid him so badly that he couldn't afford to eat – and refused to give him even pig slops.

And that's when the penny dropped – in all his years growing up alongside the father he so despised, he had never once seen him treat a worker that way. Even without pigs, on his dad's farm there were men doing the same kind of dirty, degrading work as he was now doing – but they weren't ill treated and hungry.

It was a recovered memory that drove him home – the memory of his father's generosity.

Continental

For a culture on the run from its Creator, as much as for the individual, the way home begins with remembering the generosity of God.

Coffee

Reawaken in my life, O God, the memory of your love. Bring to my mind this day the generous reality of Jesus.

GK

Orange Juice

Whoever claims to live in him must walk as Jesus did.

1 John 2:6

Exchange Your Nikes

The Big Breakfast

If you sing the songs on a Sunday you've got to walk to his tune on a Monday. Hypocrisy stinks. Jesus had some strong words to say to hypocrites. He used the kind of language that wouldn't get him invited back to preach in their churches. But frankly, he didn't care about that. It's amazing how gentle and graceful Jesus was with adulterers and swindlers, yet how righteously rude he was to the religious rulers.

The question that often haunts me as a Christ follower, a parent, a husband and a leader is this: Can God trust me? Am I a responsible ambassador? Do I love as Jesus loved, care as Jesus cared and walk where Jesus walked? "Whoever claims to live in him must walk as Jesus did." I so often stake the claim, yet so rarely walk the walk.

He walked tall – proud of his heritage. He walked far – going the extra mile. He walked humbly – not with the rich but the poor. But what I love about him most is that he walked *his* way – never sticking to the prescribed paths.

Yesterday I met a friend I hadn't seen for years. We hugged evangelically (one foot on the ground). Then he asked pointedly, "How is your walk?" Hum ... good question ...

Continental

Go on ... I to 10 ... how is your walk? A strong 10, a mediocre 5 or a flagging I? Or have you gone the whole hog and turned "March for Jesus" into "Sit Still for Jesus"? Maybe today you need to exchange your Nikes for his sandals. Spend the day in his shoes – you'll find they fit better than you think.

Coffee

When C.S. Lewis was asked for his views on hypocrisy he answered, "How difficult it is to avoid having a special standard for oneself!" How self-revealing are you? Could you share your inconsistencies with a friend and begin to deal with them?

DB

Orange Juice

He said to them, "When you pray, say: '...your kingdom come.'"

Luke 11:2

When the Revolution Comes

The Big Breakfast

When I walk down the High Street on a Saturday afternoon, I often come across one of those "street preachers" – a wee man with a microphone in one hand and a big black book in the other. Sometimes he'll have a placard saying, "Repent, for the kingdom of God is at hand!" He's trying to let people know that they need Jesus in their lives.

The words on his placard interest me: "The kingdom of God is at hand." What does that mean? It makes me think of these words in the prayer Jesus taught us. We're to pray that God's kingdom will come. Is God planning a coup? Are we to be the army that makes it happen?

It seems to me that what Jesus wants us to pray for isn't some mad revolution that will take people by force. Rather, he wants us to pray that they will change their allegiance because they want to. It will be a revolution in their hearts, and it will change things forever.

Continental

We are Jesus' followers, and he is asking us to pray that this heart revolution will happen for other people. Think about it: our best weapon in the fight for lives is prayer.

Coffee

Lord Jesus, if I'm honest, I usually pray for my own concerns. It's a bit like bringing you my shopping list. Teach me how to pray for *your* concerns.

RS

Orange Juice
Your rod and your staff, they comfort me.

Psalm 23:4 NIV

Clack, Clack, Poke, Poke

The Big Breakfast
The antidote to the fears that have us running from shadows is to know the presence of God.

The rod and staff remind the sheep that the shepherd has not left them to their fears. When darkness overwhelms them, and they can see neither the ground under their feet, nor their shepherd up ahead, the "clack, clack" of staff on rock tells them they are not alone – and gives direction.

When they are paralysed by their terror, caught between a rock and a hard place and without the strength to move, the "poke, poke" of a rod in the ribs brings them to their senses, breaking the thrall of fear.

In the dark night of the soul, when my certainties have gone down with the sun and I see monsters in the shadows on the wall, "clack, clack, poke, poke" may well be all I know of God. But I cling to these small mercies, and listen hard.

Continental
I am safe because the shepherd has chosen this route. Though I fear the worst, and though the worst I fear may come to pass, I trust myself into his care.

Coffee
Teach me, Father, to listen for the quiet echo of your presence. Help me to recognize the imperative of your love in the shocks and pains you let me feel to save me from myself.

GK

Orange Juice

Then they said to each other, "We're not doing right. This is a day of good news and we are keeping it to ourselves … Let's go at once and report this."

2 Kings 7:9 NIV

The Best-Kept Secret

The Big Breakfast

It would have taken a whole herd of wild horses to drag me away from the delivery room the day my first son was born. Eventually, the midwife put Matthew into my arms and I couldn't take my eyes off him. So cute and cuddly, so perfectly formed, so handsome, so much like his dad!

I was forced to pass him back to the nurse to get him cleaned up and dressed. Debbie looked at me with one of those "isn't-there-something-you-ought-to-be-doing?" stares. I had clean forgotten. This was the best news the family had ever had and we were keeping it to ourselves. There were parents to tell, friends to inform and a church keen to hear.

If only we could re-imagine the enormity of our new birth in Christ we would be rushing to the phone, fax or email systems at our disposal to tell the world the good news. But we seem to have lost the sense of urgency. I spoke to a good friend yesterday who was giving the remainder of his ministry to turning his church from maintenance to mission. It wasn't easy, and some had left. His concluding comment was, "Life's too short to waste it on church politics when there's a world hungry for our news."

Continental

I once heard a brilliant seminar on evangelism. The whole session took only two minutes and consisted of just one sentence. It was the most freeing and profound teaching I had ever heard on the subject. Here is the entire seminar for you, free of charge: "Find out what you really enjoy doing and go and do it with the unchurched."

Coffee

C.S. Lewis said, "God used an ass to convert a prophet; perhaps if we do our poor best we shall be allowed a stall near it in the celestial stable." Don't buy the lie – God will even use donkeys like you and me!

DB

Orange Juice

In a certain town there was a judge who neither feared God nor cared what people thought.

Luke 18:2

Survival of the Fittest

The Big Breakfast

When we come to read the Bible, we need to remember that the whole story God wants us to hear will really only make sense when we read the whole book. All 66 books will take us the whole way, just like the highway Interstate 66 in the USA.

The followers listening to Jesus as he told this story in Luke 18 would have understood what he was getting at because they'd been on the Interstate, so to speak. They would have known that the job of a judge was to act as God's representative, and therefore he was expected to be 100 per cent honest and fair. He was there to care for people, to look out for them, to make sure the weak and vulnerable were looked after, that the underprivileged got a just deal. Under no circumstances was he ever to take a bribe or be corrupted by another human being (see 2 Chronicles 19:4-6). A judge who didn't respect God and who didn't value the people's opinion was a sign of huge trouble. It would have been no surprise, however. Corruption was expected. The bribe was normal. It was another case of the survival of the fittest.

Continental

In many countries today the people with the power to protect and care for people can't be trusted. Bribery is common. The result is that ordinary people never get justice.

Coffee

Part of our job as Christians is to fight for the rights of those who can't fight for themselves. How could you play your part in this fight?

RS

Orange Juice

... all flocks and herds, and the beasts of the field, the birds of the air, and the fish of the sea, all that swim the paths of the seas.

Psalm 8:7-8 NIV

Place Your Order

The Big Breakfast

Underwater swimming is an exhilarating and stimulating experience. Whether you dabble in the shallows of a holiday beach, or plunge deeper where only an aqualung can take you, you sense the wonder of being in another world.

There are fish to see, and crabs, rocks and shells and plants. One thing that you won't see, oddly enough, is paths marked out for fish to follow. But the psalmist who wrote these words is not, by that token, completely mad. What is being described here is the sense of order at the heart of the creation.

The diversity of species, the complexity of food chains and weather systems, the patterns and structures from rock strata to relationships – all of these reflect the beauty of God's design. Where once there was chaos, where the Spirit of a brooding God has hovered, there is now order. Not the sterile order of the factory or army, but the wild, organic order of a peacock's tail.

From molecules and microbes to the furthest-flung galaxy, the creation is an orchestra tuned to the praise of God.

Continental

Studies in chaos theory have helped us to see that there is beautiful coherence at the heart of creation.

Coffee

We stand before your beauty, Lord, as we stand before an ocean. Far beyond our vision or imagination, there is no end of you.

GK

Orange Juice

God has chosen to make known among the Gentiles the glorious riches of this mystery, which is Christ in you, the hope of glory.

Colossians 1:27

Closer Than You Think

The Big Breakfast

I have to admit to being a bit of a *Star Trek* fan, though it's really only the old 1960s series that gets me switching on the TV set. I love the dramatic music, the rubber aliens, the painted polystyrene sets. My heart always breaks for the newest member of the landing party: it's clear that the alien slime will get them first and that they're never coming back. After the programme I go to bed dreaming of a fictitious world where we can flip open a communicator (that looks mysteriously like a woman's makeup compact) and get Scotty to beam us anywhere we fancy.

Just imagine that fiction became reality for one moment. Imagine Scotty pushing up his faders and beaming you right into the courtyards of heaven. Do you think you would be closer to God than you are now? Not according to the apostle Paul. The mystery that was once a secret is now revealed – "Christ lives in you". You are just as close to him now as you would be holding an audience with God in heaven. Maybe there wouldn't be as many distractions then, but remember this truth: God has taken up residence deep within you. So you don't need to come into his presence today. You never left it!

Continental

If we have all fallen short of the glory of God, is there any hope of ever reaching it? Answer: yes – Christ lives in you, and he is your hope of sharing in God's glory. The only hope you have of reaching the standard God sets is if the indwelling Christ meets it for you. It has to be an inside job.

Coffee

The Message manages to put this verse so bluntly and memorably: "The mystery in a nutshell is just this: Christ is in you, therefore you can look forward to sharing in God's glory. It's that simple."

DB

Orange Juice

O Lord, our Lord, how majestic is your name in all the earth!... O Lord, our Lord, how majestic is your name in all the earth!

Psalm 8:1, 9 NIV

Bookends

The Big Breakfast

There is something satisfying about a journey that ends where it began. The bookends that begin and end this poem of praise are these same words describing the majesty of God. The images that populate the verses in between are held by these words, like water held in two hands cupped together.

In that sense the psalm is a picture of the whole created universe. Before anything was, there was the glory of God, and at the end of all things is that glory. Our world will end as it began – in the bosom of the majesty of God. The presence and love of a personal God is the frame within which creation exists – all of time and eternity are book-ended by his character.

Before all was, he is; after all is, he will be. He is the outset of every adventure and the goal of every quest. He is the opening chapter of every story, and the end toward which it moves. Starting-pistol and finishing-tape – God is our beginning and our end.

Continental

The two sentences "In the beginning" and "At the end" can both be completed with the same two words: "God is."

Coffee

Glory to the Father, and to the Son, and to the Holy Spirit: as it was in the beginning, is now and shall be forever, world without end. Amen.

GK

About the Authors

Duncan Banks. The words *fluffy, cuddly* and *squidgy* are rarely levelled at Duncan's door, except by his wife of course. However, he suggests the words *mega-star, legend* and *deep humility* may well be suitable. Duncan writes things, speaks at conferences and leads a fantastic church in Banbury, Oxfordshire. But he confesses all that is a stroll in the park compared to parenting his three boys, Matthew, Nathan and Joe. He once met the Queen of England but had only seen her on a postage stamp before so he didn't know whether to shake her hand or lick the back of her head. Duncan loves Jesus with a passion and is a sports fanatic. His favourite theologian is Homer Simpson.

Simon Hall is a Baptist minister and a leader of Revive, a church reaching out to the pub and nightclub scene of his home city of Leeds. He teaches youth ministry and worship at London Bible College and the Centre for Youth Ministry, and writes regularly about the church and pop culture. His passions include soccer, computer games and introducing people to Jesus. He is married to Anna and they have three preschool children and a dog.

Gerard Kelly is a director of Café-net: fostering innovation and creativity in Christian mission in contemporary Europe. He is a local church elder, a member of the Leadership Team of Spring Harvest and a visiting lecturer at Redcliffe College, Gloucester. In former lives he has been a performance poet, Bible college student, petrol pump attendant, pizza chef and Personnel and Training Manager. For ten years he was on the staff of British Youth for Christ, and was seconded for two years to France. He is married to Chrissie, co-director of Café-net, and they have four children. Home base is Stourbridge in the West Midlands, where Gerard and Chrissie are both involved in the leadership of Chawn Hill Christian Centre.

Gerard speaks widely on issues of mission and culture, and his books have appeared in Britain, the United States, France and Finland. He can be contacted at gerard@future-leader.com.

Roz Stirling is the Director of Youth Ministry for the Presbyterian Church in Ireland, a position she has held for ten years. Her passions within this role is to see the church become a relevant and engaging place for young people where they feel they belong and have a spiritual home. Roz loves to keep up with the movie scene and analyses the latest releases with friends over a good meal. She is also a major U2 fan, with major respect for Bono. Roz has ambitions to write a series of guides on Christian spirituality for 21st-century teenagers, addressing the longings for connection and belonging that is part of their angst and has often been totally misunderstood and ignored by adult Christians.

IF YOU ENJOY HAVING BREAKFAST WITH GOD, DON'T STOP NOW!

You'll love these four original volumes of *Breakfast with God*.

These individual books are perfect for your on-the-go lifestyle, and with their bold colors and easy-to-use format, they also make excellent gifts. Filled with 120 readings each – all of the originals – this big, bright series takes daily Bible reading to a new, funkier and much more relevant level.

Breakfast with God–
Volume 1
Duncan Banks
Softcover: 0-551-03250-2

Breakfast with God–
Volume 2
Gerard Kelly
Softcover: 0-551-03259-6

Breakfast with God–
Volume 3
Roz Stirling
Softcover: 0-551-03260-X

Breakfast with God–
Volume 4
Simon Hall
Softcover: 0-551-03261-8

Pick up a copy today at your favorite bookstore!

We want to hear from you. Please send your comments about this book to us in care of zreview@zondervan.com. Thank you.

ZONDERVAN.com/
AUTHORTRACKER
follow your favorite authors